VISUAL QUICKSTART GUIDE

FrontPage 97

FOR WINDOWS

Phyllis Davis

Peachpit Press

Visual QuickStart Guide
FrontPage 97 for Windows
Phyllis Davis

Peachpit Press
2414 Sixth Street
Berkeley, CA 94710
510-548-4393
800-283-9444
510-548-5991 (fax)

Find us on the World Wide Web at:
http://www.peachpit.com

Peachpit Press is a division of Addison Wesley Longman

Cover design: The Visual Group
Interior design and production: Phyllis Davis

ISBN 0-201-69628-2

9 8 7 6 5 4 3 2

Printed and bound in the United States of America

This book is dedicated to my mother,

Barbara Owens Hopper

Heartfelt thanks to

♡ Nancy Davis, the nicest and best editor a writer could ever hope to have.

and

♡ Roslyn Bullas and Matt Wagner for their trust in me. Without them, this book would have never happened.

and

♡ Kate Reber for her wise suggestions about layout and production.

Table of Contents

Table of Contents

Table of Contents

The Basics

Welcome to FrontPage 97! If you want to design and create your own Web site, you've come to the right place. FrontPage 97 is an innovative Web site creation program that helps you build Web sites using templates or from the ground up. *And*, you don't need to know one bit of HTML programming to use FrontPage 97. FrontPage takes care of the nitty gritty business that goes on behind the scenes, leaving you free to easily add the content you want to your Web pages.

My purpose in writing this book is to show just how easy it is to create a professional Web site using the tools that FrontPage offers. In keeping with the *Visual QuickStart Guide* format, my aim is to present easy, step-by-step directions with illustrations to take the mystery out of designing and creating Web sites.

FrontPage 97 offers a complete set of tools for building any kind of Web site you can image, from a sweet home page and personal Web site to a classically styled corporate Web presence complete with press releases, newsletters, and a table of contents. This program has incredible power and loads of features, all incorporated into a user interface that will be familiar to those who've used word processing programs. As sophisticated as it is, it's also easy to use. You can run with it as far as you please. With FrontPage 97 and your imagination, the sky's the limit.

Have a great time building your Web site!

How does FrontPage work?

FrontPage 97 is made up of two programs, FrontPage Explorer and FrontPage Editor. FrontPage Explorer, or just Explorer, is used to create and maintain Web sites. FrontPage Editor, or the Editor for short, is used to work with the individual Web pages that make up the sites.

With FrontPage Explorer, you can create many kinds of Web sites using predesigned templates and wizards, then modify these sites to suit your taste, or you can build a Web site from the ground up. Using Explorer commands, you can create new sites, open existing ones, and delete sites. You can view a Web site in *Folder View* or *Hyperlink View*, check spelling throughout an entire Web site, and verify and recalculate *hyperlinks*. In addition, if you are an administrator working with a team, you can use Explorer to set up *permissions*, setting the type of access rights each team member has.

With FrontPage Editor you can add many types of new pages to a Web site using page templates and wizards, then modify them as you please, or add a blank Web page and design it yourself. Using Editor commands, you can create new pages, open existing ones, and add great content, such as images, sounds, and videos, as well as hyperlinks to other pages in your

site or to other sites on the World Wide Web.

The Editor comes with five special toolbars that help you get the job done quickly. With the toolbars you can change text formatting, create interactive forms, add *hotspots* to images, and insert tables and *WebBots*.

WebBots are programs that perform various tasks for you such as creating a table of contents for a site, adding a timestamp, including the same information on several Web pages, or scheduling text or images that will appear during a specific time period.

When you've finished creating a Web page, the Editor makes it easy to view it in a browser of your choice and at different *screen resolutions*. You can also view a page in print preview mode and print it.

The FrontPage To Do List helps you keep track of tasks that need to be completed and lets you assign a priority for each task. With the To Do List, you can add tasks, modify existing ones, remove tasks, and mark them as finished.

When you finish your Web site and thoroughly test all its pages and hyperlinks, it's time to take it "live." Using the Explorer you can quickly *publish* the site to a *Web server* that supports the *FrontPage Server Extensions* or to an intranet.

How Does FrontPage 97 Work?

SOME FRONTPAGE AND WEB TERMINOLOGY

cell   The smallest part of a table. In a table, a column contains one or more cells.

content   All items placed on or associated with a Web page, such as text, images, sounds, hyperlinks, forms, and tables.

external hyperlink   A hyperlink to a file, Web page, or Web site located outside of the Web site that is currently open.

form   A set of form fields on a Web page whose information is processed by a Web server. The information on a form is sent to a server when the user submits the form by clicking a button or image.

form field   Any of the controls in a form that the user enters information into, such as text boxes, radio buttons, check boxes, drop-down menus, and push buttons.

HTML (Hypertext Markup Language) A computer language used for describing the contents of Web pages. FrontPage Editor reads and writes HTML files, taking care of the coding for you. You don't need to know HTML to use FrontPage.

hotspot   A specially defined area on an image that contains a clickable hyperlink.

hyperlink   An image or text that is clicked by the user to jump to another Web page in the same Web site or to another Web site.

ISP (Internet Service Provider)   An ISP is a business that provides the service of connecting users to the Internet, usually through telephone dial-up access.

protocol   An agreement about how to communicate. Some examples of protocols are TCP/IP (Transfer Control Protocol/Internet Protocol), HTTP (Hypertext Transfer Protocol), and FTP (File Transfer Protocol).

table   One or more columns and/or rows of cells on a Web page that is used to organize data or line up images and other page content.

URL (Uniform Resource Locator) An address of a Web site or other resource on the World Wide Web combined with a protocol. Some examples of typical URLs are:
- http://www.yahoo.com
- http://www.microsoft.com

FrontPage and Web Terminology

The FrontPage Explorer Screen (Figure 1)

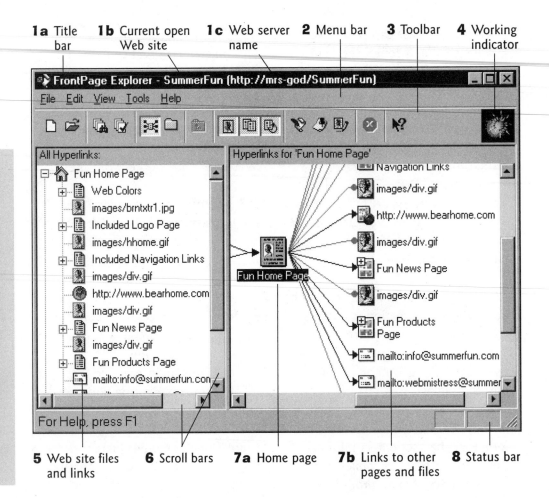

1a Title bar   **1b** Current open Web site   **1c** Web server name   **2** Menu bar   **3** Toolbar   **4** Working indicator

5 Web site files and links   **6** Scroll bars   **7a** Home page   **7b** Links to other pages and files   **8** Status bar

Key to the Explorer Screen

1a, b, c *Title bar*

Displays the program name, current open Web site, and location of the site—whether it's saved on a Web server or regular computer folder.

2 *Menu bar*

Click any menu title to access commands, fly-outs, dialog boxes, special tools, and other programs such as the FrontPage Editor.

The FrontPage Explorer Screen

3 *Toolbar*

The Explorer gives you quick access to such commands as creating a new Web site, opening an existing Web site, using hyperlink view and folder view, and showing FrontPage Editor.

4 *Working indicator*

When a command makes the Web server work, this gold star pulses, showing you the server is busy.

5 *Left view pane*

The left side of the Explorer window in hyperlink view shows all the files contained in the Web site, including Web pages, image and multimedia files, other associated files such as Microsoft Word documents and Excel spreadsheets, and hyperlinks to World Wide Web pages and e-mail.

6 *Scroll bars*

Scroll bars are used to navigate around the Explorer panes. If you click the down arrow on a vertical scroll bar, the Explorer pane will move up. If you click the right arrow on a horizontal scroll bar, the page will move left.

7a, b *Right view pane*

The right side of the Explorer window in hyperlink view graphically shows Web pages with their links. Links to a page come in from the left, whereas links to other pages and files go to the right. Double-click on any Web page icon to open it in the Editor.

8 *Status bar*

Displays information about the currently selected command or an operation in progress.

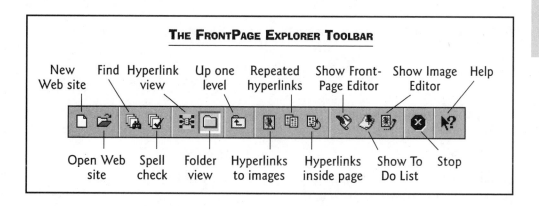

THE FRONTPAGE EXPLORER TOOLBAR

New Web site | Find | Hyperlink view | Up one level | Repeated hyperlinks | Show FrontPage Editor | Show Image Editor | Help

Open Web site | Spell check | Folder view | Hyperlinks to images | Hyperlinks inside page | Show To Do List | Stop

The FrontPage Explorer Screen

The FrontPage Editor Screen (Figure 2)

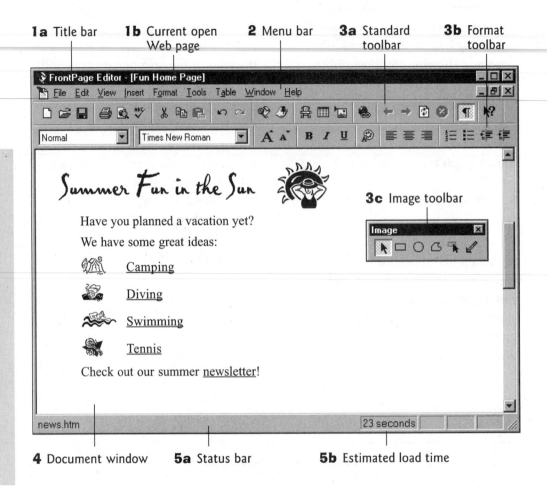

1a Title bar   **1b** Current open Web page   **2** Menu bar   **3a** Standard toolbar   **3b** Format toolbar

3c Image toolbar

4 Document window   **5a** Status bar   **5b** Estimated load time

Key to the Editor Screen

1a, b *Title bar*

Displays the program name and the page title of the currently open Web page in square brackets.

2 *Menu bar*

Click any of the nine menu titles to access commands, fly-outs, dialog boxes, and special tools.

3 a, b, c *Toolbars*

FrontPage Editor comes equipped with five toolbars that give you quick access to almost everything you need to create Web pages. The Standard toolbar gives access to basic commands such as creating a new Web page, opening an existing Web page, saving, printing, inserting a WebBot, and creating a hyperlink. The Format toolbar lets you quickly format text with predefined text styles, change text size, alignment, and color. The Image toolbar appears when an image is selected in the document window and lets you add hotspots to images and make a GIF image *transparent*. The Forms toolbar has everything you need to create interactive forms. The Advanced toolbar lets you insert ActiveX controls, scripts, plug-ins, and Java applets.

4 *Document window*

This is where you design and add content to Web pages. Since the Editor is WYSIWYG (What You See Is What You Get), the Web page you see in the Editor window appears almost as it will in a browser. This is a great development for those Web veterans who had to constantly switch between the HTML code and a browser to see what effect new code had on page layout.

5 a, b *Status bar*

Displays information about the currently selected commands, hyperlinks, operations in progress, and the estimated amount of time it will take for the Web page to load on a computer equipped with a 28.8kb modem.

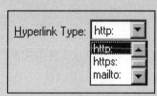
The FrontPage Editor Screen

THE FRONTPAGE EDITOR TOOLBARS

FrontPage Editor comes with five toolbars used for adding content to Web pages. To access any of these toolbars, open the View menu and choose the toolbar of your choice (**Figure 3**). A check mark next to a toolbar item on the View menu indicates that the toolbar is already open. The number/letter combinations to the right of the View menu in Figure 3 indicate the corresponding toolbar figures on pages 8 and 9.

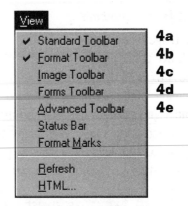

Figure 3. *To view a toolbar, choose the toolbar item you want to see.*

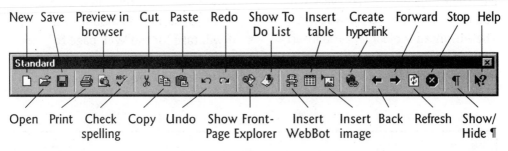

Figure 4a. *The Standard toolbar.*

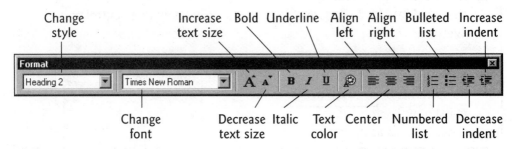

Figure 4b. *The Format toolbar.*

The FrontPage Editor Toolbars

Select Circle   Highlight
                hotspots

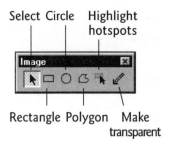

Rectangle Polygon   Make
                    transparent

Figure 4c. *The Image toolbar.*

One-line Check Drop-down
text box box   menu

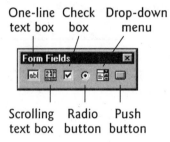

Scrolling Radio Push
text box   button button

Figure 4d. *The Forms toolbar.*

Insert Database Insert
HTML   Wizard   plug-in

Insert   Insert Insert
ActiveX   Java   script
control   applet

Figure 4e. *The Advanced toolbar.*

Figure 5. *Menus in some figures have been cropped using a jagged edge.*

Large menus and dialog boxes

FrontPage menus and dialog boxes contain many commands and items to select. Consequently, some of them are quite large. Several of the figures in this *Visual QuickStart Guide* are too big to display in their entirety or become very small when sized to fit the page. In order to fit these large items, some menus have been shortened using a jagged edge (**Figure 5**). The menu item being selected is shown, but lower or middle menu items are removed to conserve space. In a large dialog box, a circle has been drawn around the area under discussion (**Figure 6**).

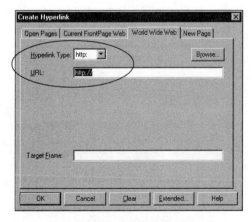

Figure 6. *A circle appears around the area under discussion in a large dialog box.*

TERMS USED IN THIS BOOK

- *Click* means to quickly press and release the left mouse button.
- *Double-click* means to quickly press and release the left mouse button twice.
- *Right click* means to quickly press and release the right mouse button.
- *Choose* means to use the mouse pointer to highlight a menu item and click.

HARDWARE CONSIDERATIONS

Microsoft recommends the following as the minimum system requirements for running FrontPage 97:

- A computer with a 486 or higher processor.
- 8 MB RAM if running Windows 95 or 16 MB RAM if running Windows NT and/or the Microsoft Personal Web Server.
- A VGA or higher graphics card.

This book was created using a 100 MHz Pentium with 32 MB RAM and an SVGA graphics card with 4 MB RAM. When testing FrontPage 97 and working with large Web sites, this hardware was fine.

SUMMARY

In this chapter you learned about:

- The way FrontPage works
- FrontPage and Web terms
- The Explorer screen
- The Explorer toolbar
- The Editor screen
- The five Editor toolbars
- Terms used in this book
- System requirements

Web Concepts

The Internet was started in the 1960s as a way for scientists at universities to communicate (and by the military for national defense purposes). Mostly, the early Internet was used to send e-mail (electronic mail) back and forth. Things didn't really start to get exciting until the concepts underlying the World Wide Web—the Web, or WWW, for short—were introduced a few years ago.

The Web introduced a visual, easy-to-understand interface that anyone with a computer and modem can use to connect to the Internet. It also provides a way for all of us to create Web page *content* that can be placed on the Internet for others to view and use—this is what FrontPage 97 is all about.

The great joy of FrontPage 97 is that when you use it to create world class Web pages and sites, you don't need to know anything about underlying Web concepts and mechanisms. The FrontPage interface is intuitive and straightforward. If you've already used any one of the Microsoft Office applications, particularly Microsoft Word, you shouldn't have too much trouble with it. But sometimes, a little bit of insight about what is going on under the hood helps clarify things. This chapter explains the basic mechanisms of the Web. If you don't want to be bothered with this stuff, you can just skip it for now and come back later if you need a concept clarified.

The Internet and the Web

Protocols

A *protocol*, in computer networking lingo, is an agreement about how to communicate. For instance, Paul Revere established a very simple protocol when he agreed to communicate if the Redcoats were coming by placing lanterns on a church steeple ("One if by land, and two if by sea!").

TCP/IP—short for *Transfer Control Protocol/Internet Protocol*—is the protocol used by all computers on the Internet to send and receive data. Actually, TCP/IP is a whole bunch of protocols stuck together that handle all the nitty-gritty details of breaking up out-going TCP/IP communications into *packets* and pasting them back together at the other end. You don't have to know too much about TCP/IP to create great Web pages, but you probably will want to know something about the protocols that are "pasted" on top of TCP/IP because you may wish to include some of them in your FrontPage Web pages.

ADDRESSES ON THE WEB

An address, used to find a resource such as a site or a page on the Internet, is referred to as a *URL—or Uniform Resource Locator—* and pronounced "you are ell."

The first part of a URL, ending with ://, is always the protocol used. The URL for World Wide Web sites always starts *http://*. Usually—but not always—*www* follows as the next part of the URL. For example: *http://www.netscape.com*.

In the latest versions of Netscape Navigator and Microsoft Internet Explorer, you don't have to enter the protocol. www.netscape.com gets you to the same place (opens the same Web page) as http://www.netscape.com.

HTTP—meaning *Hypertext Transfer Protocol*—is the most important protocol for World Wide Web users. When a browser is told to open a Web address—or URL—that begins with http://, it knows that the connection is to a Web site, and that the requested page on the site should be displayed. For example, http://www.bearhome.com displays the indicated page in a browser (**Figure 1**).

Figure 1. *When you enter a URL in a browser, the corresponding Web page is displayed.*

FTP—*File Transfer Protocol*—is used to send and receive files from other computers on the Internet. Archives holding files on the Internet that you can download are called *FTP sites*. A URL that starts with ftp:// will either download a specific file to your system or open an FTP site that you can select a file from. For example, you can connect to the Tucows FTP site—one of the largest software archives of all categories available for download on the Internet—by entering ftp://tucows.com.

> You can access the vast collection of software available for Windows 95 and Windows NT from the Tucows collection using your browser by visiting http://www.tucows.com.

Protocols: HTTP and FTP

File—file:/// is used at the beginning of a URL to indicate a file on a local disk, such as a hard drive, should be opened. For example, file:///c:\program files\test\test.htm.

Mailto:—If a URL begins mailto: it means that the rest of the URL is an e-mail address. When a browser hits a hyperlink containing a mailto URL— for example, mailto:phyllis@bearhome.com—the e-mail program on your computer will launch, ready to send mail to that address.

HTML

When a browser requests a Web page across the Internet from a Web server using the HTTP protocol, for instance http://www.bearhome.com/mypage.htm, the Web server expects to deliver (and the Web browser expects to receive) a page written in a particular language, *HTML*. HTML—*Hypertext Markup Language*—is **the** language of the Web.

When you surf the Web, the browser you use knows how to convert the HTML pages it receives from Web servers into recognizable Web pages.

The name of HTML tells one a lot about the kind of language it is. "Hypertext" means that it can be used to create *hyperlinks*, or *jumps*, from one page to another. Hyperlinks are activated by clicking on underlined text, or on a graphical hotspot in an HTML page.

You may not realize that when you ask your browser to open a Web site, such as http://www.bearhome.com/, http://www.microsoft.com/, or http://www.netscape.com, you are actually opening a specific page on the site. Exactly which page depends on the settings in the Web server software, but it is usually something like default.htm or index.html.

Actually, the process of surfing the Web means choosing one hyperlink after another in your browser. Depending on the URL of the hyperlink, the Web server you access uses the TCP/IP and HTTP protocols to send the specified HTML page back to your browser. (This process, the reverse of surfing, is called serving. Think of it this way: some folks serve so others can surf.)

VIEWING HTML SOURCE CODE

When you use FrontPage 97 to create Web pages, you don't ever have to look at HTML codes, unless you want to.

Should you decide at some point that you have a burning to desire to see what's really going on behind that beautiful FrontPage exterior, you can view the HTML source code for any Web page open in the FrontPage Editor by choosing HTML from the View menu (**Figure 2**).

Most browsers will also allow you to look at the HTML source code for World Wide Web pages open in a browser. Looking at professional Web page code can be very educational. For instance, to view a document's HTML source in Microsoft Internet Explorer, choose Source from the View menu. To view HTML source code in Netscape Navigator, choose View Source from the View menu.

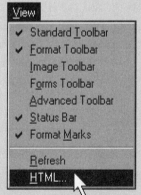

Figure 2. *In the Editor, choose HTML from the View menu.*

HTML

"Markup" means that the language is marked up, in much the same way that an editor marks up a manuscript. In the case of HTML, *tags* are codes used to mark up the HTML page. These tags are used to tell the browser what the related text is supposed to be. The browser uses this information to decide how to actually present the content.

HTML tags are always enclosed in angle brackets (<>). For example, <a> is the tag that means anchor. Most tags come in pairs with a beginning tag and an end tag. The end tag is indicated with a slash (/) and comes at the end of the text that the tags mark up. For example, <a>I'm anchored!</a>.

Many tags have *attributes*, also sometimes called *parameters*. Attributes are used to give more information to the browser about what the tag does. For example, the attribute *href* can be used with the <a> (anchor) tag, to embed a hyperlink in the anchor, <a href="http://www.bearhome.com"> I am anchored!</a>.

You can use any simple text editor to create HTML files, for instance, Notepad (**Figure 3**). But the FrontPage Editor does an excellent job of visual HTML page creation. After you've used it, it's unlikely that you'd want to deal with hand coding HTML.

Here's a very simple HTML file that you can save as a text file and open in your browser (**Figure 4**). (It's probably as complex as you'd want to get doing it by hand!)

In case you want to know, you'll find information about the hypertext tags used to create effects throughout *FrontPage 97 for Windows: Visual Quick Start Guide* in the "What's My Tag?" sidebars.

```
<html>
  <head>
    <title>A very simple Web page!
    </title>
  </head>
  <body>
  You can make your own Web pages.<br>
  <a href="http://www.bearhome.com">
  I am anchored!</a>
  </body>
</html>
```

Like the animals in Noah's ark, you can see from this HTML page that most tags come in pairs. Think of them as parentheses: one to open an HTML phrase, the other to close it.

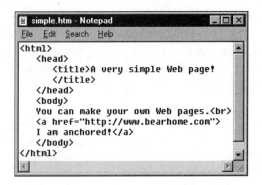

Figure 3. *You can use a simple text editor such as Notepad to create a Web page.*

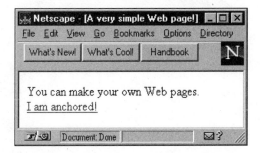

Figure 4. *The same simple Web page created in Notepad, viewed in a browser.*

HTML Tags

Clients and Servers on the Web

You may have worked at an office that is net-worked. This might mean that desktop PCs are connected to each other, to peripheral devices such as scanners and printers, and maybe even to databases on a larger computer (**Figure 5**). In this kind of network, the larger computer is called a *server* and the desktop computers are called *clients*.

When your computer is connected to the Internet, a computer on the World Wide Web using the HTTP protocol becomes a server and your browser is a client, similar to the set up of an office net-work (**Figure 6**). When you have loaded an HTML page in your browser (the client), the HTTP server has different contributions to make to the appear-ance of the Web page. You can think of it this way: during the conversation between a browser and a Web server, the browser is pulling things off the server—but the server is also pushing things into the browser.

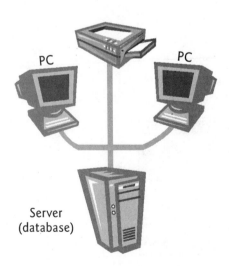

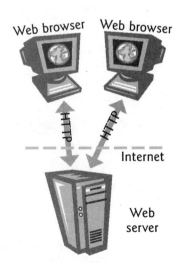

Figure 5. *A network can contain PCs and peripheral devices connected to a server.*

Figure 6. *Web browsers connected to the Internet are clients connected to a Web server.*

The browser handles client-side duties, including translating HTML codes and *scripts*. Scripts are instructions telling the browser to do something and are written in *JavaScript* or *VBScript*.

The Web server delivers programs that do things within the browser, programs such as FrontPage *WebBots*, *Java Applets*, and *ActiveX controls*. The server is also responsible for answering requests made by the browser, such as starting a *CGI* program.

Downloading Current Web Browsers

It's important that you view your Web pages in a number of different browsers. HTML tags only describe a Web page's content—they do not tell the browser how to display it. This means that there can be considerable difference between the appearance of a page in different browsers.

The two most popular browsers are Microsoft Internet Explorer and Netscape Navigator. Version 3.01 of Internet Explorer comes with the FrontPage 97 bonus pack. You can install the browser using the FrontPage CD-ROM. The most recent updates to Internet Explorer can be downloaded from http://www.microsoft.com/ie/.

You can download current versions of Netscape Navigator from Netscape's World Wide Web home page, http://www.netscape.com.

Among the many varieties of browser animals out there is Lynx—a text-only browser that runs primarily on Unix platforms. Lynx makes a compelling case for providing text alternatives to any graphics on a Web page: otherwise you risk producing pages that not all browsers can read. As for why anyone would want to use a text-only browser, have a look at the cute and silly Ode to Lynx page, http://www.batch.com/ode-to-lynx.

Downloading Web Browsers

Build It and They Will Come

The question, on the Web, is, how will they find you? This is not only a question of publicity, promotion, and advertising—those things come later. The first question is, when someone connected to the Internet enters your URL in their browser, how does the browser know to load your Web page from your Web site? Because the first part of the URL is http://, the browser knows it's supposed to be using Hypertext Transfer Protocol to load an HTML page from the *domain* in the URL.

But, how does the browser find your domain? This depends on how your Web page—and site—is connected to the Internet.

Every Web server connected to the Internet is assigned an *Internet Protocol* (or *IP*) address. An IP address is an unwieldy quadruplet of numbers separated by periods, for example, 207.71.18.55 (sometimes called a *dotted quad*). These numbers represent a *node* on the Internet. You could open a Web site in a browser using its IP address, but domain names are usually used instead since they are easier for human beings—as opposed to computers—to understand.

An *Internet Service Provider* (or *ISP*) is a business that provides the service of connecting users to the Internet, usually through telephone dial-up access.

Most Internet dial-up access accounts do not assign you a fixed IP number (called a *static* IP). Instead, you are given a new IP (called a *dynamic* IP) each time you call into your ISP.

A dynamic IP, by itself, doesn't provide a means for other browsers to find your Web page because the location of your server on the Internet will be different each time you log on. One answer is to arrange to have an ISP assign you a static IP.

You can obtain your own domain name which can be used to access your Web site and pages. Domain names are translated into IP addresses using a utility known as *Domain Name System* (or *DNS*). Each ISP maintains a DNS server that translates registered domain names into IP addresses.

Hosting a Web Site

It's a fact of life that you will probably not want to connect a Web server directly to the Internet. These days, this is something that only hard-core propeller-heads, and/or large, well-funded organizations with high-speed Internet connections, should attempt.

But, don't worry! If you're using FrontPage 97 in an environment that is not already connected to the Web, you can easily arrange for an ISP or other organization to *host* your Web pages and site for

---

GETTING YOUR OWN DOMAIN NAME

A company named InterNIC is currently charged with handling domain name registrations. InterNIC can be found on the Web at http://www.internic.net. You can browse their site to find out if the name you want is already taken or to start the registration process. (Most likely, if an ISP or other organization is hosting your Web site, they will handle this for you.)

InterNIC currently handles United States domain name requests ending in .com, .edu, .gov, .net, and .org. (International domain names tend to use the country of origin; for example, .ca means Canada and .uk means United Kingdom.)

Proposals are in discussion to help alleviate domain name crowding by adding seven new domain names: .arts, .info, .firm, .nom, .rec, .store, and .web. Further information about these proposed new domains can be found on the Internet Society's site, http://www.iahc.org.

Hosting a Web Site

you. (A Web site host is also sometimes called a *Web Presence Provider*.) This usually can be done quite inexpensively and is far and away the easiest way to put a site up on the Web.

You should know that there is a special requirement for Web Presence Providers who host Web sites created using FrontPage 97: they must have the *FrontPage Server Extensions* installed. The FrontPage Server Extensions are special programs that allow you to take full advantage of FrontPage's capabilities when you create your Web (to learn more about the Server Extensions, see page 38).

You'll find an extensive list of registered Web Presence Providers who specialize in hosting sites created with FrontPage on Microsoft's site, http://microsoft.saltmine.com/frontpage/wpp/list/. As you'd expect, these Web Presence Providers all have the FrontPage Server Extensions installed.

WHAT IS A FRONTPAGE WEB?

When you import a World Wide Web site into FrontPage or start a new Web site in FrontPage, behind-the-scenes scaffolding is added to the Web site to support FrontPage's special features. A Web site that has had this scaffolding added to it is referred to as a *FrontPage Web*.

SUMMARY

In this chapter you learned about:

- Protocols
- Addresses on the Web and URLs
- HTTP servers
- HTML code and tags
- Downloading current browsers
- Obtaining domain names

Principles of Good Web Design

Web sites—and Web pages—can be designed well or poorly. FrontPage 97 makes it easy to throw many different kinds of elements into a Web page; the results can often be a confusing hodge-podge (**Figure 1**). In Web page design, as in design in general, less is often more.

It's important to maintain a consistent look and feel across an entire Web site. Maintaining visual standards for all the pages in a site gives a Web site cohesion (**Figure 2**), and differentiates it from the World Wide Web at large.

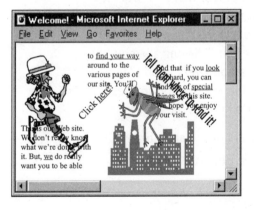

Figure 1. *A jumble of elements can make a Web page confusing and difficult to read.*

Figure 2. *A well-designed Web page is easy to understand and looks good.*

Of course, it is essential that Web pages and sites should present information in an easy-to-comprehend fashion. Sites should be navigable without confusion, and users should be able to easily find what they are looking for on a site. And, in the best of all possible worlds, Web page design uses the architectural principle that form should follow function. In other words, there should be a relationship between a Web site's visual appearance and what it is supposed to do.

This chapter explains how you can use FrontPage 97 to implement principles of good Web design. With FrontPage it's easy to create a consistent, sophisticated, professional-looking Web site.

Naming Web Pages

After you've created a Web page, you'll need to save it. When you save a Web page, you'll have to name the file that makes it up. FrontPage 97 will let you name files pretty much anything you'd like. If you wanted, you could save a Web page as "This is my Pretty little Web page.htm." Saving a Web page with a name like this is not a very good idea. The fact is, you'll avoid trouble by sticking to these simple file-naming rules for all your Web pages:

- Use only lowercase letters of the alphabet.
- Do not include numbers, punctuation marks, or spaces.
- Name the file extension .htm.
- Stick to a maximum of eight characters in the file name, followed by a period and the three-character file extension. This is the old DOS way of naming files, sometimes referred to as the "eight plus three" file-naming convention.

Here are some examples of "good" Web page file names: home.htm, denali.htm, and concord.htm.

TITLING A WEB PAGE

Besides the file name it is saved with, every Web page should also have a title. When you save a Web page in FrontPage, you are given a chance to enter the page's title (**Figure 3**).

When the Web page is viewed in a browser, its title is displayed in the title bar of the browser (**Figure 4**). Because it is given such prominent attention, Web page titles are important. They are used to navigate your site, and search engines use them to determine the contents of your site. Therefore, you should think carefully about the titles of your Web pages. Try to give them titles that are related to what they contain.

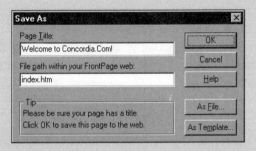

Figure 3. *When you save a new Web page, you can give it an informative page title.*

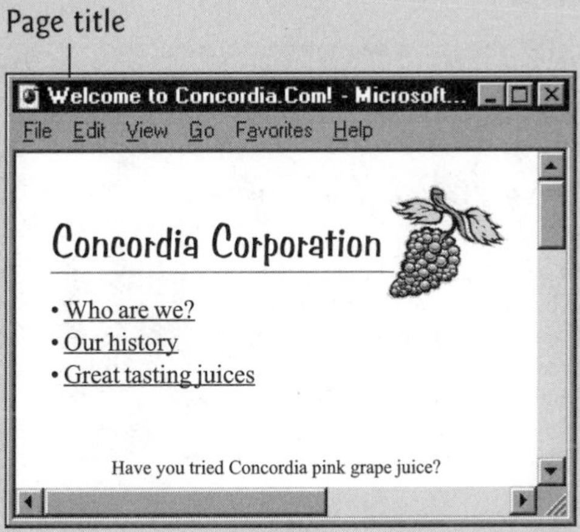

Page title

Figure 4. *The page title appears in the browser's title bar.*

Planning Web Site Flow

If you want to complete a complex task, good planning helps. You'll find that this is very true when it comes to designing Web site flow.

Web site flow is the way users will move around your site. Often, this involves navigation through hierarchical information. For example, if part of your site were used to display photographs from around the world, there might be a link to the photo page from your site's main page.

> Your Web site's main page is usually—but not always—the page that your Web server opens first when a browser accesses your site. Sometimes the main page is called a *home* page.

The main photo page might contain a link to an Italy photo page. The Italy photo page might contain links to pages of Italian cities, such as Rome, Florence, and so on (**Figure 5**).

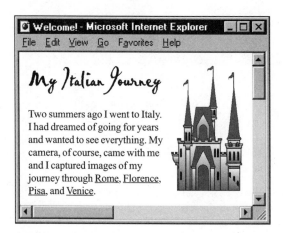

Figure 5. *A Web site's pages should be interconnected with links.*

If there are parallel branches to this hierarchical structure—for example, a France photo page with links to the Paris and Chartres pages, and a China photo page that is reached from the main photo page—this can get pretty complicated very fast.

It's a great idea to plan this hierarchical structure in advance. When you do, be sure to keep in mind how users will navigate your site.

One way to plan a Web site is to create a diagram similar to a flow chart showing the connections between all the pages (**Figure 6**). (This can be done using pencil and paper or a flow-charting program.)

The FrontPage 97 Explorer shows the links between the pages in your Web site. You can use the Explorer to understand the hierarchical relationships in your Web site better.

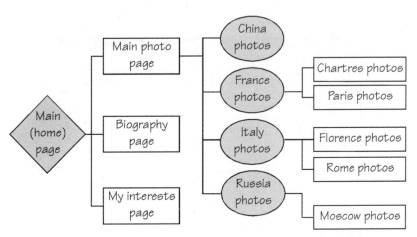

Figure 6. *You can use a pencil and paper or flow-charting program to create a diagram of your Web site.*

Planning Web Site Flow

Some Web designers prefer to create a hierarchical outline so they can understand the relationship between the pages in their Web site. You can use Microsoft Word in Outline View for this purpose (**Figure 7**).

It's important to provide a consistent way to move through your site, using, for example, a button bar or hyperlinks repeated on every page. The user should be able to easily reach all important pages from any page (and, certainly, the main page should be accessible).

For example, the user might reach the Paris photo page, and decide they really want to see photos of Africa. It would be great if there were a navigation link over to the Africa photo page so the user didn't have to navigate back through the France photo page and the main photo page.

Not only is it courteous to provide consistent links to other parts of your site, it also helps with the effort of providing one overall look and feel for your entire site.

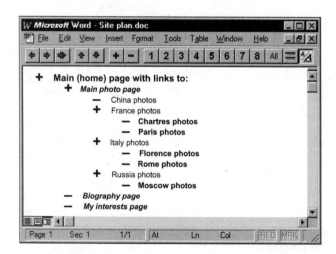

Figure 7. *You can use Microsoft Word in Outline View to create a plan for your Web site.*

Consistent links within a site can be provided as hyperlinks placed within a table or as a graphic *image map*, perhaps looking like the subject (**Figure 8**).

Figure 8. *There are many ways to organize links throughout a Web site. Two often-used methods are to arrange links in a table or use an image with hotspots.*

Through the Generations with Web Sites

Some observers of the World Wide Web have said that Web sites can be categorized as first generation, second generation, or third generation. Here's what they mean:

- ⑨ First-generation Web sites are text only. These are just-plain-vanilla Web sites, primarily designed to distribute information.

- ⑨ Second-generation Web sites provide fancy graphics and interactive features. Users decide how to navigate through these sites. Web sites created using FrontPage 97 are normally second-generation sites.

- ⑨ Third-generation Web sites guide users through the site with a gentle, but firm invisible hand. FrontPage can be used to create third-generation sites.

Third-Generation Web Sites

Third-generation sites are more like a fun house than a place to dig for information. There is an expected flow to what is presented on the site, just like in a movie.

When a third-generation site is planned, it usually includes an ante-room with only one way into the site (**Figure 9**). From this entrance room, the user is gently (but firmly) guided through a progression of pages. Finally, an Exit page is reached. This will often give the user the chance to exit to related sites, or start at the beginning again.

FrontPage 97 can certainly be used to create third-generation Web sites. If this kind of site conceptually suits the logic of your Web project, by all means go for it! You should understand, however, that controlling the user requires more work than simply providing a clear menu of choices.

Figure 9. *A third-generation site uses an ante-room to welcome you to the Web site.*

Being Visually Consistent

Visual consistency within a Web site is very important. If you are creating a personal Web site, you can choose images and colors that suit your personality, but aren't necessarily consistent from page to page. Sites created in a business context give the wrong impression if they are not internally consistent. A Web site is an extension of the business it represents. It is inappropriate to create business sites that do not maintain a consistent look and feel, even if the look and feel is one of zany wackiness.

In order to maintain visual consistency between Web pages in a site, you should establish standardized fonts, colors, graphic styles used, and site navigation tools.

The FrontPage Wizards make it very easy to create consistent Web sites. For example, the Corporate Presence Wizard, available in FrontPage Explorer, gives you a very good start on a corporate Web site. To find out how to start a site using a Wizard, take a look at page 56.

Page Wizards, available in the FrontPage Editor, allow you to create Web pages that start with consistent elements every time. For details on how to start a page with a page wizard, see page 76.

In addition, you can save any Web page as a template. New Web pages based on your custom template start with exactly the same visual elements. To find out how to create a page template, see page 80.

Another way to keep pages consistent is to use one Web page as the basis for colors on other pages. FrontPage makes it easy to set a Web page's colors using another Web page. For details on how to do this, see page 134.

Being Visually Consistent

Using Clip Art

The Web is a very visual medium. It's important to add art to your pages. Don't hesitate to be creative!

As part of the FrontPage 97 Bonus Pack, included on the FrontPage 97 CD-ROM, you'll find a sophisticated, yet easy to use drawing and image creation program, Image Composer 1.0. You can use this program to create your own art for the Web.

The Image Composer contains an extensive clip art library arranged in category collections, such as retro, techno, and western. If you find a particular category that pleases you, that category collection will provide you with all the necessary graphics, such as backgrounds, buttons, panels, and bullets. To access the clip art collection that comes with Image Composer, launch Image Composer, then choose From File from the Image menu. In the Insert From File dialog box that opens, move to the hard drive where Image Composer was installed, then open Multimedia Files\Graphics\Web\ Microsoft Image Composer Themes.

FrontPage 97 also includes a nice collection of clip art you can use in your Web pages. This clip art consists of many things you'll need when creating a Web page such as backgrounds, animations, logos, bullets, and buttons. For details on how to add FrontPage clip art to your Web pages, take a look at page 138.

If you need additional styles of clip art, you should be able to find commercially released clip art collections on the Web or in software catalogs.

Whether you create your own art, or use existing clip art, it's important to use only one style of art

Using Clipart

in a Web site. For example, if your site uses high-tech space ships and deep space stations as illustrations, you probably should not also include pen and ink drawings styled after Disney cartoons.

It's important in Web page design to place art precisely, rather than just plopping it anywhere. The easiest way to precisely place art is to put it in a table. Take a look at Chapter 12 for more about tables.

Background Patterns and Colors

Background patterns and colors offer a thorny path for you to follow.

On the one hand, as Spike Lee sort of said, you gotta have 'em. Web pages with a gray background are just not acceptable any more.

On the other hand, nothing does more damage to a Web page than an inappropriate background choice. A page that is hard to read because the text and the background blend together is one that will most likely remain unread.

The golden rule here is that if it looks even slightly difficult for you to read, it's much too hard for anyone else. (After all, you know what it is supposed to say before you try reading it.)

You should also try to avoid garish color combinations. Text in shocking pink and a background in fluorescent green can be rather jarring as well as eye straining. The watch words for color combinations in your Web pages should be mellow, complementary, low key, and supportive of the page's content. Anything else, and you risk having your page look like a house whose colors were chosen because the paint was on sale.

Background Patterns and Colors

Understanding Spatial Relationships

Designing Web pages should be regarded as a two-dimensional design exercise. As such, there are some standard principles that apply.

You need to understand the spatial relationships between the objects on your page. The size of the objects—and how they are positioned—should, in some way, reflect their relationships.

In order to understand the spatial relationships between objects, it helps to evaluate the *white space* (sometimes called *negative space*) on a page. White space is the area not taken up by objects (**Figure 10**). (It's called "white space" even if the background is yellow or another color.) You will see how objects spatially relate to one another more clearly if you look at the white space rather than the objects themselves.

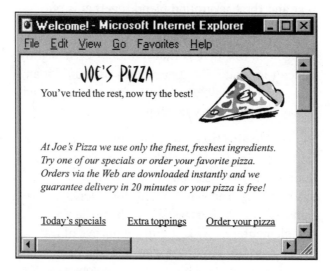

Figure 10. *White space gives a Web page and the user's eyes room to breathe.*

One common—and sound—principle for organizing spatial relationships is to divide your page into groups of related objects. The folks who browse your page should be able to quickly grasp the organization of the page. Grouping related objects together helps accomplish this.

Pages should be clean, and never cluttered. A cluttered Web page is like a messy room: no one wants to visit. Make sure to leave plenty of white space, so that the eye "has room to breathe."

Neatness and white space, while a good start, are not quite enough. Your pages should also use contrast to make the page more visually interesting and to highlight important elements.

Visual contrast can be generated in many ways, such as by manipulating spatial relationships, using placement and weight of fonts, and much more.

The Importance of Narrative

Have you ever noticed how important the story is to a novel or movie? If you have a good story, sometimes the writing can be terrible or the film-making bad but you still want to stay to the end.

It's the same way with a well-designed Web site: it should tell a story. Some Web sites—for example, some third-generation sites—are explicitly designed to tell a story with a beginning, middle and end. For these sites, the narrative is quite clear.

But even sites that don't have an obvious story are narrating something. If visitors to your Web site get the impression that there is no direction to the site, that your site is made up of random collections of pages, they will probably become confused and leave quickly.

When you first start to plan your Web site, try to determine what story you are trying to tell or what you want your readers to know when they leave your site. This may be quite obvious. For example, "Paul's Deli: we sell Pastrami mail-order and were the first Kosher Deli over 12,000 feet in the Rockies" has a story from the start. Other times, the story you are telling may not be so clear.

If you can figure out the narrative thread behind your Web site, use this information. It is precious! Each page should, in some way, further the thrust of your narrative. Perhaps the page helps to set the stage for the rest of your Web site. Perhaps the page serves to answer a question a viewer might have. But every page, in some way or other, should play a narrative role.

GOOD WEB DESIGN BOOKS

◉ *<designing web graphics>* by Lynda Weinman (New Riders)

◉ *Elements of Web Design* by Darcy DiNucci, Maria Giudice, and Lynne Stiles (Peachpit Press)

◉ *The Non-Designer's Web Book* by Robin Williams (Peachpit Press)

SUMMARY

In this chapter you learned about:

◉ Naming and titling Web pages

◉ Planning Web site flow

◉ Third-generation Web sites

◉ Visual consistency

◉ Background patterns and colors

◉ Spatial relationships and your Web page

◉ Web site narrative

Installing FrontPage 97

This chapter gets you started with FrontPage 97 by showing you how to install FrontPage 97, the FrontPage Personal Web Server, the Microsoft Personal Web Server, and how to use the FrontPage Server Administrator to set up your Personal Web Server. (Yes! FrontPage Personal Web Server and Microsoft Personal Web Server *are* two different programs.)

The FrontPage Personal Web Server is a computer program that helps you set up and test the Web sites you create with FrontPage. This server is only for testing simple Web sites that do not use advanced features such as database connectivity. In addition, it is not meant for use as a World Wide Web server. It uses the same protocol as a standard Web server, HTTP via TCP/IP, but it cannot handle multiple simultaneous Web connections or *hits*.

The Microsoft Personal Web Server is a different program than the FrontPage Personal Web Server. The Microsoft Personal Web Server is a bit more robust and should be used to test Web sites that include advanced features. It can be used as a Web server, but according to Microsoft's documentation it is limited to ten simultaneous hits.

The FrontPage Server Administrator is used to set up the FrontPage Server Extensions on your computer. The Administrator is also used to make a FrontPage Web site available to a server and set up passwords for those folks who will be working on Web sites loaded on a server.

Personal Web Servers

WHAT ARE THE FRONTPAGE SERVER EXTENSIONS?

The FrontPage Server Extensions are programs that let Web servers, such as the FrontPage Personal Web Server, talk to FrontPage Web sites. In order for a server to talk to FrontPage and vice versa, the server must be setup to use a specific *port* on your computer. You can think of a port as the "telephone line" that the server and FrontPage use to talk to each other. The default port is 80.

If an ISP will be hosting your FrontPage Web site, the ISP *must* have the FrontPage Server Extensions installed. For information about where to find an ISP that can host FrontPage Web sites, see page 22.

DO I NEED TO INSTALL MICROSOFT PERSONAL WEB SERVER?

If you are going to post your Web site to an Internet Service Provider (ISP) host's computer, the host will be running an "industrial strength" server program that can handle many, many hits at once. In this case, you probably do not need to install the Microsoft Personal Web Server on your machine.

YOU CAN ALWAYS GO BACK WHEN INSTALLING FRONTPAGE

When you install FrontPage 97 on your computer, an installation wizard will guide you through the process. Just like any other wizard, you will click Next to move forward from panel to panel. If you decide that you want to change something on a previous panel, just click the Back button to move back to that panel. From there, you can change what you want, then click the Next button to return to the panel from which you came.

Figure 1. *The Microsoft FrontPage 97 with Bonus Pack window.*

CD-ROM icon

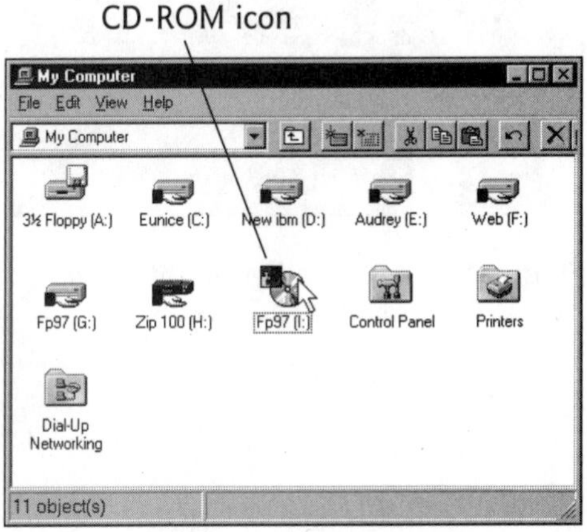

Figure 2. *Double-click on the CD-ROM icon to open the Microsoft FrontPage 97 with Bonus Pack window.*

The steps for installing FrontPage may seem complicated at first, but if you follow them along, you'll find that the installation is not hard at all. After you have installed FrontPage, you'll discover just how easy it is to create your own Web sites!

To install FrontPage 97:

1. Close any applications you might have open on your computer.

2. Insert the FrontPage 97 CD-ROM into your computer's CD-ROM drive.

3. After a moment, the Microsoft FrontPage 97 with Bonus Pack window will open (**Figure 1**).

   or

   If this window does not appear, double-click on the My Computer icon. The My Computer dialog box will open (**Figure 2**). Find the icon for your CD-ROM drive and double-click on it. The Microsoft FrontPage 97 with Bonus Pack window will appear (**Figure 1**).

   Using this window you can choose to install:

   ◉ Microsoft FrontPage 97 (and the FrontPage Personal Web Server).

   ◉ Microsoft Image Composer, an easy-to-use program for creating graphics for your Web site.

Install FrontPage 97

- Microsoft Personal Web Server, a low-volume Web server.
- Microsoft Internet Explorer 3.0, a browser.
- The Web Publishing Wizard, a program that lets you post your Web site to a server not running the FrontPage server extensions.

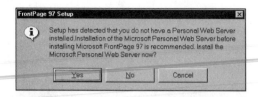

Figure 3. *The installation routine will ask whether you want to install the Microsoft Personal Web Server.*

4. Click the FrontPage 97 Installation button. Set up for the installation will begin.

5. If no server is installed on your computer, a FrontPage Setup dialog box will appear, asking whether you want to install the Microsoft Personal Web Server (**Figure 3**).

6. Click No if all you need is a Web server to test your Web sites. The FrontPage Personal Web Server will be installed on your computer later.

   or

   Click Yes if you need a low-volume Web server for use on the World Wide Web. A License Agreement dialog box will appear on the screen (**Figure 4**). Now, do the following:

   a. After reading the license agreement, if you accept the agreement, click the I Agree button. The Microsoft Personal Web Server will be installed on your computer.

Figure 4. *The License Agreement for the Microsoft Personal Web Server.*

Figure 5. *Click Yes to restart your computer.*

Install FrontPage 97

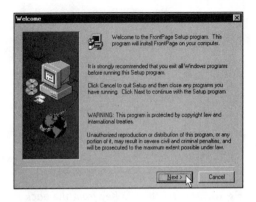

Figure 6. *The Welcome panel of the installation wizard.*

Figure 7. *Enter your name and company in the text boxes on the FrontPage Registration panel.*

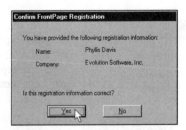

Figure 8. *The Confirm FrontPage Registration dialog box.*

When installation is complete, a Personal Web Server dialog box will appear, telling you that you must restart your computer (**Figure 5**).

b. Click Yes. Your computer will reboot.

c. When your machine is back at the Windows 95/NT desktop, return to the Microsoft Front-Page 97 with Bonus Pack window (**Figure 1**), using either method described in step 3 above.

d. Click the FrontPage 97 Installation button again. A set up screen will appear.

7. The Welcome panel of the installation wizard will appear (**Figure 6**).

8. Click Next to move to the FrontPage Registration panel (**Figure 7**).

9. Type your name and company name in the appropriate text boxes.

10. Click Next to move on to the Confirm FrontPage Registration dialog box (**Figure 8**).

Install FrontPage 97

11. If the information in the dialog box is correct, click Yes. The Microsoft FrontPage 97 CD Key dialog box will appear (**Figure 9**). If the information is not correct, click No. The FrontPage Registration panel will reappear (**Figure 6**).

12. Type in the 11-digit CD Key number in the text boxes from the sticker on the back of your CD case.

13. Click OK. The Destination Path panel of the installation wizard will appear (**Figure 10**). This panel is used to set the location on your hard drive where the FrontPage program will be installed. The default location is C:\Program Files\ Microsoft FrontPage. If you want to put the program in a different location, such as on another hard drive, click the Browse button and select a new location from the Choose Directory dialog box (**Figure 11**). When you are finished with the dialog box, click OK to return to the Destination Path panel.

Figure 9. *Enter the CD Key from the back of the CD case.*

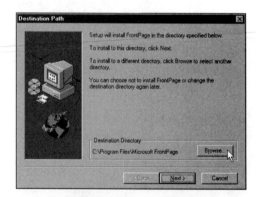

Figure 10. *Use the Destination Path panel to tell the installation program where to install FrontPage.*

Figure 11. *Use the Choose Directory dialog box to select a different location for the files.*

Figure 12. *Select Custom, then click Next.*

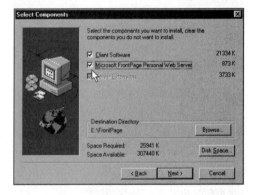

Figure 13. *The Select Components panel.*

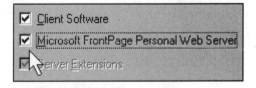

Figure 14. *Make sure both Client Software and Microsoft FrontPage Personal Web Server are checked.*

14. Click Next. The Setup Type panel of the installation wizard will appear (**Figure 12**). With this panel, you can choose either a Typical installation or a Custom installation.

15. A Typical installation will not install everything you will need, for instance the FrontPage Personal Web Server, so select Custom, then click Next. The Select Components panel of the installation wizard will appear (**Figure 13**).

16. Make sure that *both* the Client Software and Microsoft FrontPage Personal Web Server check boxes have checks in them (**Figure 14**).

17. Click Next. The Choose Microsoft FrontPage Personal Web Server Directory panel of the installation wizard will appear (**Figure 15**). This panel is used to set where the FrontPage Personal Web Server program will be installed on your hard drive. The default location is C:\FrontPage Webs. If you want to put the program in a different location, such as on an-other hard drive, click the Browse button and select a new location from the Choose Directory dialog box (**Figure 11**). When you are finished with the dialog box, click OK to return to the wizard panel.

Install FrontPage 97

18. Click Next. The FrontPage Personal Web Server panel of the installation wizard will appear (**Figure 16**). This panel detects whether there is another server on your computer and sets the FrontPage Personal Web Server to run on a specific TCP/IP port, usually 80.

19. Click Next. One of the following will happen:

⑨ If the setup program has found another Web server on your computer, such as the Microsoft Personal Web Server, the Installed Servers Detected panel of the installation wizard will appear (**Figure 17**). This panel is used to select which FrontPage server extensions will be installed. Select the Web servers that you want to include from the list box. Click Next to move to the Start Copying Files panel of the installation wizard (**Figure 18**).

or

⑨ The Start Copying Files panel of the installation wizard will appear (**Figure 18**). This panel gives a summary of what types of files will be installed to what destination.

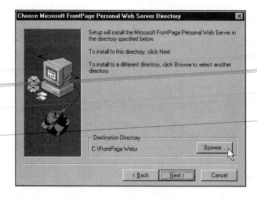

Figure 15. *If you would like the FrontPage Personal Web Server installed in another location, click Browse.*

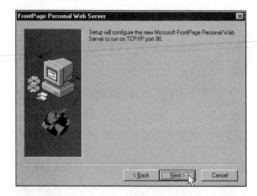

Figure 16. *This panel tells you what port the server will communicate on.*

Figure 17. *Select the servers you want to install extensions for.*

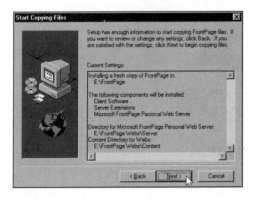

Figure 18. *The Start Copying Files panel tells you what files will be copied where.*

Figure 19. *The files you selected are installed onto your computer.*

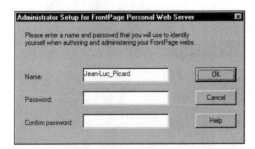

Figure 20. *Enter your name and a password in the Administrator Setup dialog box.*

20. Click Next. The setup program will install the items you selected (**Figure 19**). When it is almost finished the following *might* appear:

⑤ An Administrator Setup for FrontPage Personal Web Server dialog box might appear (**Figure 20**). Enter your name with no spaces (you can use an underscore to connect a first and last name) in the name text box, a password in the Password text box, and the password again in the Confirm password text box. The password is *case sensitive*. This means that FrontPage sees *Pasha* and *pasha* as two different passwords. When you are finished, click OK.

⑤ A dialog box asking if you want to restart the server to complete installation of the WWW Service of the Microsoft Personal Web Server. Click *Yes*.

⑤ A dialog box recommending that you restart Windows to finish the installation. Click *Yes*.

Install FrontPage 97

21. If you don't need to restart your computer, the Setup Complete panel of the installation wizard will appear (**Figure 21**).

22. If you want to launch FrontPage 97 right away, click Finish. Otherwise, remove the check mark from the Start the FrontPage Explorer now check box, then click Finish. *Congratulations!* The installation is complete.

Figure 21. *The Setup Complete panel appears when installation is finished.*

SETTING UP THE FRONTPAGE SERVER EXTENSIONS IS IMPORTANT

The FrontPage Server Extensions are programs that let a Web server and FrontPage Web site talk to each other through a port on your computer. The FrontPage Server Administrator tells the server what port to use. It's as if you wanted to telephone your best friend to talk to her, but didn't know the phone number.

If you don't tell the server what port to use and you try to create or open a FrontPage Web site on a server, the dialog box shown in **Figure 22** will appear.

Figure 22. *If you don't tell the Web server what port number to use, it won't know how to communicate with FrontPage.*

Figure 23. *Select Windows Explorer from the Programs fly-out.*

Figure 24. *Use the Windows Explorer to move to the folder where FrontPage was installed.*

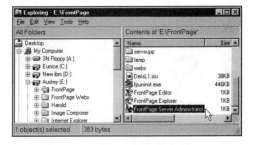

Figure 25. *Click the FrontPage folder icon in the left pane, then double-click on the FrontPage Server Administrator shortcut in the right pane.*

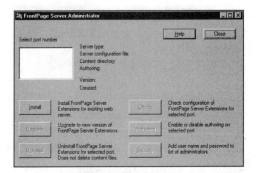

Figure 26. *The FrontPage Server Administrator is used to set up Web server port connections and password access.*

To work with the FrontPage Personal Web Server or the Microsoft Personal Web Server that you just installed, you will need to use the FrontPage Server Administrator to set up the FrontPage Server Extensions for your server.

To launch the FrontPage Server Administrator:

1. Launch Windows Explorer by selecting it from the Programs fly-out located on the Windows 95/NT Start button (**Figure 23**). The Windows Explorer window will open (**Figure 24**).

2. Use the left pane of Windows Explorer to move to the folder where FrontPage was installed. (By default this is C:\Program Files\Microsoft FrontPage.)

3. In the left pane, click the FrontPage folder icon. The contents of the FrontPage folder will appear in the right pane (**Figure 25**).

4. Locate the FrontPage Server Administrator shortcut and double-click on it. The FrontPage Server Administrator will launch with most of its buttons disabled (**Figure 26**).

Launch the Server Administrator

47

To install the server extension for FrontPage Personal Web Server:

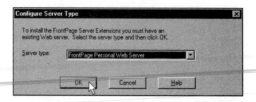

Figure 27. *Use the Server type drop-down list to select FrontPage Personal Web Server, then click OK.*

1. Launch the FrontPage Server Administrator, if you haven't already done so.

2. Click Install. The Configure Server Type dialog box will appear (**Figure 27**).

3. Select FrontPage Personal Web Server using the Server type drop-down list.

4. Click OK. The Server Configuration dialog box will appear (**Figure 28**).

Figure 28. *Click the Browse button in the Server Configuration dialog box.*

5. Click the Browse button. The Server Config dialog box will open (**Figure 29**). You will need to find a configuration file named httpd.cnf. This file is located by default in the C:\FrontPage Webs\Server\Conf folder. If you installed the FrontPage Personal Web Server to a different location, look there.

WHAT'S IN A NAME?

The default name given to a FrontPage Personal Web Server is "default."

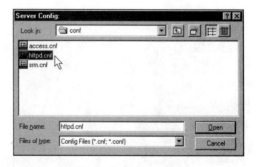

Figure 29. *Use the Server Config dialog box to find the httpd.cnf configuration file. The default location for this file is the C:\FrontPage Webs\Server\Conf folder.*

Install FrontPage Server Extensions

Figure 30. *When you click Open in the Server Config dialog box, the path for the configuration file will appear in the Server Config text box in the Server Configuration dialog box.*

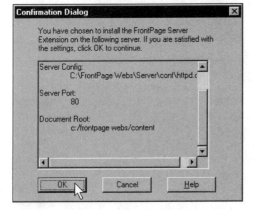

Figure 31. *The Confirmation Dialog tells you which FrontPage Server Extension will be installed.*

Figure 32. *Enter your name and a password in the Administrator Setup dialog box.*

6. When you have found the httpd.cnf file, select it, then click Open. The Server Config dialog box will close and the path for the configuration file will appear in the Server Config text box in the Server Configuration dialog box (**Figure 30**).

7. Click OK. The Confirmation Dialog will open (**Figure 31**), indicating what will be installed where, the server port number, and the document root folder where FrontPage Web sites will be stored.

8. Click OK. If the FrontPage installation program did not let you set up an administration name and password, the Administrator Setup for FrontPage Personal Web Server will appear (**Figure 32**). Enter your name and a password in the appropriate text boxes. Then enter the password again in the Confirm password text box. No spaces are allowed between a first and last name, so you might want to use an underscore to connect them, for example, Jean-Luc_Picard. In addition, the password is case sensitive, meaning that *Klingon* and *klingon* are two different passwords. Click OK.

9. The Server Administrator will install the server extensions and tell you when it is finished (**Figure 33**). The upper half of the FrontPage Server Administrator window will now show what port is being used, the server type, and other information (**Figure 34**).

Figure 33. *The Server Administrator tells you when it has finished the installation.*

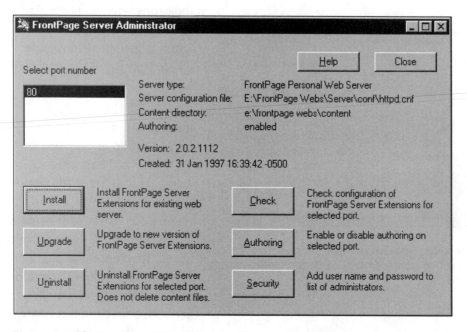

Figure 34. *The FrontPage Server Administrator now shows Web server information.*

I FORGOT MY PASSWORD!

If you forget the password you selected, don't panic! There's an easy way to set a new password. Launch the FrontPage Server Administrator and click the Security button (**Figure 34**). The Administrator name and password dialog box will open (**Figure 32**). Enter your name (with no spaces) and a new password. Then enter the password again in the Confirm password text box. Click OK. You're all set!

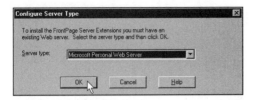

Figure 35. *Select Microsoft Personal Web Server from the Server type drop-down list, then click OK.*

Figure 36. *If the Microsoft Personal Web Server is not running, the Server Administrator will start it for you.*

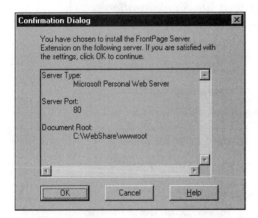

Figure 37. *The Confirmation Dialog tells you which FrontPage Server Extension is being installed.*

To install the server extension for Microsoft Personal Web Server:

1. Launch the FrontPage Server Administrator.

2. Click the Install button. The Configure Server Type dialog box will appear (**Figure 35**).

3. Select Microsoft Personal Web Server from the Server type drop-down list.

4. Click OK. One of two things will happen:

   - If the Microsoft Personal Web Server is not running, the Server Administrator dialog box will appear (**Figure 36**). Click OK to start the Microsoft Personal Web Server. Repeat steps 2 through 4.

   or

   - The Confirmation Dialog will appear (**Figure 37**).

Install FrontPage Server Extensions

5. Click OK. The server extension for the Microsoft Personal Web Server will be installed. Another Server Administrator dialog box will appear (**Figure 38**).

6. Click Yes to complete the installation.

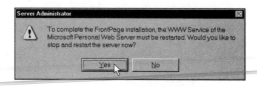

Figure 38. *Click Yes in the Server Administrator dialog box to complete the installation.*

Tip:

◎ FrontPage Server Extensions are available for many commercial Web servers. If you need to install the extension for a different server, just select that server from the Server type drop-down list.

WEB SITE ADMINISTRATION AND FRONTPAGE 97

There are many more administration features built into FrontPage, including *permissions*. To learn more about these features, check out Chapter 16, *Web Site Administration*.

SUMMARY

In this chapter you learned how to:

◎ Install FrontPage 97

◎ Install the FrontPage Personal Web Server

◎ Install the Microsoft Personal Web Server

◎ Change your password

◎ Setup the FrontPage Server Extensions for the FrontPage and Microsoft Personal Web Servers

---

Getting Started with Explorer

Designing a Web site may seem like a complex task at first, but FrontPage 97 makes it simple with FrontPage Explorer, FrontPage Editor, and the To Do List.

This chapter gets you started on the road to creating professional Web sites with FrontPage Explorer. Explorer is used to create a Web site and organize the different files that make up a Web site, as well as manage links, and perform operations across an entire site.

In this chapter you will launch FrontPage Explorer, create a new site, and open an existing one. After a brief discussion of the templates and wizards that come with FrontPage, you'll find out how to use the Explorer, and look at a Web site in both *Hyperlink* and *Folder* views. From there, you'll learn how to import and export a Web site, delete a Web site, and exit Explorer.

MICROSOFT LIKES TO GO EXPLORING

You may have already noticed that several "Explorers" are being used in this book: FrontPage 97 Explorer, Windows 95/NT Explorer, and Microsoft Internet Explorer. As explained above, FrontPage 97 Explorer is used to view a Web site's files. You use Windows 95/NT Explorer to view a computer's hard drives and files. Internet Explorer is a browser, used to view Web pages on the World Wide Web.

To keep confusion at bay, FrontPage 97 Explorer will just be called "Explorer," and the others "Windows Explorer" and "Internet Explorer."

To launch Explorer:

1. On the Windows 95/NT desktop, click the Start button on the Status Bar.

2. Move the mouse up to Programs to open that fly-out.

3. Click the Microsoft FrontPage icon near the bottom of the Programs fly-out (**Figure 1**).

To put a shortcut to Explorer on the Windows 95/NT desktop:

1. Right mouse click on the Start button and select Explore from the pop-up menu (**Figure 2**). This will open the Windows Explorer with the Start Menu folder near the bottom of the left pane (**Figure 3**).

2. Click the word "Programs." The folders and shortcuts available in this folder will display in the right Windows Explorer pane.

3. Position the mouse over the Microsoft FrontPage shortcut in the right pane. Press the right mouse button and drag the shortcut from Windows Explorer to the Windows 95/NT desktop.

4. Release the mouse button. A pop-up menu will appear on the desktop (**Figure 4**).

5. Click Create Shortcut(s) Here. The Microsoft FrontPage shortcut will appear on the desktop (**Figure 5**).

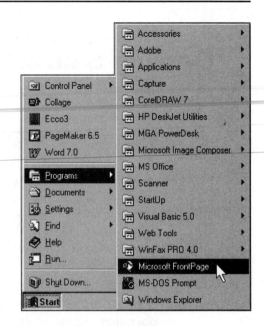

Figure 1. *Launching FrontPage 97.*

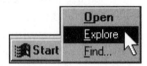

Figure 2. *Right click on the Start button, then choose Explore from the pop-up menu.*

Figure 3. *Click the word "Programs." Several folders and shortcuts will appear in the right pane.*

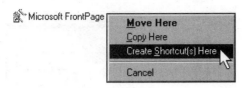

Figure 4. *Click Create Shortcut(s) Here on the pop-up menu.*

Figure 5. *The Microsoft FrontPage shortcut appears on the Windows desktop.*

When you launch FrontPage 97 for the first time, you will see the Getting Started with Microsoft FrontPage dialog box (**Figure 6**). This window displays five options from which to select:

- Open the last Web site you worked on
- Open an existing Web site
- Start a new Web site using a template or wizard
- Create a new Web site by importing files
- Create a new Web site containing one blank Web page

To choose one of these options, select the radio button next to the desired item, then click OK.

If you do not want to see this dialog box every time you launch FrontPage, remove the check from the check box next to Show Getting Started Dialog. If you uncheck the box, Explorer will open without loading a Web site (this is the same as clicking the Cancel button on the Getting Started with Microsoft FrontPage dialog box).

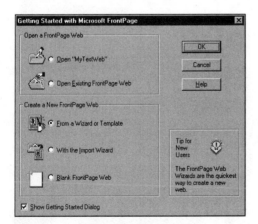

Figure 6. *The Getting Started with Microsoft FrontPage dialog box.*

The Getting Started Dialog Box

$\mathcal{T}$he easiest way to go about creating your own Web site is to use one of the templates or wizards that come with FrontPage 97.

To start a new Web site:

1. Launch FrontPage 97. The Getting Started with Microsoft FrontPage dialog box will appear (**Figure 6**).

2. In the Create a New FrontPage Web area, select the From a Wizard or Template radio button.

3. Click OK. The New FrontPage Web dialog box will open (**Figure 7**).

4. Select a wizard or template from the Template or Wizard list in the New FrontPage Web dialog box. (See the next page for a descrip-tion of the wizards and templates.)

Figure 7. *Use the New FrontPage Web dialog box to select a wizard or template.*

STARTING A NEW SITE IN EXPLORER

If you are already working on a Web site in Explorer or if you removed the Getting Started with Microsoft Front-Page dialog box as described on the previous page and you want to create a new site, choose FrontPage Web from the New fly-out on the File menu (**Figure 8**) or press Ctrl+N on the keyboard. The New FrontPage Web dialog box will appear (**Figure 7**).

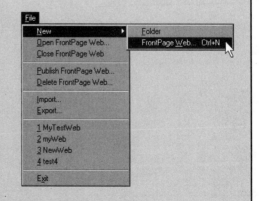

Figure 8. *Choose FrontPage Web from the New fly-out on the File menu.*

Figure 9. *This dialog box is used to set the location and name of the new Web site.*

5. Click OK. A dialog box named for the template or wizard you selected will appear (**Figure 9**). In the case of the Normal Web, this dialog box is titled Normal Web Template. This dialog box is used to set the location and name of the new Web site.

FRONTPAGE WEB SITE WIZARDS AND TEMPLATES

The New FrontPage Web dialog box offers several templates and wizards from which to choose. They are as follows:

- ◎ *Normal Web* This template creates a new Web site with one blank page.
- ◎ *Corporate Presence Wizard* This wizard gets you started with creating a business Web site.
- ◎ *Customer Support Web* This template quickly creates a business site for customer support.
- ◎ *Discussion Web Wizard* This wizard makes a Web site for discussions that includes a table of contents and text searching.
- ◎ *Empty Web* This template creates a new site with no Web pages.
- ◎ *Import Web Wizard* This wizard helps you import existing Web sites into Explorer.
- ◎ *Learning FrontPage* This template is for use with the FrontPage tutorial available in the *Getting Started with Microsoft FrontPage 97* manual.
- ◎ *Personal Web* This template gets you started on a personal Web site that you can fill with such information as who you are, what interests you, and what you do.
- ◎ *Project Web* This template creates a Web site that helps you manage projects, including scheduling, who is involved, and more.

You can use any of these templates and wizards to quickly create a professional Web site that suits your needs.

Web Site Wizards and Templates

6. In the Web Server or File Location drop-down list, select either the name of the Web server where the site will be located or type in a directory path, if you want to place the site on a hard drive (**Figure 10**). In Figure 10, the path that has been typed in is C:\MyWeb. If you enter a path name that does not exist, FrontPage will create it for you.

7. In the Name of New FrontPage Web text box, type a name for your Web site (**Figure 11**). The name can include characters and numbers, but no spaces. In Figure 11, the name for the new Web site is MyFirstWeb.

8. Click OK. FrontPage will create your new Web site, adding all the files you will need. The new Web site will appear in Explorer (**Figure 12**). If you selected a wizard, FrontPage will ask you various questions first, so it can customize your site before generating it.

Tips:

- You can also click the New FrontPage Web button on the Toolbar to start a new Web site.

- Depending on the speed of your computer, it may take a few minutes for FrontPage to create your Web site.

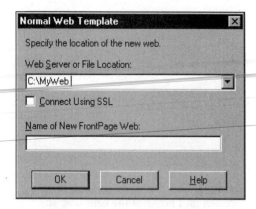

Figure 10. *In the Web Server or File Location drop-down list, type the path or the name of the server where you want to place the new Web site.*

Figure 11. *In the Name of New FrontPage Web text box, type a name for the site.*

Figure 12. *After you click OK, FrontPage creates the Web site.*

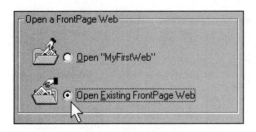

Figure 13. *Select the Open Existing FrontPage Web radio button, then click OK.*

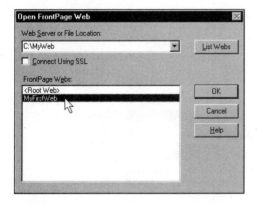

Figure 14. *Use the Open FrontPage Web dialog box to select the location of the Web site and the Web site itself.*

Figure 15. *Choose Open FrontPage Web from the File menu to open the Open FrontPage Web dialog box.*

To open an existing FrontPage Web site:

1. Launch FrontPage. The Getting Started with Microsoft FrontPage dialog box will open.

2. In the Open a FrontPage Web area, select the Open Existing FrontPage Web radio button (**Figure 13**).

3. Click OK. The Open FrontPage Web dialog box will appear (**Figure 14**).

4. Use the Web Server or File Location drop-down list to select the Web site's location or type the name of the Web server or directory path where the site is located.

5. Click the List Webs button. FrontPage will search the file location or Web server you specified and display a list of sites in the FrontPage Webs list box.

6. Select a Web site, then click OK. The site you selected will open in Explorer.

Tip:

◉ If you are already working in Explorer, click the Open FrontPage Web button on the toolbar or choose Open FrontPage Web from the File menu (**Figure 15**). The Open FrontPage Web dialog box will appear (**Figure 14**). Continue from step 4 above.

Open an Existing Web Site

Now that you've created a Web site and opened an existing one, it's time to see how the Explorer works. There are two ways to view a Web site in Front-Page Explorer—Hyperlink view and Folder view. The way you want to view your Web sites is up to you. Each view shows all files and links, but in different fashions.

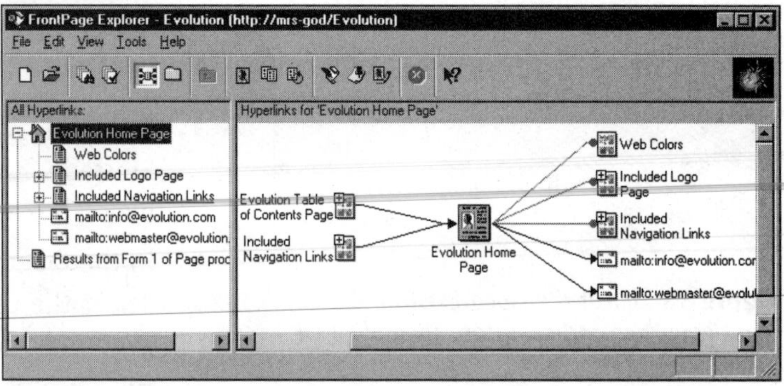

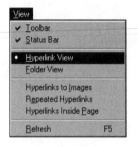

Figure 16. *A Web site displayed in Hyperlink view.*

Hyperlink view (**Figure 16**) displays a Web site graphically. The left pane shows an outline of all the files contained in the Web site and the right pane displays these files as icons, linked together with arrows.

Figure 17. *Choose Hyperlink View from the View menu.*

To show a Web site in Hyperlink view:

1. Open or create a Web site in Explorer.

2. Choose Hyperlink View from the View menu (**Figure 17**) or click the Hyperlink View button on the toolbar (**Figure 18**).

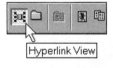

Figure 18. *Click the Hyperlink View button on the toolbar.*

HYPERLINK VIEW ICONS

Centered Page	 Page, Sound, or Video file	 Page with broken link	 Graphics file	 Link to another Web site	 E-mail link

---

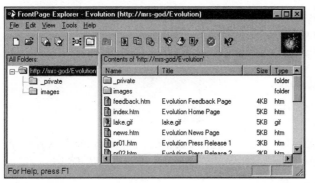

Folder view is very similar to Windows Explorer (**Figure 19**). The left pane shows the folder structure for the Web site. FrontPage automatically creates this folder structure when you use a wizard or template to create a Web site. The right pane displays the contents of the folder that is selected in the left pane. Just like the Details view in Windows Explorer, the right pane shows a file's or folder's name, size, type, and other information.

Figure 19. *A Web site displayed in Folder View.*

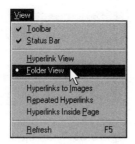

Figure 20. *Choose Folder View from the View menu.*

To display a Web site in Folder view:

1. Open or create a Web site in Explorer.

2. Choose Folder View from the View menu (**Figure 20**) or click the Folder View button on the toolbar (**Figure 21**).

Figure 21. *Click the Folder View button on the toolbar.*

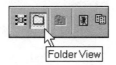

FOLDER VIEW ICONS

Closed folder

Open folder

Page file

Sound or video file

Graphics file

If you created Web sites before you started using FrontPage, you can turn them into FrontPage Web sites using the Import Web Wizard. You can also import older FrontPage Web sites, built with previous versions of FrontPage.

To import a Web site:

1. Launch FrontPage. The Getting Started with Microsoft FrontPage dialog box will open (**Figure 22**).

2. In the Create a New FrontPage Web area, select the With the Import Wizard radio button, then click OK. The Import Web Wizard dialog box will open (**Figure 23**).

3. In the Web Server or File Location drop-down list, type the name of the server or location for the new Web site, or select the server or file location from the drop-down list, if it's available.

4. Type a name for the Web site in the Name of New FrontPage Web text box.

5. Click OK. The Import Web Wizard – Choose Directory panel will appear (**Figure 24**).

6. Click the Browse button to locate the folder where the Web site you want to import currently resides. If there are subfolders under the folder you've selected that you want to import, put a check in the Include subdirectories check box.

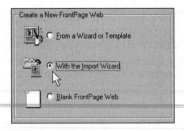

Figure 22. *Select the With the Import Wizard radio button, then click OK.*

Figure 23. *Enter the server or location and name for the new Web site, then click OK.*

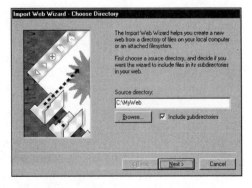

Figure 24. *On the Choose Directory panel, click the Browse button to locate the folder where the Web site resides.*

Import a Web Site

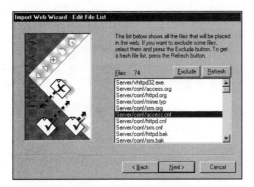

Figure 25. *Use the Edit File List panel to select files that will be imported.*

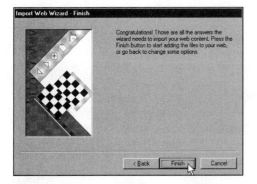

Figure 26. *Click Finish to import the files you selected.*

THERE'S ALWAYS A WAY OUT!

If you find yourself in a window you did not mean to use, don't panic! Remember that you can always press the Cancel button.

---

7. Click Next. The wizard will move to the next panel, Import Web Wizard – Edit File List (**Figure 25**). This panel contains a list of all the files contained in the folder (and subfolders) that you selected. It is used to select the specific file you want to import.

8. To exclude a file from being imported, select it with the mouse, then click the Exclude button. If you remove some files, but realize you don't want to exclude them, click Refresh. The original list will appear again.

9. When you have finished excluding files, click Next. The Import Web Wizard – Finish panel will appear (**Figure 26**).

10. Click Finish. The Web site will be imported.

Tips:

◉ If you want to change some information on a wizard panel after you've moved to another panel, just click Back to move to that panel.

◉ If you are already working in FrontPage and want to import a Web site, choose New from the File menu, then choose Import Web Wizard from the list of templates in the New FrontPage Web dialog box. Continue from step 3.

Import a Web Site

To import a file into a Web site:

1. Launch Explorer and open the site to which you want to add the file.

2. Change to Folder View.

3. Click the folder to which you want to add the file.

4. Choose Import from the File menu (**Figure 27**). The Import File to FrontPage Web dialog box will open (**Figure 28**).

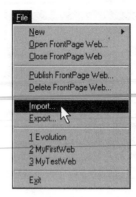

Figure 27. *Choose Import from the File menu.*

WHAT'S SSL?

In many of the dialog boxes shown in this chapter (for example, see Figures 9 and 23), there's a check box option "Connect Using SSL." SSL stands for Secure Socket Layer. SSL is a security protocol that encrypts the data passing between a client computer and a server computer. Most Web servers need to be specially configured to use SSL.

Generally, SSL should be used on Web sites that involve data transmission that requires protection, such as credit card numbers or private financial information.

Not all browsers support SSL. However, the current versions of Microsoft Internet Explorer and Netscape Navigator do.

If you need to work with an SSL server and

- You are using a corporate server, talk to your Webmaster or Web site administrator to see if your server has been configured for SSL.

- You will be posting your Web site to an Internet Service Provider (ISP) host equipped with the FrontPage Server Extensions, follow the instructions provided by the ISP to enable SSL.

- You are maintaining your own Web server connected directly to the Internet, follow the steps outlined in the server software documentation to enable SSL.

Import a File into a Web Site

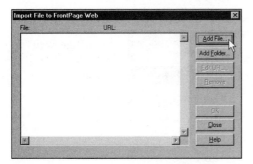

Figure 28. *The Import File to FrontPage Web dialog box.*

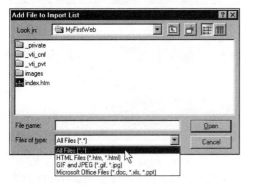

Figure 29. *Use the Add File to Import List dialog box to select files.*

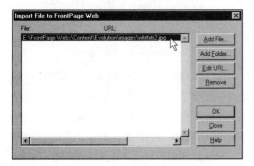

Figure 30. *Once you've selected the files you want to import, click OK.*

5. Click the Add File button. The Add File to Import List dialog box will appear (**Figure 29**).

6. Use the Files of type drop-down list near the bottom of the dialog box to select the type of file you want to import. If you don't know what kind of file it is, select All Files (*.*).

7. Move to the folder where the file is stored and select the file.

8. Click Open. The Add File to Import List dialog box will close and the file you selected will appear in the Import File to FrontPage Web dialog box (**Figure 30**).

9. If you want to add files from other folder locations, repeat steps 3 through 6.

10. Click OK. The file(s) will be added to your Web site.

Tips:

- When selecting a file in any given folder in the Add File to Import List dialog box, you can select more than one file at a time by pressing the Shift key when clicking the mouse.

- After you click OK in the Import File to FrontPage Web dialog box, the OK button changes to a Stop button. So if you need to, you can click Stop to halt the files being imported.

Import a File into a Web Site

To export a Web site:

1. Open the Web site you want to move in Explorer.

2. Choose Publish FrontPage Web from the File menu (**Figure 31**). The Publish FrontPage Web dialog box will open (**Figure 32**).

3. In the Destination Web Server or File Location drop-down list, select a server or directory path where you want to place the exported Web site, or type in the name of a server or directory path.

4. In the Name of Destination FrontPage Web text box, type a name for the exported Web site.

5. You can use the options area to:

   ◉ Copy changed pages only: If your Web site is already in the location you've specified, this option will update the site only with pages that have changed.

   ◉ Add to an existing FrontPage web: This lets you combine the copy you are creating with another Web site.

   ◉ Copy child webs (for Root Web only): This option is only available if you copy a root Web site. It lets you automatically copy all other sites that have links from that root Web site.

6. Click OK. FrontPage will copy the Web site, then let you know when the process is complete (**Figure 33**).

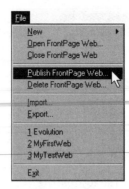

Figure 31. *Choose Publish FrontPage Web from the File menu.*

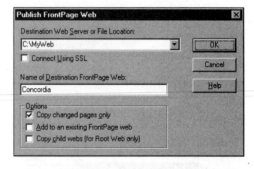

Figure 32. *Use the Publish FrontPage Web dialog box to select an export location and to name the exported Web site.*

WHY EXPORT A WEB SITE?

◉ To move your site to another Web server to go "live."

◉ To save a copy of a site for safe keeping as a back up.

FrontPage also refers to exporting as *publishing*. Take a look at Chapter 19 for details on publishing and testing a Web site.

Export a Web Site

Figure 33. *FrontPage tells you when it has finished exporting a Web site.*

Figure 34.
Choose Export from the File menu.

To export a file from a Web site:

1. Using Explorer, open the site that contains the file you want to export.

2. Select the file you want to export by clicking on it.

3. Choose Export from the File menu (**Figure 34**). The Export Selected As dialog box will open (**Figure 35**).

4. Move to the folder where you want to place the file.

5. If you want to rename the file, type a new name in the File name text box.

6. Click Save.

Tips:

- ⊚ You can export more than one file at a time. Just hold down the Shift key while clicking the mouse to select files that are next to each other or hold down the Ctrl key while clicking to select files that are not next to each other.

- ⊚ When you export a file, it is not actually removed from the Web site. Instead, a copy of the file is exported. To completely remove a file from a site, you have to delete it (see page 68).

Figure 35. *Use the Export Selected As dialog box to select the location where the exported files will reside.*

Export a File from a Web Site

To close a Web site:

Choose Close FrontPage Web from the File menu (**Figure 36**).

Tip:

◎ FrontPage can only display one Web site at a time, so if you create a new site or open an existing one, FrontPage will automatically close the current site.

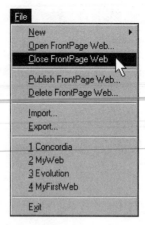

Figure 36. *Choose Close FrontPage Web from the File menu.*

To delete a Web site:

1. Open the site you want to delete in Explorer.

2. Choose Delete FrontPage Web from the File menu (**Figure 37**). A Confirm Delete dialog box will appear on the screen (**Figure 38**).

3. Click Yes to delete the Web site.

Tips:

◎ If you want to delete a Web site from a server, you must have administrative access. For more about user permissions and Web site administration, see Chapter 16.

◎ Once you've deleted a site using the steps above, *it's gone*. You won't find it in the Windows Recycle Bin, so look before you leap!

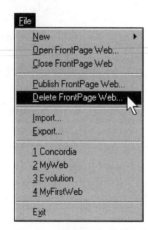

Figure 37. *Choose Delete FrontPage Web from the File menu.*

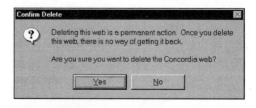

Figure 38. *The Confirm Delete dialog box lets you make sure you really want to delete the Web site.*

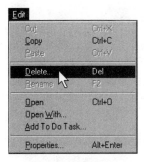

Figure 39. *Choose Delete from the Edit menu.*

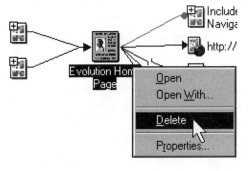

Figure 40. *Right mouse click on the file, then select Delete from the pop-up menu.*

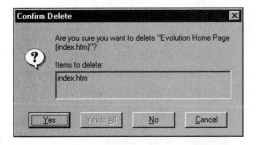

Figure 41. *The Confirm Delete dialog box lets you reconsider your course of action.*

To delete a file from a Web site:

1. Open the Web site in Explorer.

2. Using either view, select the file with the mouse.

3. Choose Delete from the Edit menu (**Figure 39**).

   or

   Press the Delete key on the keyboard.

   or

   Right mouse click on the file and select Delete from the pop-up menu (**Figure 40**).

4. Click Yes in the Confirm Delete dialog box that appears (**Figure 41**).

Tips:

◉ You can select several files to delete at one time by holding down the Shift key while clicking the mouse.

◉ When you delete a file from a Web site, it's gone forever. You won't find it in the Windows Recycle Bin.

Delete a File from a Web Site

To exit FrontPage 97 Explorer:

Choose Exit from the File menu (**Figure 42**).

or

Press Alt+F4 on the keyboard.

or

Click the Close button in the extreme upper-right corner of the screen (**Figure 43**).

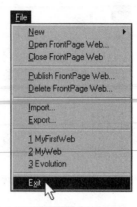

Figure 42. *Choose Exit from the File menu.*

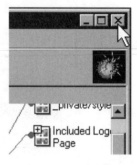

Figure 43. *Click the Close button at the upper-right corner of the screen.*

Exit FrontPage Explorer

SUMMARY

In this chapter you learned how to:

- Launch FrontPage 97
- Create a new Web site
- Open an existing Web site
- Show a Web site in Folder and Hyperlink views
- Import a Web site or file
- Export a site or file
- Close a Web site
- Delete a site or file
- Exit Explorer

Using FrontPage Editor

*C*hapter 4 showed you how to create Web sites with FrontPage 97 Explorer. Now it's time to take a look at those pages with FrontPage 97 Editor.

FrontPage Editor is used to open Web pages and add new pages to a site. It is also used to add to and edit the content of Web pages. The Editor is easy to use because it displays the page you are designing almost as it will appear on the Web. FrontPage Editor uses a WYSIWYG interface, meaning What You See Is What You Get. You won't have to switch back and forth between FrontPage and a browser to see what you've done.

In this chapter, you will open a FrontPage Web page in the Editor, then discover how to open other types of files, such as WordPerfect and Word documents, and pages on the Web itself. Next, you'll add a Web page to a site and save your work. Finally, you will discover how to create a custom Web page template and close the Editor.

FrontPage 97 Editor

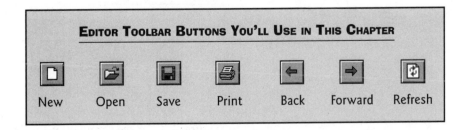

EDITOR TOOLBAR BUTTONS YOU'LL USE IN THIS CHAPTER

| New | Open | Save | Print | Back | Forward | Refresh |

Open a FrontPage Web Page

With FrontPage Explorer, you can open many types of files, including FrontPage Web pages, other document files, such as a Word document or Excel spreadsheet, and even Web site pages on an intranet or the World Wide Web.

To open a FrontPage Web page:

1. Launch FrontPage Explorer.

2. Create a new Web site or open an existing one.

3. Double-click on a Web page icon or right mouse click on a Web page icon and select Open from the pop-up menu (**Figure 1**). FrontPage Editor will launch and open the Web page that you clicked (**Figure 2**).

or

1. If you are already working in Editor, choose Open from the File menu (**Figure 3**), or press Ctrl+O on the keyboard, or click the Open button on the toolbar (**Figure 4**). The Open File dialog box will appear (**Figure 5**).

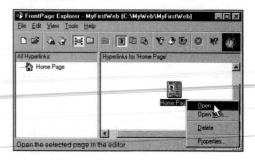

Figure 1. *Select Open from the pop-up menu.*

Figure 2. *The Web page open in FrontPage Editor.*

Figure 3. *Choose Open from the File menu.*

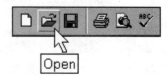

Figure 4. *Click the Open button on the Editor toolbar.*

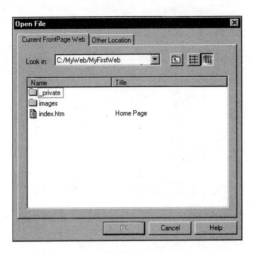

Figure 5. *The Open File dialog box.*

Figure 6. *Choose Show FrontPage Editor from the Tools menu.*

Figure 7. *Click the Show FrontPage Editor button on the Explorer toolbar.*

Back   Forward

Figure 8. *Use the Back and Forward buttons to move between pages.*

2. Use the Current FrontPage tab page to open a file in the Web site you are working in or use the Other Location tab page to open a file that's not part of the currently open Web site.

3. Click OK. The Web page you selected will open in the Editor.

Tips:

◉ You can also open the Editor from Explorer by choosing Show FrontPage Editor from the Tools menu (**Figure 6**) or clicking the ShowFrontPage Editor button on the toolbar (**Figure 7**). This will launch Editor without a Web page open. To open a Web page, use the second method above.

◉ You can open several Web pages in Editor at the same time. To quickly move between these pages, click the Forward and Back buttons on the toolbar (**Figure 8**) or select the page from the Window menu (**Figure 9**).

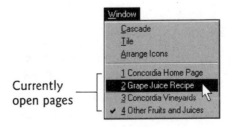

Currently open pages

Figure 9. *Use the Window menu to move from page to page.*

Open a FrontPage Web Page

To open another type of document:

1. In the Editor, choose Open from the File menu (**Figure 3**) or click the Open button on the toolbar (**Figure 4**). The Open File dialog box will appear (**Figure 5**).

2. Click the Other Location tab to move to that tab page (**Figure 10**).

3. Select the From File radio button.

4. Type in the path name of the file in the From File text box, then click OK.

   or

   Click the Browse button. The Open File dialog box will appear (**Figure 11**). Use this dialog box to locate the file. If you don't know the extension of your file, select All Files (*.*) from the Files of type drop-down list. When you find the file, select it, then click Open.

5. FrontPage will translate the file into HTML code and open it in the Editor (**Figure 12**). You can now work with it like any other FrontPage file.

Tip:

◉ You can open many types of files in the Editor, including Word and WordPerfect documents (.doc and .wpd), Excel worksheets (.xls and .xlw), and HTML files (.htm and .html) not created in FrontPage.

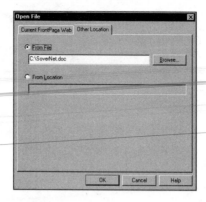

Figure 10. *Use the Other Location tab page to specify a file and location.*

Figure 11. *After clicking Browse, use the Open file dialog box to find the file.*

Figure 12. *FrontPage translates the document into HTML and loads it into the Editor.*

Figure 13. *Type the URL of the page you want to open.*

Figure 14. *A page on the Web opened in the Editor.*

To open a Web page that's on an intranet or the Web:

1. In the Editor, choose Open from the File menu (**Figure 3**) or click the Open button on the toolbar (**Figure 4**). The Open File dialog box will appear (**Figure 5**).

2. Click the Other Location tab to move to that tab page (**Figure 13**).

3. Select the From Location radio button.

4. Type the URL of the page you want to open in the From Location text box.

5. Click OK. The page will load into the Editor (**Figure 14**).

Tip:

- If you are trying to open a page on the Web and you get error messages (**Figures 15a–b**), check to see if your connection to the Web is still live. Then, make sure the connection is working by viewing the page you want to open with a browser.

Figure 15a. *This is the first error message you will see if you are not connected to the World Wide Web.*

Figure 15b. *The second error message tells you FrontPage cannot open the page.*

Open a Page from the Web

To add a new Web page to a site:

1. Open the Web site in Explorer, then move to the Editor by double-clicking on a page file or clicking the Show FrontPage Editor button on the toolbar.

2. In the Editor, choose New from the File menu (**Figure 16**), or press Ctrl+N on the keyboard, or click the New button on the toolbar (**Figure 17**). The New Page dialog box will appear (**Figure 18**). The Template or Wizard list box displays an extensive list of many types of Web pages (see the next page for a brief description of many of the templates and wizards).

3. Select a template or wizard from the list box.

4. Click OK. The new page will open in the Editor. If you selected a wizard, FrontPage will ask you various questions first, so it can customize your new page before creating it.

Tip:

⑨ When you add a new page to a site, it is not automatically saved with the site. To make sure you don't lose any work, save your changes frequently! See page 79 for details on saving a Web page.

Figure 16. *Choose New from the File menu.*

Figure 17. *Click the New button on the toolbar.*

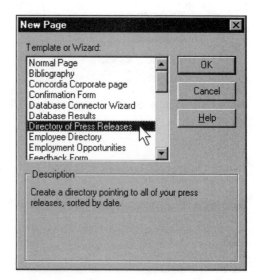

Figure 18. *The New Page dialog box offers many templates and wizards from which to choose.*

Add a New Page to a Web Site

FRONTPAGE WEB PAGE WIZARDS AND TEMPLATES

The New Page dialog box offers many templates and wizards from which to choose. These wizards and templates are used to create Web specific kinds of Web pages, based on your input. You'll probably understand what each wizard and template is supposed to do just by looking at its title. Here's a sampling of what's available:

- **Normal Page**   This template creates a blank page.
- **Bibliography**   If you need to create a bibliography page for your site, this template will get you started with some examples.
- **Confirmation Form**   If your Web site will be collecting data from users, this template will create a page that displays the information entered by the users.
- **Database Connector Wizard**   This wizard guides you through creating an Internet Database Connector (IDC) file, which contains query and database connection information.
- **Frequently Asked Questions**   Also known as a FAQ sheet or page, this template creates a page where users can get answers to questions.
- **Office Directory**   This template is used to create a complete directory of a company's employees and their locations.
- **Search Page**   If you want users of your site to be able to search for keywords throughout the entire site, this template is for you.
- **What's New**   This template gets you started on creating a page that lists changes to your site by date.

If you don't see a template or wizard on the list that fits your needs or if you will be creating several pages with the same look, you can create a custom template. For directions on how to do this, see page 80.

Web Page Wizards and Templates

To save your work:

In the Editor, choose Save from the File menu (**Figure 19**) or press Ctrl+S on the keyboard or click the Save button on the toolbar (**Figure 20**).

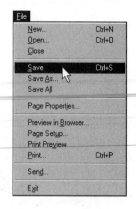

Figure 19.
Choose Save from the File menu.

Tips:

◉ If you have added a new page to your site, the Save As dialog box will open (**Figure 21**). This dialog box is used to give the page a title and set the location where it's saved. For a complete description of how to use this dialog box, see "To save a copy of a page" on the next page.

Figure 20. *Click the Save button on the toolbar.*

◉ If you have added a graphic or multimedia file to your site, special Save As dialog boxes will open. For a description of these dialog boxes, see Chapter 10.

Figure 21. *The Save As dialog box.*

To save changes to all open pages:

Choose Save All from the Edit menu (**Figure 22**).

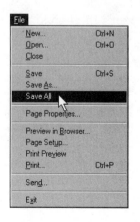

Figure 22.
Choose Save All from the Edit menu.

Figure 23.
Choose Save As from the File menu.

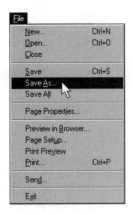

To save a copy of a page:

1. Open the page in the Editor.

2. Choose Save As from the File menu (**Figure 23**). The Save As dialog box will open (**Figure 24**).

3. Type a title for your new page in the Page Title text box.

4. In the File path within your FrontPage web text box, type a file name for your new page.

5. You can save the page in two ways:

   ◉ If you have a Web site open that is loaded on a server, the page will automatically be saved with that Web site. Click OK to save the Web page.

   ◉ If you want to save the Web page on a hard drive instead of a server, click the As File button. Use the Save As File dialog box that opens (**Figure 25**) to move to a location for the file, enter a name in the File name text box, then click Save.

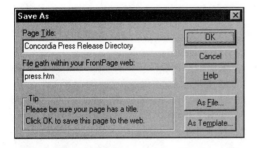

Figure 24. *The Save As dialog box is used to give a title and name to a new Web page.*

Tip:

◉ If you want to experiment with the design of a page, but aren't sure if you'll like the changes, save a copy of the page. This is a safe way to go since you'll always have a backup of the original page.

Figure 25. *The Save As File dialog box lets you save a Web page on a hard drive.*

Save a Copy of a Web Page

Part of the beauty of FrontPage is being able to quickly create Web pages. If you don't see a Web page template that contains what you need, you can create your own custom template. For instance, if you are part of a team designing a Web site and all of you need to create pages with the same background color, fonts, and company logos, then a template will minimize the work and help create a consistent look.

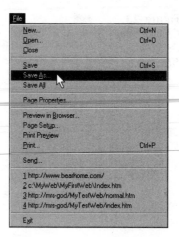

Figure 26. *Choose Save As from the File menu.*

To create a Web page template:

1. In the Editor, create a new Web page using the template that is closest to the template you want to create.

2. Customize the Web page with the content, such as logos, custom navigation buttons, disclaimer text, etc., that you want to appear when a Web page is created with your template.

3. Choose Save As from the File menu (**Figure 26**). The Save As dialog box will open (**Figure 27**).

4. Click the As Template button. The Save As Template dialog box will open (**Figure 28**).

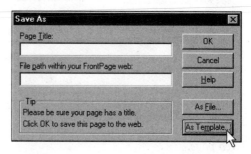

Figure 27. *Don't enter a title or path in the Save As dialog box, just click the As Template button.*

Figure 28. *Enter a title, name and description for your cutom template.*

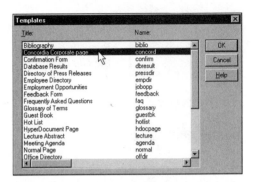

Figure 29. *Choose a template in the Templates dialog box that you want to replace.*

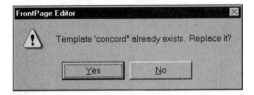

Figure 30. *Click Yes to replace an existing template.*

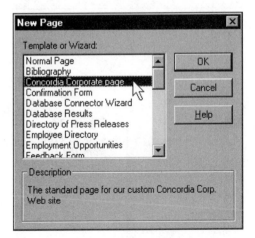

Figure 31. *The next time you create a new Page, your custom template will be available in the New Page dialog box.*

5. Type in a Title, Name, and Description for the custom template.

6. To save the template in place of another template, click the Browse button. The Templates dialog box will open (**Figure 29**).

7. Select the template you want to replace, then click OK to close the Templates dialog box.

8. Click OK. If you selected a template for replacement in the Templates dialog box, FrontPage will ask you if are sure about that change (**Figure 30**). Click Yes. FrontPage will save the Web page as a template. The next time you create a new Web page, you will see your custom template in the New Page dialog box (**Figure 31**).

Tip:

⑨ If none of the existing templates use the elements you need for your custom template, start with a Normal Page template. This will create a blank Web page that you can modify to suit your needs.

L ooking at a hard copy of a Web page can be helpful. Many times you will see things differently on a hard copy than you will on a computer monitor. Also, there are always folks who print Web pages for later reading. So, if you print copies of your Web pages, you can see what they will look like to others.

To see what a Web page will look like before you print it, use the Editor's Print Preview command.

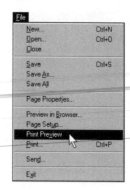

Figure 32.
Choose Print Preview from the File menu.

To view a Web page in Print Preview:

1. Open the page you want to preview in the Editor.

2. Choose Print Preview from the File menu (**Figure 32**). The Web page will appear in a Print Preview window (**Figure 33**).

3. To print the page from this window, click Print. To close the window and make adjustments to the Web page, click Close.

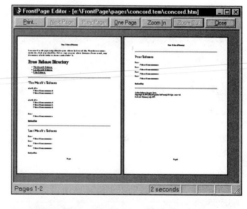

Figure 33. *A Web page displayed in the Print Preview window.*

Tip:

⊚ What you see in Print Preview is not what the user will see in a browser. Check out page 115 for information about viewing your Web pages in the browser(s) you have installed on your computer.

Figure 34.
Choose Print from the File menu.

Figure 35. *Click Print on the toolbar.*

To print a Web page:

1. Open the Web page you want to print in the Explorer.

2. Choose Print from the File menu (**Figure 34**), or press Ctrl+P on the keyboard, or click the Print button on the toolbar (**Figure 35**). The standard Windows 95/NT Print dialog box will open (**Figure 36**).

3. Click OK. The Web page will print.

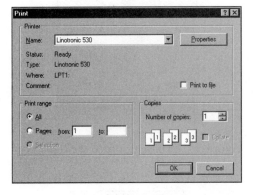

Figure 36. *The standard Windows Print dialog box lets you change settings for your printer. To print the Web page, click OK.*

Tips:

- ☺ If you need to change the settings for your printer (for instance, you want to print the page in a landscape orientation), click the Properties button in the Print dialog box.

- ☺ If your Web page is longer than the paper you are printing on, FrontPage Editor will split the Web page onto multiple printed pages.

Figure 37. *Click Refresh on the toolbar.*

Figure 38. *Choose Refresh from the View menu.*

REFRESHING YOUR PAGES

If you are working on a page and want to revert to the last saved version of that page, click the Refresh button on the toolbar (**Figure 37**) or choose Refresh from the View menu (**Figure 38**). Refreshing a page is also handy for displaying changes made to a page by another person.

Print a Web Page

To exit FrontPage Editor:

Choose Exit from the File menu (**Figure 39**).

or

Press Alt+F4 or Ctrl+F4 on the keyboard.

or

Click the Close button at the extreme upper-right corner of the Editor window (**Figure 40**).

Tip:

⑨ If you don't have any Web sites open in Explorer and you've made changes to a Web page that need to be saved, you will have to open the site in Explorer first, then save the page using the Editor.

Figure 39. *Choose Exit from the File menu.*

File	
New...	Ctrl+N
Open...	Ctrl+O
Close	
Save	Ctrl+S
Save As...	
Save All	
Page Properties...	
Preview in Browser...	
Page Setup...	
Print Preview	
Print...	Ctrl+P
Send...	
Exit	

Figure 40. *Click the Close button in the extreme upper-right corner of the Editor window.*

SUMMARY

In this chapter you learned how to:

⑨ Launch FrontPage Editor

⑨ Open a Web page

⑨ Open other documents

⑨ Create a new Web page

⑨ Save your work

⑨ Create a custom template

⑨ Print a Web page

⑨ Exit the Editor

Exit FrontPage Editor

Working with Text

Now that you know how to create Web sites with Explorer and Web pages with the Editor, it's time to start adding content to your Web pages.

If you are familiar with Microsoft Word, you have probably already noticed that FrontPage Editor resembles Word. In fact, it works in a very similar fashion and uses Word's twenty-five most popular keyboard shortcuts. FrontPage Editor works just like a word processing program using menus, toolbar buttons, and a work space, where you add content to and design your Web pages.

This chapter shows you how to add text, comments, and special characters to a Web page. Then, you'll find out how to select a portion of text and select everything on a page. Next you'll discover how to delete, move, and copy text, find and replace words, and check the spelling on a Web page. Finally, you will move back to the FrontPage Explorer and learn how easy it is to find and replace words and spell check an entire Web site.

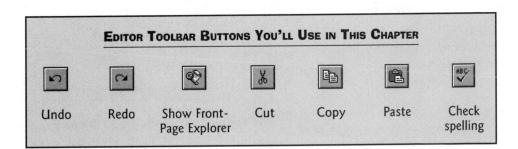

EDITOR TOOLBAR BUTTONS YOU'LL USE IN THIS CHAPTER

Undo	Redo	Show Front-Page Explorer	Cut	Copy	Paste	Check spelling

To enter text on a Web page:

1. Click on the place where you want the text to start (**Figure 1**). A vertical, blinking line will appear where you clicked. This is called the *insertion marker*.

2. Type your text. As you type, corresponding characters will appear on the screen (**Figure 2**).

Tip:

⑨ Since the Editor works like a word processor, the text will automatically wrap when you reach the end of a line.

There are two ways to add breaks between lines of text. Creating a new paragraph adds a blank line between paragraphs. A *line break* starts a new line without adding any blank lines in between.

To start a new paragraph:

1. Move the insertion marker to the place where you want to end a paragraph.

2. Press the Enter key on the keyboard. The insertion marker will move down two lines (**Figure 3**).

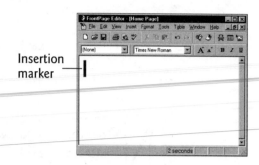

Insertion marker

Figure 1. *Click where you want the text to start.*

Figure 2. *As you type, the characters appear in the Editor.*

Figure 3. *When you press the Enter key, the insertion marker moves down two lines.*

Figure 4. *Choose Break from the Insert menu.*

Break Properties

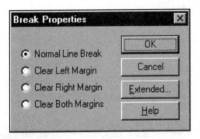

Figure 5. *Select the Normal Line Break radio button, then click OK.*

To add a line break:

1. Move the insertion marker to the place where you want to add the line break.

2. Choose Break from the Insert menu (**Figure 4**). The Break Properties dialog box will open (**Figure 5**).

3. Select the Normal Line Break radio button.

4. Click OK. A left pointing arrow will appear at the end of the line to mark the line break and the insertion marker will move down one line. As you type more text, you will see that there's no extra space between the lines (**Figure 6**).

Tip:

☺ You can also press Shift+Enter on the keyboard to insert a line break.

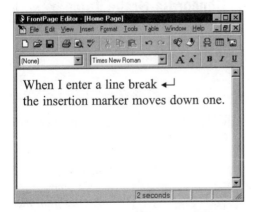

Figure 6. *A line break moves the insertion marker to the next line down.*

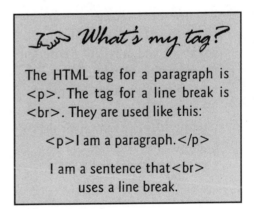

What's my tag?

The HTML tag for a paragraph is <p>. The tag for a line break is <br>. They are used like this:

<p>I am a paragraph.</p>

I am a sentence that
 uses a line break.

Add a Line Break

Comments are the electronic version of "sticky notes." You can add comments to your Web pages using the Editor as a reminder to yourself or for someone else working on the Web page. You will be able to see them in the Editor window, but they will be invisible to folks browsing your pages on the Web.

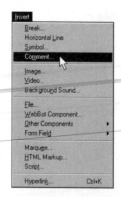

Figure 7. *Choose Comment from the Insert menu.*

To add a comment:

1. Move the insertion marker to the place where you want to add a comment.

2. Choose Comment from the Insert menu (**Figure 7**). The Comment dialog box will appear (**Figure 8**).

3. Type your comment in the large text box.

4. Click OK. Your comment will be added to the Web page (**Figure 9**).

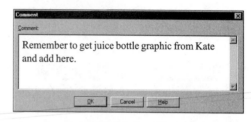

Figure 8. *Enter your comment in the dialog box, then click OK.*

Tip:

⑨ If you want to change a comment's text, select the comment and press Alt+Enter on the keyboard or right click on the comment and select Comment Properties from the pop-up menu (**Figure 10**). The Comment dialog box will open. Change the comment, then click OK.

Figure 9. *The comment will appear on the Editor Web page.*

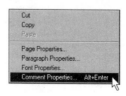

Figure 10. *Select Comment Properties from the pop-up menu.*

Figure 11. *Choose Symbol from the Insert menu.*

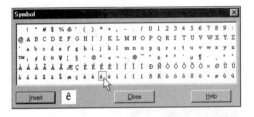

Figure 12. *Select the character you want to add, then click Insert.*

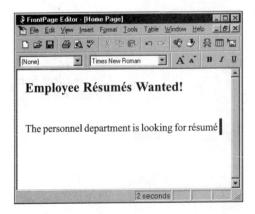

Figure 13. *When you click Insert, the symbol is added to your Web page.*

M any Web sites contain foreign words and measurements that use *special characters*. Special characters are those symbols, such as ©, é, and ¼, that do not appear on a standard keyboard.

To insert a special character:

1. Move the insertion marker to the place where you want to insert a special character.

2. Choose Symbol from the Insert menu (**Figure 11**). The Symbol dialog box will open (**Figure 12**).

3. In the list box, click the symbol you want to insert. It will appear in the small window to the right of the Insert button.

4. Click Insert. The character will be added to your Web page (**Figure 13**). If you want to add another symbol, repeat steps 2 through 4.

5. Click Close. The dialog box will close and you can continue working on your Web page.

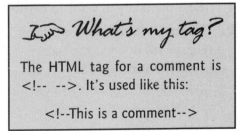

What's my tag?

The HTML tag for a comment is <!-- -->. It's used like this:

<!--This is a comment-->

To select text:

1. Position the insertion marker to the left of the text you want to select.

2. Press the left mouse button and drag. The text will become highlighted as it is selected (**Figure 14**).

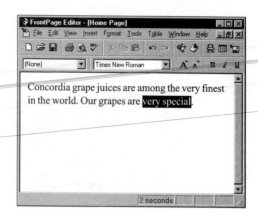

Figure 14. *Select text by dragging the mouse.*

Tips:

- ◉ To quickly select a word, double-click on it.

- ◉ To select an entire paragraph, hold down the Alt key, then click once.

To deselect text:

Move the mouse outside the selected text area and click.

To select everything on a page:

Choose Select All from the Edit Menu (**Figure 15**) or press Ctrl+A on the keyboard.

Figure 15. *Choose Select All from the Edit menu.*

To delete text:

1. Select the text you want to delete.

2. Choose Clear from the Edit menu (**Figure 16**) or press the Delete key or the Backspace key on the keyboard.

Figure 16. *Choose Clear from the Edit menu.*

Figure 17.
Choose Undo from the Edit menu.

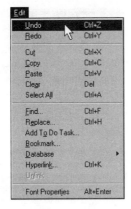

Figure 18.
Click the Undo button on the toolbar.

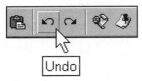

Figure 19.
Choose Redo from the Edit menu.

Figure 20.
Click the Redo button on the toolbar.

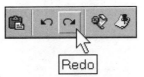

*U*ndo is a favorite command of many users. If you happen to delete or move something you don't mean to, don't panic! You can always undo.

To undo an action:

Choose Undo from the Edit menu **(Figure 17)** or press Ctrl+Z on the keyboard or click the Undo button on the toolbar **(Figure 18)**.

Tip:

◉ In FrontPage Editor, you can undo up to the last 30 actions!

To redo an action:

Choose Redo from the Edit menu **(Figure 19)** or press Ctrl+Y on the keyboard or click the Redo button on the toolbar **(Figure 20)**.

Tip:

◉ You can redo up to the last 30 Undo commands.

Undo an Action; Redo an Action

To move text:

1. Select the text you want to move (**Figure 21**).

2. Position the mouse pointer over the selected text.

3. Press the left mouse button and drag the mouse to the new location. As you drag, the pointer will change to an arrow with a gray rectangle attached to it and the insertion marker will change to a gray line.

4. Release the mouse button. The selected text will spring to its new location (**Figure 22**).

or

1. Select the text you want to move.

2. Choose Cut from the Edit menu (**Figure 23**) or press Ctrl+X on the keyboard or click the Cut button on the toolbar (**Figure 24**).

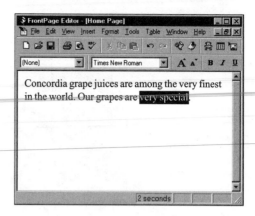

Figure 21. *Select the text you want to move.*

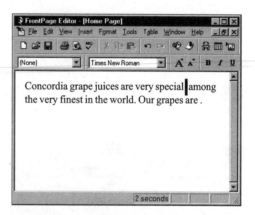

Figure 22. *When you release the mouse, the text moves to its new position.*

Figure 23. *Choose Cut from the Edit menu.*

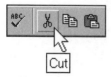

Figure 24. *Click the Cut button on the toolbar.*

Move Text

Figure 25.
Choose Paste from the Edit menu.

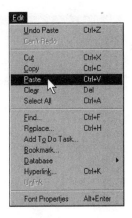

3. Position the insertion marker at the place where you want to move the text.

4. Choose Paste from the Edit menu (**Figure 25**) or press Ctrl+V on the keyboard or press the Paste button on the toolbar (**Figure 26**).

Tip:

- You can also right click on the selected text and choose Cut from the pop-up menu (**Figure 27**), then move the insertion point to where you want to place the text, right click, and choose Paste from the pop-up menu.

Figure 26. *Click the Paste button on the toolbar.*

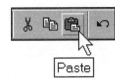

Figure 27. *Choose Cut from the pop-up menu.*

HIDING FORMAT MARKS

When you add a line break, a special line break format mark, ↵, is added at the end of the line. If you don't want to see this mark, just click the Show/Hide Paragraph button on the toolbar. To show the mark again, just click the button.

Move Text

To copy text:

1. Select the text you want to copy (**Figure 28**).

2. Position the mouse pointer over the selected text.

3. Press the Ctrl key and the left mouse button. The mouse pointer will change to an arrow with a little plus sign attached to it.

4. Move the mouse to the new location for the copied text (**Figure 29**).

5. Release the mouse button and *then* the Ctrl key. (If you release the Ctrl key *before* the mouse button, the text will be moved instead of copied.) The copied text will appear in the new location.

or

1. Select the text you want to copy.

2. Click the Copy button on the toolbar (**Figure 30**) or press Ctrl+C on the keyboard or choose Copy from the Edit menu (**Figure 31**).

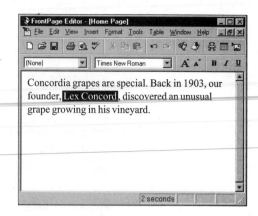

Figure 28. *Select the text you want to copy.*

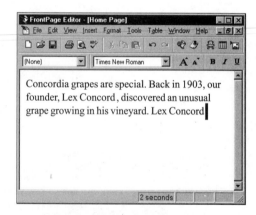

Figure 29. *When you release first the mouse button and then the Ctrl key, the copied text is added to the new position.*

Figure 30. *Click the Copy button on the toolbar.*

Figure 31.
Choose Copy from the Edit menu.

3. Position the insertion marker where you want to place the text.

4. Choose Paste from the Edit menu (**Figure 25**) or press Ctrl+V on the keyboard or click the Paste button on the toolbar (**Figure 32**). The copied text will appear in the new location.

Tip:

ⓨ You can also right click on the selected text and choose Copy from the pop-up menu (**Figure 33**), then move the insertion point to where you want to place the text, right click, and choose Paste from the pop-up menu.

Figure 32.
Click the Paste button on the toolbar.

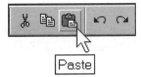

Figure 33.
Choose Copy from the pop-up menu.

THE WINDOWS CLIPBOARD

When you copy or cut text, it is held in the Windows Clipboard. The text will remain in the Clipboard until you cut or copy other text.

You can cut or paste text between two FrontPage Web pages by opening both pages in the Editor and toggling between them—cutting or copying text from one page and pasting it to another.

In addition, you can copy or cut text from other types of documents, such as a Word or WordPerfect document, then paste it into a FrontPage Web page.

Copy and Paste Text

FrontPage 97 makes it easy to find and/or replace any kind of text on your Web page.

To find text on a Web page:

1. In the Editor, choose Find from the Edit menu (**Figure 34**) or press Ctrl+F on the keyboard. The Find dialog box will open (**Figure 35**).

2. In the Find what text box type in the text you want to search for.

3. Using the radio buttons, select a direction for your search, up or down through the text.

4. Click Find Next. When FrontPage finds an instance of the text, it will highlight it (**Figure 36**). To find the next occurrence of the word, click Find Next again.

5. When you have finished searching the text, click Cancel or the Close button to close the dialog box.

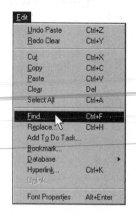

Figure 34. *Choose Find from the Edit menu.*

Figure 35. *Type the text you want to find in the Find what text box, then click Find Next.*

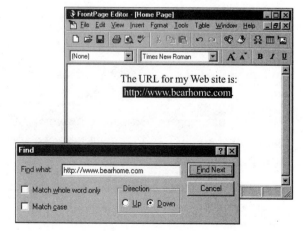

Figure 36. *When FrontPage finds a match, it highlights the text. To find the next match, click Find Next.*

Figure 37.
Choose Replace from the Edit menu.

To replace text on a Web page:

1. In the Editor, choose Replace from the Edit menu (**Figure 37**) or press Ctrl+H on the keyboard. The Replace dialog box will appear (**Figure 38**).

2. In the Find what text box, type the text you want to replace.

3. In the Replace with text box, type in the text with which you want to replace the found text.

4. To replace all occurrences of the text on a page, click Replace All, or to locate the first matching occurrence, click Find Next. When the Editor finds the text, it will highlight it (**Figure 39**). You can then click Replace to change the text or click Find Next to move on to the next instance.

5. When you have finished replacing text, click Cancel or the Close button to close the dialog box.

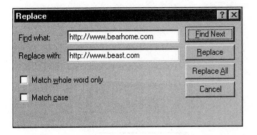

Figure 38. *Enter the text you want to replace in the Find what text box. Next, enter the replacement text in the Replace with text box.*

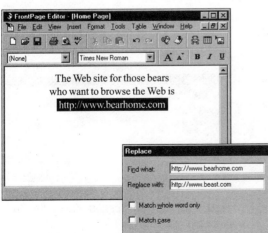

Figure 39. *When FrontPage finds a match, it highlights the text. To replace the text, click Replace. To move on to the next match, click Find Next.*

Replace Text on a Web Page

Spelling is very important. How many times have you browsed a Web site and seen spelling errors? To avoid typos, let the Editor check your Web pages.

To spell check a Web page:

1. Open the page you want to check in the Editor.

2. Choose Spelling from the Tools menu (**Figure 40**), or press F7 on the keyboard, or click the Check Spelling button on the toolbar (**Figure 41**). The Spelling dialog box will open (**Figure 42**) and FrontPage will start spell checking.

3. If FrontPage finds a misspelling, the word will appear in the Not in Dictionary list box and offer a suggestion in the Change To text box. You can click:

   - Ignore: to ignore the current word

   - Ignore All: to ignore all instances of the word on the Web page

   - Change: to change the current word

   - Change All: to change all instances of the word on the Web page

   - Add: to add the word to the dictionary

   - Suggest: for a list of suggested words

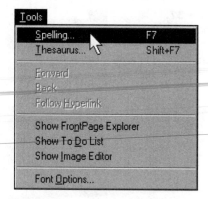

Figure 40. *Choose Spelling from the Tools menu.*

Figure 41. *Click the Check Spelling button on the toolbar.*

Figure 42. *Use the Spelling dialog box to change misspellings or add specialized words to the FrontPage dictionary.*

Spell Check a Web Page

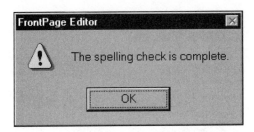

Figure 43. *When FrontPage is finished checking a Web page, it will tell you so.*

Figure 44. *Choose Show FrontPage Explorer from the Tools menu.*

Figure 45. *Click the Show FrontPage Explorer button on the toolbar.*

4. When FrontPage is finished spell checking the page, it will tell you so (**Figure 43**). If you want to stop spell checking before it is finished, click Cancel.

Tip:

🌀 If you want to spell check a few words or a paragraph, select the text, then choose Spelling from the Tools menu.

To move from Editor back to Explorer:

Choose Show FrontPage Explorer from the Tools menu (**Figure 44**) or click the Show FrontPage Explorer button on the toolbar (**Figure 45**).

Tip:

🌀 If you minimized FrontPage Explorer when you opened the Editor, you can restore the Explorer by clicking the FrontPage Explorer button on the Windows 95/NT status bar.

Spell Check a Page; Move to Explorer

Quickly finding and replacing text and spell checking throughout an entire Web site uses very similar dialog boxes as finding and replacing text on a Web page. The only difference is that Explorer performs the tasks over a Web site, whereas the Editor performs the tasks on a single Web page.

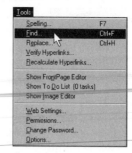

Figure 46.
Choose Find from the Explorer's Tools menu.

To find text throughout an entire Web site:

1. Open the Web site you want to search in Explorer.

2. Choose Find from the Tools menu (**Figure 46**) or press Ctrl+F on the keyboard or click the Cross File Find button on the toolbar (**Figure 47**). The Find in Front-Page Web dialog box will appear (**Figure 48**).

3. In the Find what text box, type the text you want to find.

4. In the Find in area, select either the All pages radio button or the Selected pages radio button. If you choose Selected pages, the finder will only search the pages that are selected in Explorer.

5. Click OK. FrontPage will perform the search. When it has finished, a Find occurrences dialog box will appear (**Figure 49**). If instances of the text have been found, you will see how many times on how many pages at the bottom left of

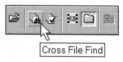

Figure 47. *Click the Cross File Find button on the Explorer's toolbar.*

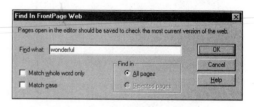

Figure 48. *Type the text you want to find in the Find what text box, then click OK.*

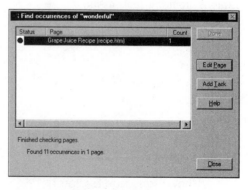

Figure 49. *When FrontPage has found the text, the Find occurrences dialog box lists how many occurrences and on what pages.*

Find Text Throughout a Web Site

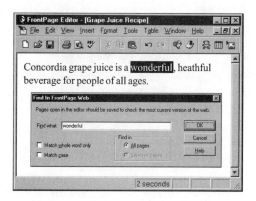

Figure 50. *When FrontPage finds a match, it highlights the text.*

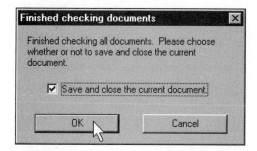

Figure 51. *Click Next Document to continue finding text.*

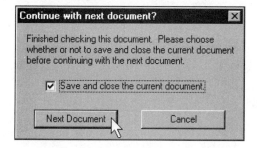

Figure 52. *Click OK to save the changes made to the current Web page and close it.*

the Find occurrences dialog box. The pages where the text was found will be shown in the list box.

6. To edit the Web pages in the Editor, click Edit Page. The first page listed in the Find occurrences dialog box will open in the Editor. In addition, the Find dialog box will open and the first matched text highlighted (**Figure 50**). Edit the page as you choose.

7. Click Find Next to move to the next match (**Figure 35**).

8. If more than one page was listed in the Find occurrences dialog box and FrontPage has finished searching the first page in the Editor, the Continue with next document dialog box will open (**Figure 51**). Click Next Document to continue finding text on the next page or click Cancel to return to the Find occurrences dialog box.

9. When FrontPage has finished finding word matches on all the Web pages listed in the Find occurrences dialog box, the Finished checking documents dialog box will open (**Figure 52**).

10. Click OK to save and close the current page, then close the Editor to return to the Find occurrences dialog box and the Explorer.

Find Text Throughout a Web Site

To replace text throughout an entire Web site:

1. Open the Web site in Explorer.

2. Choose Replace from the Tools menu (**Figure 53**) or press Ctrl+H on the keyboard. The Replace In FrontPage Web dialog box will open (**Figure 54**).

3. Type the text you want to replace in the Find what text box.

4. In the Replace with text box, enter the text with which you want to replace the found text.

5. Select either the All pages radio button or the Selected pages radio button in the Find in area. If you choose Selected pages, only those pages selected in Explorer will be searched.

6. Click OK. FrontPage will perform the search for the text and the Find occurrences dialog box will open (**Figure 55**). If instances of the text have been found, you will see how many occurrences on how many pages at the bottom left of the Find occurrences dialog box. The pages where the text was found will be shown in the list box.

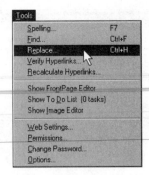

Figure 53. *Choose Replace from the Explorer's Tools menu.*

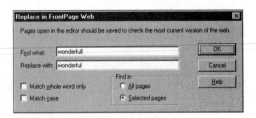

Figure 54. *After entering text in the Find what and Replace with text boxes, click OK.*

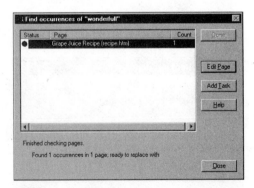

Figure 55. *When FrontPage has found the text, the Find occurrences dialog box lists how many occurrences and on what pages.*

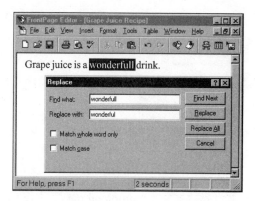

Figure 56. *When FrontPage finds a match, it highlights the text.*

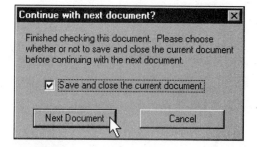

Figure 57. *Click Next Document to continue replacing text.*

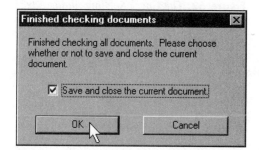

Figure 58. *Click OK to save the changes made to the current Web page and close it.*

7. To edit the Web pages in the Editor, click Edit Page. The first page listed in the Find occurrences dialog box will open in the Editor. In addition, the Replace dialog box will open and the first matched text highlighted (**Figure 56**). Edit the page as you choose.

8. Click Find Next to move to the next match.

9. If more than one page was listed in the Find occurrences dialog box and FrontPage has finished searching the first page in the Editor, the Continue with next document dialog box will open (**Figure 57**). Click Next Document to continue replacing words on the next page or click Cancel to return to the Find occurrences dialog box.

10. When FrontPage has finished finding word matches on all the Web pages listed in the Find occurrences dialog box, the Finished checking documents dialog box will open (**Figure 58**).

11. Click OK to save and close the current page, then close the Editor to return to the Find occurrences dialog box and the Explorer.

Replace Text Throughout a Web Site

To spell check an entire Web site:

1. Open the Web site in Explorer.

2. Choose Spelling from the Tools menu (**Figure 59**), or press F7 on the keyboard, or click the Cross File Spelling button on the toolbar (**Figure 60**). The Spelling dialog box will open (**Figure 61**).

3. In the Check spelling of area, select whether you want to spell check the entire Web site or just pages you have selected in Explorer.

4. Click Start. FrontPage will start the check and open a Check Spelling dialog box (**Figure 62**). You can use this dialog box to select a specific page and edit it by clicking Edit Page, or save the task for later and put it on the To Do List by clicking Add Task (to find out more about the To Do List, take a look at Chapter 13).

5. When you are finished editing pages, click Close to return to Explorer.

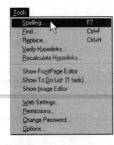

Figure 59. *Choose Spelling from the Explorer's Tools menu.*

Figure 60. *Click the Cross File Spelling button on the Explorer's toolbar.*

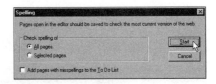

Figure 61. *Select the pages you want to search, then click Start.*

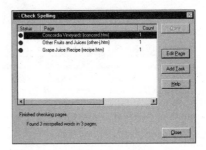

Figure 62. *The Check Spelling dialog box tells you where the mistakes are.*

SUMMARY

In this chapter you learned how to:

- Add text, line breaks, and comments
- Select and delete text
- Move and copy text
- Spell check a Web page and an entire site

Fun with Text

A large part of the content of many Web pages is text. Text doesn't have to be boring! Now that you know how to add text in the Front-Page Editor, it's time to jazz it up using styles, different fonts, and colors.

The size of text on Web pages is measured in increments from 1 to 7. These sizes move from smallest to largest. Size 1 is text that is a bit less than 1/8" high. Size 7 is text that is 1/2" high.

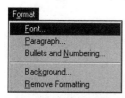

Figure 1.
Choose Font from the Format menu.

To change text size:

1. Select the text you want to change.

2. Choose Font from the Format menu (**Figure 1**). The Font dialog box will open (**Figure 2**). Use the Size list box to select a new size, then click OK.

or

Click the Increase Text Size button or Decrease Text Size button on the Format toolbar (**Figure 3**).

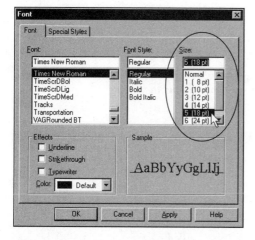

Figure 2. *Use the Size list box in the Font dialog box to select a new font size.*

Increase   Decrease
Text Size   Text Size

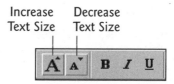

Figure 3. *Click the Decrease Text Size or Increase Text Size buttons.*

Change Text Formatting

You can easily add more emphasis to text by changing its formatting and making it bold and/or italic, or adding an underline.

Bold Italic Underline

Figure 4. *Click the Bold, Italic, or Underline buttons on the Format toolbar.*

To change text formatting:

1. Select the text you want to change.

2. Click the Bold, Italic, or Underline buttons on the Format toolbar (**Figure 4**).

    or

    Choose Font from the Format menu (**Figure 1**). The Font dialog box will open (**Figure 5**). Use the Font Style list box to select Bold, Italic, or Bold Italic, or use the Effects area to put a check mark next to Underline, Strikethrough, or Typewriter. Click OK.

    The selected text will be reformatted (**Figure 6**).

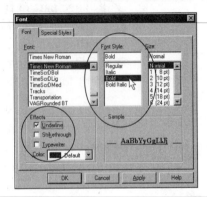

Figure 5. *Use the Font Style list box and the Effects area to select the formatting you want to use.*

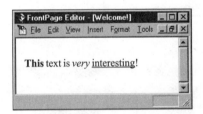

Figure 6. *When you format text, the Editor window shows the effects.*

Tips:

- You can select more than one formatting option at a time. For instance, you could make some selected text bold and italic and underlined.

- When formatting text, don't use too many styles and effects at the same time because the text can become hard to read.

- The Typewriter effect makes the selected text one size smaller.

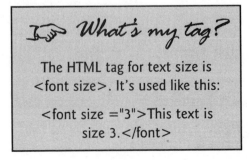

☞ *What's my tag?*

The HTML tag for text size is <font size>. It's used like this:

<font size ="3">This text is size 3.</font>

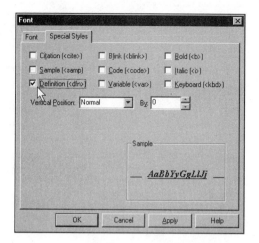

Figure 7. *Use the Special Styles tab of the Font dialog box to pick special effects such as blinking text.*

In addition to standard text formatting, such as bold or italic, there are *special styles*. These styles include Citation, an italic that can be used for the name of a book, Keyboard, a typewriter-like font that can be used to indicate text the user should type, and Blink, which makes text blink. Not all browsers support these special styles. For instance, blinking text is only supported by Netscape Navigator.

To use a special style:

1. Select the text you want to change.

2. Choose Font from the Format menu (**Figure 1**). The Font dialog box will appear (**Figure 5**).

3. Click the Special Styles tab to bring that tab page forward (**Figure 7**).

4. Select the style you want to use by clicking the appropriate text box.

5. Click OK. The text you selected will change to that style in the Editor.

Tips:

- Blinking text is a novelty and draws attention to something, but it can quickly become annoying. Use blinking text *sparingly*.

- The HTML tag for each special style is listed next to the style on the Special Styles tab in the Font dialog box.

☞ *What's my tag?*

There are two HTML tags for bold, <b> and <strong>.
They are used like this:

<b>Bold text</b> is very <strong>distinct</strong>.

There are two tags for italic, <i> and <em>.
They are used like this:

I <i>am</i> very <em>emphasized</em>!

The tag for underline is <u>.
It's used like this:

<u>Please</u> be careful!

Use Special Styles

*B*ack in the old days of the Web (not *that* long ago!), the only typefaces or *fonts* that most browsers would display were Times and Courier.

These days, you can use any font that you have to design your Web pages. *However*, if you use a special font, the folks browsing your Web page must also have that font loaded on their computer. Otherwise, the text will appear in their browser's default font, most likely Times.

For instance, if you created a Web page using the Snap ITC font, it would look something like **Figure 8** on your computer. But, when folks browse your Web site using computers that do not have the Snap ITC font installed on them, your page would look something like **Figure 9**.

With that in mind, use special fonts carefully. Don't hesitate to use them for special emphasis, but design your pages so they will look good with either the special font or a default font such as Times.

Figure 8. *A Web page shown in FrontPage Editor that uses the Snap ITC font.*

Figure 9. *The same Web page viewed in a browser on a computer that does not have the Snap ITC font installed on it.*

DEFAULT FONTS AND BROWSERS

Some browsers let users set their own default fonts. For instance, default fonts can be set in Netscape Navigator by selecting General Preferences from the Options menu, then using the Font tab page in the Preferences dialog box that opens.

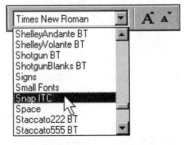

Figure 10. *Use the Change Font drop-down list to select a new font.*

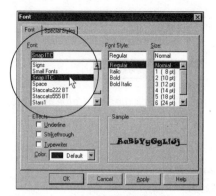

Figure 11. *Select a new font from the Font list box in the Font dialog box, then click OK.*

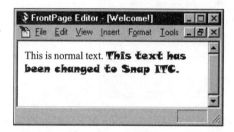

Figure 12. *In the Editor window, the text changes to the font you selected.*

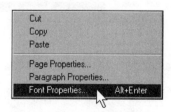

Figure 13. *Choose Font Properties from the pop-up menu.*

To change fonts:

1. Select the text you want to change or position the insertion marker at the place where you would like the new font to begin.

2. Use the Change Font drop-down list on the Format toolbar to select a new font (**Figure 10**).

   or

   Choose Font from the Format menu (**Figure 1**). The Font dialog box will open (**Figure 11**). Use the Font list box to select a new font, then click OK.

   The text will change to the font you selected (**Figure 12**).

Tips:

- You can see a preview of the font you've selected in the Sample area in the Font dialog box.

- If you need to use a special font and want to make sure it shows up correctly in any browser, convert the text to a graphic using a graphics program such as Photoshop or the Image Composer program included with the FrontPage Bonus Pack on the FrontPage 97 CD-ROM.

Change Fonts

MORE WAYS TO OPEN THE FONT DIALOG BOX

With the text selected, press Alt+Enter on the keyboard or right mouse click and choose Font Properties from the pop-up menu (**Figure 13**).

---

*A*nother way to emphasize text is to change its color. You can change the color of a selected bit of text or set the default text color for an entire Web page.

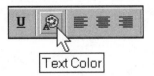

Figure 14. *Click the Text Color button on the Format toolbar.*

To change selected text's color:

1. Select the text you want to change.

2. Click the Text Color button on the Format toolbar (**Figure 14**). The Color dialog box will open (**Figure 15**).

3. Click one of the *color wells* to select a color.

4. Click OK. The selected text will change to the color you chose in the Editor window.

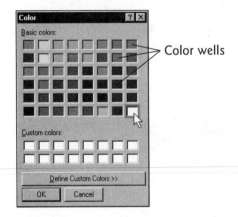

Color wells

Figure 15. *Select a color by clicking on one of the color wells, then click OK.*

or

1. Choose Font from the Format menu (**Figure 1**). The Font dialog box will open (**Figure 16**).

2. Use the Color drop-down list in the Effects area to select a color.

3. Click OK. The selected text will change color in the Editor window.

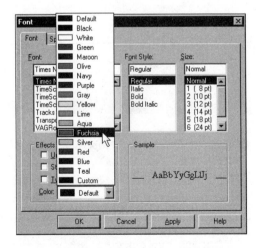

Figure 16. *In the Font dialog box, use the Color drop-down list to select a new color.*

Figure 17. *Choose Page Properties from the File menu.*

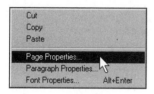

Figure 18. *Choose Page Properties from the pop-up menu.*

To set the default text color:

1. Open the Page Properties dialog box by choosing Page Properties from the File menu (**Figure 17**) or right clicking anywhere on the Editor page and choosing Page Properties from the pop-up menu (**Figure 18**).

2. Click the Background tab to bring that tab page to the front (**Figure 19**).

3. Make sure the Specify Background and Colors radio button is selected.

4. Use the Text drop-down list to select a color (**Figure 20**).

5. Click OK. Type some text. It will appear in the color you just selected.

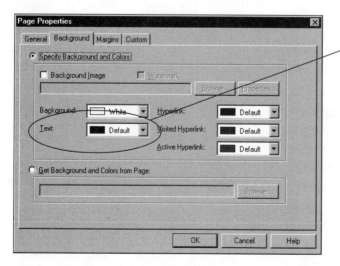

Figure 19. *Click the Background tab to move to that tab page.*

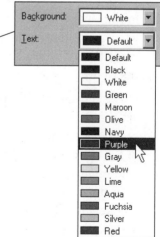

Figure 20. *Select a text color from the Text drop-down list.*

Set Default Text Color

Create a Marquee

M arquees are lines of text that scroll or slide across a page. Using a marquee is a great way to get someone browsing your Web site to notice an important message. FrontPage makes its easy to create marquees. You should know, however, that only advanced browsers support marquees. Any other browser will display it just like regular text.

To create a marquee:

1. Position the insertion marker where you want to insert the marquee.

2. Choose Marquee from the Insert menu (**Figure 21**). The Marquee Properties dialog box will open (**Figure 22**).

3. Type the text for the marquee in the Text box at the top of the dialog box.

4. In the Direction area, select whether you want the marquee to move toward the left or toward the right.

5. In the Movement Speed area set the Delay (the length in milliseconds between each movement of the marquee) and the Amount (the number of pixels between each movement of the marquee). The default values for these items are good settings.

Figure 21. *Choose Marquee from the Insert menu.*

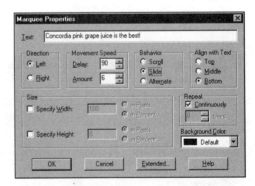

Figure 22. *The Marquee Properties dialog box is used to set up the direction and how fast the marquee will move.*

Marquee

Figure 23. *To see the marquee move, you will have to view it in an advanced browser.*

Cut

Copy

Paste

Page Properties...

Marquee Properties... Alt+Enter

Figure 24. *Choose Marquee Properties from the pop-up menu.*

CHANGING MARQUEE SETTINGS

To change any setting in a marquee, select the marquee, then press Alt+Enter on the keyboard or right mouse click and choose Marquee Properties from the pop-up menu (**Figure 24**). The Marquee Properties dialog box will appear.

---

6. In the Behavior area, select one of the following:

    ◉ Scroll: the text will appear at one end of the marquee and disappear at the other end.

    ◉ Slide: the text will appear at one end of the marquee and stop when it reaches the other end, remaining on the screen.

    ◉ Alternate: the text moves back and forth across the screen, never disappearing.

7. In the Align with Text area, select whether the marquee text will be aligned to the top, middle, or bottom of the marquee area.

8. Use the Repeat area to set whether the marquee will continuously repeat or repeat only a specified number of times.

9. Select a color in the Background Color area, if you want the marquee text to move against a colored background.

10. Click OK. The marquee will appear on the Editor page but will not move (**Figure 23**). To see it function, you will have to view the Web page using a Microsoft Explorer browser.

Create a Marquee

Web page titles are important. They appear in the title bar of the Editor. In addition, a page title is displayed in the title bar of a browser, giving the user basic information as to what the Web page is about. In the Editor, you can easily change a Web page's title.

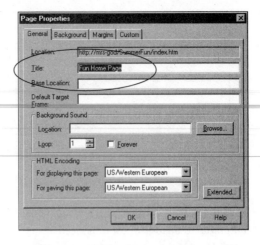

Figure 25. *Use the General tab page of the Page Properties dialog box to set a new page title.*

To change the page title:

1. Open the Page Properties dialog box by choosing Page Properties from the File menu (**Figure 17**) or right clicking anywhere on the Editor page and choosing Page Properties from the pop-up menu (**Figure 18**).

2. Click the General tab to bring that tab page to the front (**Figure 25**).

3. Enter a new page title in the Title text box (**Figure 26**).

4. Click OK to close the dialog box. The page title is shown in the title bar of a browser (**Figure 27**).

Figure 26. *Enter the new page title in the Title text box, then click OK.*

Tips:

- For more about the Editor's title bar, take a look at page 6.

- See the next page for directions about viewing your Web pages in a browser.

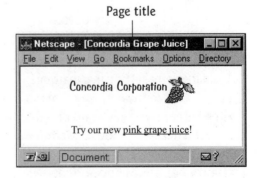

Figure 27. *The page title appears in a browser's title bar.*

Figure 28.
*Choose Preview
in Browser from
the File menu.*

Preview in Browser

Figure 29. *Click
the Preview in
Browser button
on the Standard
toolbar.*

Preview in Browser

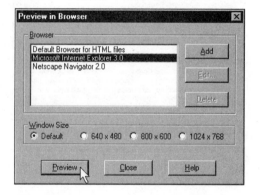

Figure 30. *Select the browser you want to
use from the Browser list box or click Add
to include another browser on the list.*

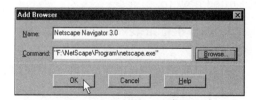

Figure 31. *Use the Add Browser dialog
box to find a new browser's program file.*

$\mathcal{N}$ ow that you've created some stunning effects with text, it's time to see what you've done by viewing it in a browser. FrontPage makes this easy with the Preview in Browser command.

To preview your Web page in a browser:

1. Choose Preview in Browser from the File menu (**Figure 28**) or click the Preview in Browser button on the Standard toolbar (**Figure 29**). The Preview in Browser dialog box will open (**Figure 30**).

2. Select the browser you want to use from the list box in the Browser area. If you don't see the browser you want to use and you know it's installed on your computer, click Add. The Add Browser dialog box will appear (**Figure 31**). Type in a name for the browser and click the Browse button to find the program file (.exe) for the browser. Click OK to return to the Preview in Browser dialog box.

3. Use the Window Size area to see what the browser window will look like to folks using other screen resolutions. In order for the different window sizes to work, your monitor must be set at the same or higher screen resolution than the one you select.

4. Click Preview. If the Web page you want to view is located on a server, the Connect To dialog box will appear (**Figure 32**). Click Connect. The Web page will appear in the browser you selected (**Figure 33**).

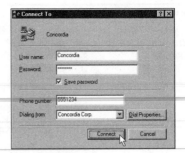

Figure 32. *If the Web site is loaded on a server, you'll need to connect to it via modem.*

Tips:

- It's a good idea to have several of the most popular browsers installed on your computer. That way, you can test to see what your Web site will look like in the different browsers.

- If you connected to the Web site via modem, don't forget to disconnect once you're finished.

Figure 33. *The Web page viewed in a browser.*

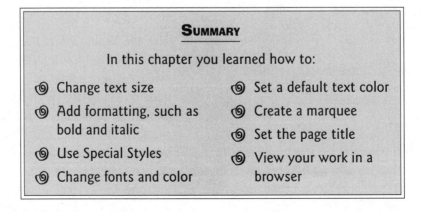

SUMMARY

In this chapter you learned how to:

- Change text size
- Add formatting, such as bold and italic
- Use Special Styles
- Change fonts and color
- Set a default text color
- Create a marquee
- Set the page title
- View your work in a browser

Preview Your Pages in a Browser

Formatting Paragraphs

hapter 8 showed you how to format individual characters and words by selecting them. It dealt with character-level formatting. This chapter will tell you all about paragraph-level formatting, such as alignment, paragraph styles, and numbered and bulleted lists.

Paragraph alignment specifies how text is positioned between the left and right sides of the browser window.

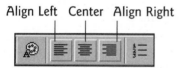

Figure 1. *Click the Align Left, Center, or Align Right buttons on the Format toolbar.*

To set paragraph alignment:

1. Select the paragraph(s) you want to change.
2. Click the Align Left, Center, or Align Right buttons on the Format toolbar (**Figure 1**).

WHAT'S MY PARAGRAPH ALIGNMENT?

I am aligned
on the
left.

I am aligned
in the
center.

I am aligned
on the
right.

Set Paragraph Alignment

When you just type along in Front-Page Editor without adding any fancy formatting, the default style that Editor places your text in is *Normal*. This Normal style is left aligned, Times text.

Formatted style creates paragraphs with a *monospaced* font, meaning that each character takes up the same amount of room. Formatted style also preserves any tabs or spaces that you create with the spacebar on the keyboard. `Courier` is generally used as a browser's default monospaced font. So, if you want to create columns using spaces or tabs, you can do so and be sure that the columns will look the same in every browser. They would line up correctly, as in **Figure 2**. (A more elegant way to create columns is to use tables, which are discussed in Chapter 12.)

To use the Formatted style:

1. Position the insertion marker where you would like the paragraph to begin or place the insertion marker in an existing paragraph to change it to Formatted style.

2. Choose Formatted from the Change Style drop-down list on the Format toolbar (**Figure 3**). Type your text.

3. When you are finished, press Ctrl+Enter on the keyboard to return to Normal style.

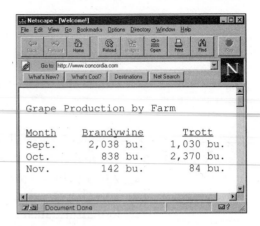

Figure 2. *The Formatted style uses a mono-spaced font, so every character and space lines up evenly.*

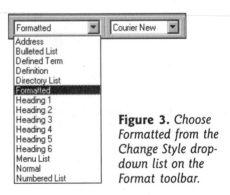

Figure 3. *Choose Formatted from the Change Style drop-down list on the Format toolbar.*

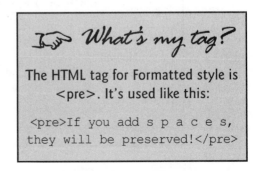

What's my tag?

The HTML tag for Formatted style is <pre>. It's used like this:

```
<pre>If you add s p a c e s,
they will be preserved!</pre>
```

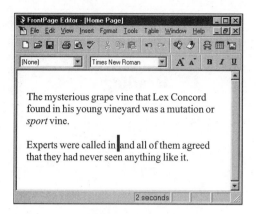

Figure 4. *Place the insertion marker inside a paragraph.*

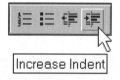

Increase Indent

Figure 5. *Click the Increase Indent button on the Format toolbar.*

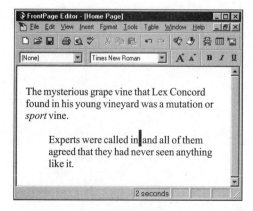

Figure 6. *When the Increase Indent button is clicked, the paragraph becomes indented.*

Using the FrontPage Editor, you can indent entire paragraphs with just the click of a button.

To indent a paragraph:

1. Place the insertion marker anywhere in the paragraph (**Figure 4**).

2. Click the Increase Indent button on the Format toolbar (**Figure 5**). The paragraph will become indented (**Figure 6**).

Tips:

- To indent several paragraphs at once, select the paragraphs before clicking the Increase Indent button.

- To remove the indent from a paragraph, place the insertion marker in the paragraph, then click the Decrease Indent button on the Format toolbar (**Figure 7**).

- Increasing and decreasing indents works only on left-aligned paragraphs.

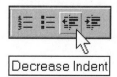

Decrease Indent

Figure 7. *Click the Decrease Indent button on the Format toolbar.*

Increase and Decrease an Indent

eadings are an important part of any Web page. Typically, a large heading will be found near the top of a page to tell the user what the page is about. Smaller headings will be used throughout the page to separate it into manageable sections. As you learned in Chapter 8, text sizes are measured in increments from 1 to 7, with 1 being the smallest and 7 the largest. Heading increments work in the opposite fashion. Headings are measured in increments from 1 to 6, but 1 is the largest size and 6 is the smallest. **Figure 8** shows the relative sizes of the six heading formats.

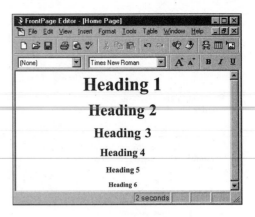

Figure 8. *The six different Heading styles.*

PARAGRAPHS VS. LINE BREAKS

Every time you press the Enter key on the keyboard, FrontPage starts a new paragraph. As the insertion marker moves down to begin the new paragraph, it adds extra space between the previous line and the new line.

To move the insertion marker down to the next line without creating a new paragraph and adding that extra space, press Shift+Enter on the keyboard. This inserts a line break.

For more information about paragraphs and line breaks, turn to pages 86 and 87 in Chapter 7.

What's my tag?

The HTML tag for paragraph alignment is <p align>. It's used like this:

```
<p align="left">I am on the left!</p>
<p align="center">I am centered!</p>
<p align="right">I am on the right!</p>
```

The tag for the Heading styles is <h>. It's used like this:

```
<h1>I am Heading 1 style</h1>
<h2>I am Heading 2 style</h2>
<h3>I am Heading 3 style</h3>
<h4>I am Heading 4 style</h4>
<h5>I am Heading 5 style</h5>
<h6>I am Heading 6 style</h6>
```

Figure 9. *Choose a Heading style from the Change Style drop-down list on the Format toolbar.*

Figure 10. *Choose Paragraph from the Format menu.*

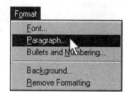

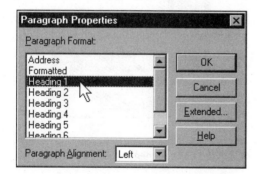

Figure 11. *Use the Paragraph Properties dialog box to select a Heading style.*

Figure 12. *Choose Paragraph Properties from the pop-up menu.*

To apply a Heading style:

1. Select the paragraph(s) you want to change.

2. Use the Change Style drop-down list on the Format toolbar to select a heading style (**Figure 9**). The text you selected will change to that heading style.

   or

   Choose Paragraph from the Format menu (**Figure 10**). The Paragraph Properties dialog box will open (**Figure 11**). Select the heading style you would like, then click OK. The text you selected will change to that heading style.

Tips:

- Another way to open the Paragraph Properties dialog box is to right click on the selected paragraph, then select Paragraph Properties from the pop-up menu (**Figure 12**).

- You can apply several types of paragraph formatting to a paragraph. For instance, you could change a paragraph to Heading 1 style, then center align it.

Apply Heading Styles

Organized lists are a great way to show information in an easy-to-read format. You can use the Editor to create bulleted and numbered lists, as well as definition lists.

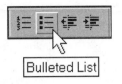

Bulleted List

Figure 13. *Click the Bulleted List button on the Format toolbar.*

To create a bulleted list:

1. Position the insertion marker where you want the bulleted list to begin. If you place the insertion marker on a line that contains text, that line will become the first item of the list.

2. Click the Bulleted List button on the Format toolbar (**Figure 13**).

   or

   Choose Bulleted List from the Change Style drop-down list on the Format toolbar (**Figure 14**).

   or

   Choose Bullets and Numbering from the Format menu (**Figure 15**). The List Properties dialog box will open with the Bulleted tab page in front (**Figure 16**). Select a bullet style by clicking on a sample, then click OK.

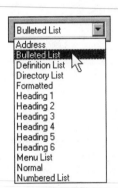

Figure 14. *Choose Bulleted List from the Change Style drop-down list on the Format toolbar.*

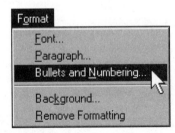

Figure 15. *Choose Bullets and Numbering from the Format menu.*

BROWSERS AND SPECIAL BULLET SHAPES

Only the Netscape Navigator browser supports bullet shapes other than a dot. If you use another bullet style on a Web page, such as a square, and the person browsing the page is not using Navigator, the bullets will appear as dots.

Create a Bulleted List

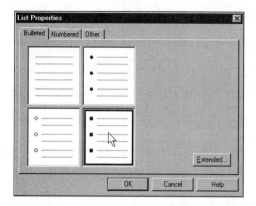

Figure 16. *Use the Bulleted tab page of the List Properties dialog box to select a bullet style, then click OK.*

3. Where the bullet appears on the page, type in your first list item.

4. When you are finished with the first item, press Enter on the keyboard to create another bullet. Continue typing and pressing Enter until your list is complete (**Figure 17**).

5. When you are finished adding the last bulleted item, press Ctrl+Enter on the keyboard to change back to the Normal style.

Tip:

⑨ You can also turn existing paragraphs into a bulleted list by selecting the paragraphs, then proceeding from step 2.

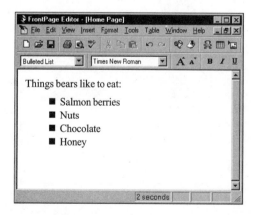

Figure 17. *As you type and press Enter, the bulleted list takes shape.*

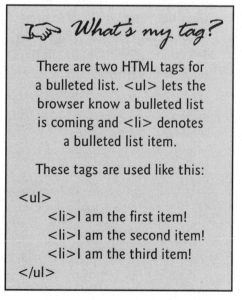

☞ *What's my tag?*

There are two HTML tags for a bulleted list. <ul> lets the browser know a bulleted list is coming and <li> denotes a bulleted list item.

These tags are used like this:

<ul>
    <li>I am the first item!
    <li>I am the second item!
    <li>I am the third item!
</ul>

Create a Bulleted List

To create a numbered list:

1. Position the insertion marker where you would like the numbered list to begin. If you place the insertion marker on a line that contains text, that line will become the first item of the list.

2. Click the Numbered List button on the Format toolbar (**Figure 18**).

   or

   Choose Numbered List from the Change Style drop-down list on the Format toolbar (**Figure 19**).

   or

   Choose Bullets and Numbering from the Format menu (**Figure 20**). The List Properties dialog box will open with the Bulleted tab page in front (**Figure 16**). Click the Numbered tab to bring that tab page forward (**Figure 21**). Select a number style by clicking on a sample, then click OK.

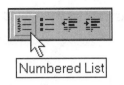

Figure 18. *Click the Numbered List button on the Format toolbar.*

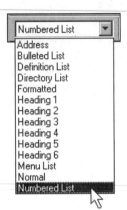

Figure 19. *Choose Numbered List from the Change Style drop-down list on the Format toolbar.*

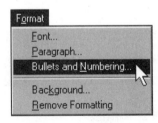

Figure 20. *Choose Bullets and Numbering from the Format menu.*

BROWSERS AND NUMBERED LISTS

When you create a numbered list using the List Properties dialog shown in Figure 21, you can select special numbering styles such as Roman numerals and letters. Only Netscape Navigator and Microsoft Internet Explorer will display these special numbers. Other browsers will ignore them and just display Arabic numerals which are the default.

Create a Numbered List

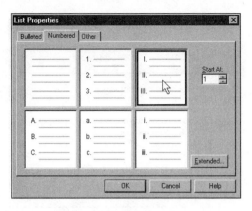

Figure 21. *Use the Numbered tab in the List Properties dialog box to select a numbered list style, then click OK.*

3. Where the number appears on the page, type in your first list item.

4. When you are finished with the first item, press Enter on the keyboard to create the next number. Continue typing and pressing Enter until your list is complete (**Figure 22**).

5. When you are finished adding the last numbered item, press Ctrl+Enter on the keyboard to change back to the Normal style.

Tip:

⊚ If you use the List Properties dialog box to create your numbered list, you can choose from different numbering styles including Roman numerals and letters.

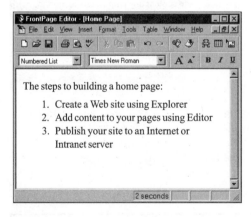

Figure 22. *As you type and press Enter, your numbered list takes shape.*

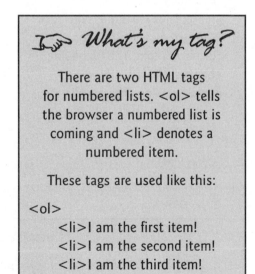

☞ *What's my tag?*

There are two HTML tags for numbered lists. <ol> tells the browser a numbered list is coming and <li> denotes a numbered item.

These tags are used like this:

```
<ol>
    <li>I am the first item!
    <li>I am the second item!
    <li>I am the third item!
</ol>
```

Create a Numbered List

You can also create nested bulleted and numbered lists. Some folks call this "a list in a list." FrontPage makes creating multilevel lists easy.

To create a nested list:

1. Create a bulleted or numbered list containing the top-level items (**Figure 23**).

2. Move the insertion marker to the end of the line above where you want to add a second-level list.

3. Press Enter on the keyboard, then click the Increase Indent button on the Format toolbar. An indented blank line will appear between the main level items (**Figure 24**).

4. Depending on the type of secondary list you want to create, click the Bulleted List or Numbered List button on the Format toolbar. The blank line changes into a bulleted or numbered line (**Figure 25**).

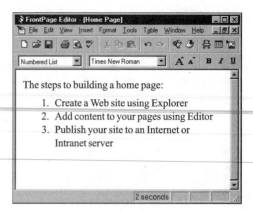

Figure 23. *Use the Editor to create a bulleted or numbered list of top-level items.*

Figure 24. *After you press Enter and click the Increase Indent button, an indented blank line appears between the top-level items.*

LISTS AND HYPERLINKS

Lists are great for presenting information in an organized way. You can use them to create a table of contents Web page with hyperlinks to related topics. For more about hyperlinks, see Chapter 14.

Create a Nested List

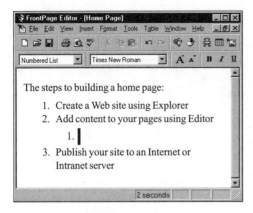

Figure 25. *When you click either the Bulleted List or Numbered List buttons, a bullet or number appears on the secondary line.*

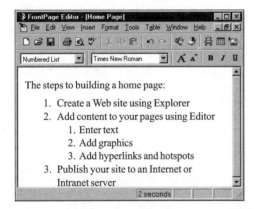

Figure 26. *The secondary list appears as you type and press Enter.*

5. Type the secondary list, pressing Enter each time you want to add a new secondary item.

6. When you are finished typing the secondary list, click anywhere on the page outside of the list (**Figure 26**).

7. To add another secondary list to another main list item, repeat steps 2 through 6.

Tips:

◉ If you want to change the bullet type (round or square) or number type (Roman numerals or letters) of a secondary list, type in your secondary list as described above. Select the secondary list and choose Bullets and Numbering from the Format menu. Use the List Properties dialog box to select the bullet or number type you would like to use.

◉ To move a secondary list item up to a main list item, select the secondary item, then click the Decrease Indent button twice.

◉ To move a main list item down to the secondary list below it, select the main item, then click the Increase Indent button twice.

Create a Nested List

𝒜 definition list presents information in a dictionary-type format. The term being defined is on the first line and the definition is indented on the next line. When you create a definition list, FrontPage automatically alternates between two styles, Defined Term and Definition.

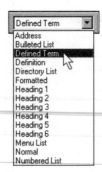

Figure 27. *Choose Defined Term from the Change Style drop-down list on the Format toolbar.*

To create a definition list:

1. Position the insertion marker where you want the list to begin.

2. Choose Defined Term from the Change Style drop-down list on the Format toolbar (**Figure 27**).

3. Type the term that you want to define (**Figure 28**).

4. Press Enter. The insertion marker will move down and the style will automatically change to Definition.

Figure 28. *Type the term you want to define, then press Enter.*

OTHER AVAILABLE LIST STYLES

You may have noticed that there are two other list styles available on the Change Style drop-down list on the Format menu. These two styles are called Directory List and Menu List. These styles are very similar to the Bulleted List style and work in exactly the same way. A few browsers, including the latest versions of Netscape Navigator and Microsoft Internet Explorer, recognize these styles and apply a special bulleted formatting to them, but many browsers will display these styles exactly the same as the Bulleted List style.

Figure 29. *Type the definition for the term, then press Enter.*

5. Type in the definition for the term (**Figure 29**).

6. Press Enter. The insertion marker will move down and the style will automatically change back to Defined Term.

7. Repeat steps 3 through 6 for every term you want to define (**Figure 30**).

8. When you are finished, either press Ctrl+Enter or press Enter twice to return to the Normal style.

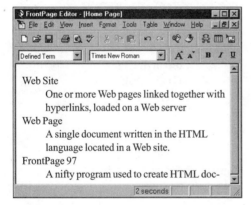

Figure 30. *As you type terms and definitions and press Enter, the definition list takes shape.*

Create a Definition List

☞ *What's my tag?*

There are three HTML tags used to create a definition list. <dl> tells the browser a definition list is coming, <dt> denotes a defined term and <dd> denotes a definition.

These tags are used like this:

```
<dl>
<dt>This is a term
    <dd>This is the definition
<dt>This is a second term
    <dd>This is the definition
</dl>
```

With FrontPage Editor, you can remove any extra formatting that you have applied to words or paragraphs using the Remove Formatting command. When you use Remove Formatting, the words or paragraphs are returned to the default setting for the style that the text is using.

Figure 31. *Select the paragraphs or characters you want to change back.*

To return a style to its default look:

1. Select the characters or para-graph(s) that you want to return to the format's default style (**Figure 31**).

2. Choose Remove Formatting from the Format menu (**Figure 32**). The characters or paragraph(s) will revert to the style's default settings (**Figure 33**).

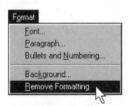

Figure 32. *Choose Remove Formatting from the Format menu.*

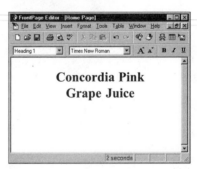

Figure 33. *The text reverts to the default formatting.*

Return a Style to its Default Look

SUMMARY

In this chapter you learned how to:

- Align paragraphs
- Apply the Formatted style
- Indent a paragraph
- Use the Heading styles
- Create bulleted and numbered lists
- Create nested lists
- Create a definition list

Fun with Graphics

O ne of the great features of the World Wide Web is the support of graphics, sounds, and videos. These multimedia elements make Web browsing fun while communicating a message to users. Adding multimedia elements to your Web pages is just a click away with FrontPage Editor.

The simplest graphical element you can add to a Web page is a horizontal line. Horizontal lines are great for separating topics and large blocks of text.

Figure 1. *Choose Horizontal Line from the Insert menu.*

To insert a horizontal line:

1. Position the insertion marker where you want the line to appear.

2. Choose Horizontal Line from the Insert menu (**Figure 1**). The line will appear on your Web page (**Figure 2**).

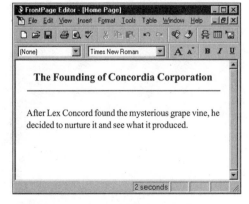

Figure 2. *The horizontal line appears on the Web page.*

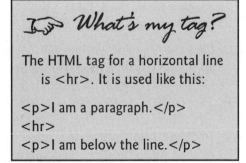

☞ *What's my tag?*

The HTML tag for a horizontal line is <hr>. It is used like this:

<p>I am a paragraph.</p>
<hr>
<p>I am below the line.</p>

You can change the way a horizontal line looks and customize it for your needs.

To format a horizontal line:

1. Right mouse click on the horizontal line. A pop-up menu will appear (**Figure 3**).

2. Choose Horizontal Line Properties from the pop-up menu. The Horizontal Line Properties dialog box will open (**Figure 4**).

3. Use the Width area to specify the length of the line as a percentage of the browser window width or as a specific length in pixels.

4. Use the Height area to specify how tall the line will be in pixels.

5. In the Alignment area, select how the line will be aligned in the browser window.

6. Use the Color drop-down list to choose a color for the line.

7. If you want the line to be all one color, instead of shaded, put a check mark in the Solid line (no shading) check box.

8. Click OK. Your custom line will appear on the Web page (**Figure 5**).

Tip:

- To delete a horizontal rule, select it, then press Delete or Backspace on the keyboard.

Figure 3. *Choose Horizontal Line Properties from the pop-up menu.*

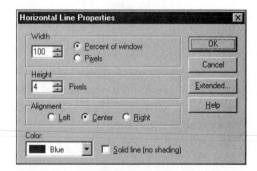

Figure 4. *Use the Horizontal Line Properties dialog box to set the width, height, alignment, and color of a horizontal line.*

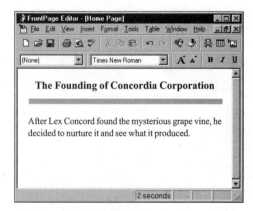

Figure 5. *The horizontal line takes on the custom qualities you selected.*

Figure 6.
*Choose Page
Properties
from the
File menu.*

Figure 7.
*Choose Page
Properties
from the pop-
up menu.*

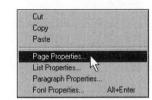

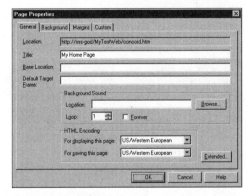

Figure 8. *The Page Properties dialog box.*

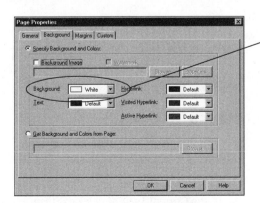

Figure 9. *The Background tab page.*

The next page element that you may want to change is the background color of your page. Whatever color you decide on, make sure the page's text is still easy to read.

To change a page's background color:

1. Open the Web page in the Editor.
2. Choose Page Properties from the File menu (**Figure 6**) or right click on the page area and select Page Properties from the pop-up menu (**Figure 7**). The Page Properties dialog box will open with the General tab page in front (**Figure 8**).
3. Click the Background tab to move to that tab page (**Figure 9**).
4. Use the Background drop-down list to choose a color (**Figure 10**).
5. Click OK. The dialog box will close and the page will redraw with the background color you selected.

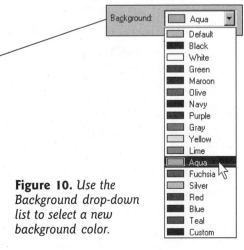

Figure 10. *Use the Background drop-down list to select a new background color.*

Change a Page's Background Color

Frontpage makes it easy to create Web pages with the same background, text, and hyperlink text colors. (Hyperlinks are discussed in Chapter 14.) All you have to do is set up one page, then use that page as the color basis for any other pages you create.

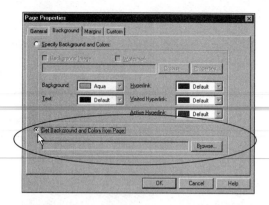

Figure 11. *The Background tab page of the Page Properties dialog box.*

To set up page colors using another Web page:

1. Use the Editor to open the page whose colors you want to change.

2. Open the Page Properties dialog box by selecting Page Properties from the File menu (**Figure 6**) or right clicking on the page area and selecting Page Properties from the pop-up menu (**Figure 7**).

3. Click the Background tab to move to that tab page (**Figure 11**).

4. Select the Get Background and Colors from Page radio button near the bottom of the Background tab page in the Page Properties dialog box (**Figure 12**).

5. Click the Browse button. The Current Web dialog box will open (**Figure 13**).

6. Choose the Web page whose colors you want to copy, then click OK.

7. Click OK to close the Page Properties dialog box. Your Web page will assume the colors specified by the Web page you selected.

Figure 12. *Select the Get Background and Colors from Page radio button, then click the Browse button.*

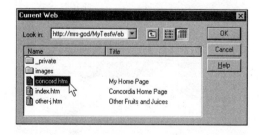

Figure 13. *Select a Web page from the list box in the Current Web dialog box, then click OK.*

Graphic File Formats and the Web

Graphics file formats for the Web come in two flavors, .gif (CompuServe bitmap) and .jpg (Joint Photographic Experts Group (JPEG)) bitmap. The JPEG file format is ideal for photographs and images with depth and small color changes such as lighting effects. The GIF file format is typically used for black and white art, line drawings, and images that are less than 256 colors.

There are two GIF Formats, 87a and 89a. 87a Format was developed in 1987 and is the standard GIF format. A special feature of this format is *interlacing*. An interlaced GIF file appears in the browser in chunks, starting at a low resolution, and progressing after several seconds to its final form.

89a Format, developed in 1989, is a descendant of the 87a Format. As with its predecessor, 89a Format offers interlaced images. The special feature of this format is *transparency*. Transparent images contain sections (usually in the background) that are invisible. This is handy when a Web page has a special background pattern. You don't have to try to match the graphic's background to the background on the Web page (an impossible task!); instead, the image's invisible background lets the Web page background shine through.

FrontPage Editor will import many kinds of image file formats, including .bmp, .tif, .wpg, .eps, .pcx, and .wmf, and automatically convert them for you to either the .gif or .jpg format.

Graphic File Formats and the Web

How to View File Extensions in Windows 95/NT

To see all file extensions, open any Windows 95/NT window—for instance, double click on My Computer to open that window—and select Options from the View menu. In the Options dialog box, click the View tab to bring that tab page to the front. For Windows 95, make sure the check box next to "Hide MS-DOS file extensions for file types that are registered" is unchecked. For Windows NT, make sure the check box next to "Hide file extensions for known file types" is unchecked.

There are several sources you can use to add an image to your Web page. You can select an image from the current Web site, from a location on your computer, from the World Wide Web itself, and from the FrontPage clip art collection. FrontPage 97 ships with an interesting library of clip art images, animations, and background textures that you can use in your Web pages.

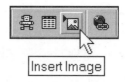

Figure 14. *Click the Insert Image button on the Standard toolbar.*

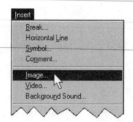

Figure 15. *Choose Image from the Insert menu.*

To insert an image from the current Web site:

1. In the Editor, place the insertion marker where you would like to insert the image.

2. Click the Insert Image button on the Standard toolbar (**Figure 14**) or choose Image from the Insert menu (**Figure 15**). The Image dialog box will open (**Figure 16**).

3. Click the Current FrontPage Web tab to bring that tab page to the front. The list box on this tab displays your Web site's images and file folders. If you don't see any image files, double-click on the images folder.

4. Select the image you want to insert, then click OK. The dialog box will close and the image will appear in your Web page (**Figure 17**).

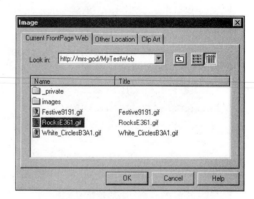

Figure 16. *Select an image from the list box on the Current FrontPage Web tab page.*

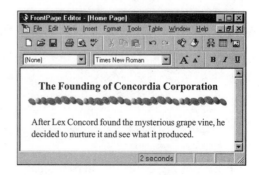

Figure 17. *The image appears on your Web page.*

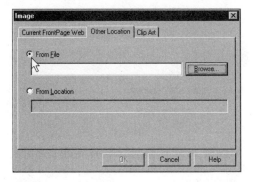

Figure 18. *Select the From File radio button on the Other Location tab page.*

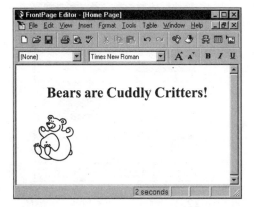

Figure 19. *After you enter the file name and click OK, the graphic appears on the Web page.*

Figure 20. *Use the Image dialog box to find the file you want to insert.*

To insert an image from a location on your computer:

1. In the Editor, place the insertion marker where you would like to insert the image.

2. Click the Insert Image button on the Standard toolbar (**Figure 14**) or choose Image from the Insert menu (**Figure 15**). The Image dialog box will open (**Figure 16**).

3. Click the Other Location tab to bring that tab page to the front (**Figure 18**).

4. Select the From File radio button, type the exact path and name of the file, and then click OK. The image will be added to the Web page (**Figure 19**).

   or

   Click the Browse button. The Image dialog box will open (**Figure 20**). Use this dialog box to locate the graphic file. When you have found it, select it, and then click Open. Both dialog boxes will close and the image will be added to the Web page (**Figure 19**).

Insert an Image from Your Computer

To insert an image from the FrontPage clip art collection:

1. In the Editor, place the insertion marker where you would like to insert the image.

2. Click the Insert Image button on the Standard toolbar (**Figure 14**) or choose Image from the Insert menu (**Figure 15**). The Image dialog box will open (**Figure 16**).

3. Click the Clip Art tab to bring that tab page to the front (**Figure 21**).

4. Use the Category drop-down list to select a group of clip art. You can choose from various bullets, buttons, backgrounds, lines, and miscellaneous images.

5. Select the image you want to insert by clicking on it in the list box (**Figure 22**).

6. Click OK. The dialog box will close and the image will appear in your Web page (**Figure 23**).

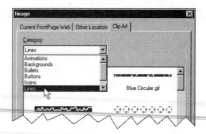

Figure 21. *Use the Category drop-down list on the Clip Art tab page to select a clip art library.*

Figure 22. *Select a graphic from the list box, then click OK.*

PERMISSION TO USE IMAGES

Before you can use images from the World Wide Web, such as the BearHome welcome screen shown in Figure 25, you must get permission to use the image from the owner.

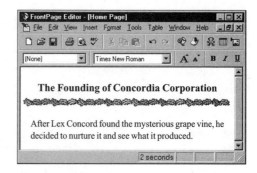

Figure 23. *The FrontPage clip art appears in your Web page.*

Insert a FrontPage Clip Art Image

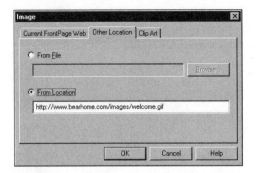

Figure 24. *Select the From Location radio button, then type in the absolue URL for the image.*

Figure 25. *The image appears in your Web page.*

Figure 26. *If you are not connected to the Web, this dialog box will appear.*

Figure 27. *The broken image icon will appear where the graphic would be.*

To insert an image from the World Wide Web:

1. Make sure you are connected to the Web via modem.

2. In the Editor, place the insertion marker where you would like to insert the image.

3. Click the Insert Image button on the Standard toolbar (**Figure 14**) or choose Image from the Insert menu (**Figure 15**). The Image dialog box will open (**Figure 16**).

4. Click the Other Location tab to bring that tab page to the front (**Figure 24**).

5. Select the From Location radio button.

6. Type the *absolute URL* of the image you want to reference. An absolute URL includes the complete address of the file. (Turn to the next page for more about finding absolute URLs.)

7. Click OK. If you are connected to the Web and the absolute URL you typed is correct, the image will appear in the Web page (**Figure 25**).

Tip:

- ✪ If you are not connected to the Web, a warning dialog box will appear (**Figure 26**) and a broken image icon will appear where the graphic should be (**Figure 27**).

Insert an Image from the Web

I f you want to insert a graphic into your Web page that is located on a site on the World Wide Web, you are going to need the absolute URL for that image.

Figure 28. *In Microsoft Internet Explorer, right mouse click on the graphic and choose Properties from the pop-up menu.*

To find the URL and add it to the Image dialog box:

1. Connect to the Web via modem.

2. Launch your favorite browser and find the graphic you want to add to your Web page. (Most browsers work like Microsoft Internet Explorer or Netscape Navigator.)

3. For Microsoft Internet Explorer:

   a. Right mouse click on the graphic and choose Properties from the pop-up menu (**Figure 28**). The Properties dialog box will open (**Figure 29**).

   b. Position the mouse at the beginning of the Address, press the left mouse button and drag to select the entire address (**Figure 30**).

   c. Press Ctrl+C on the keyboard to copy the Address. Don't disconnect your Web connection. Return to FrontPage Editor.

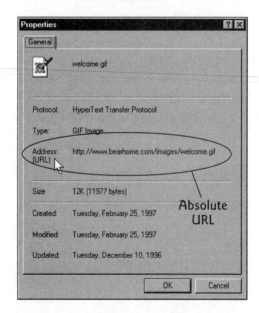

Figure 29. *Near the middle of the Properties dialog box next to Address is the absolute URL for the graphic.*

When you include an image from another Web site in your Web page, remember that the folks running that Web site may remove the image from their site or change its location. If this happens, the broken image icon will appear in your page.

Find an Absolute URL

Figure 30. *Use the mouse to select the absolute URL, then press Ctrl+C on the keyboard.*

Figure 31. *In Netscape Navigator, right click on the image and select Copy Image Location from the pop-up menu.*

Figure 32. *Place the insertion marker in the From Location text box, then press Ctrl+V on the keyboard.*

For Netscape Navigator:

a. Right mouse click on the graphic and choose Copy Image Location from the pop-up menu (**Figure 31**). Don't disconnect your Web connection. Return to FrontPage Editor.

4. Position the insertion marker where you want to place the image and open the Image dialog box by clicking the Insert Image button on the Standard toolbar (**Figure 14**) or choosing Image from the Insert menu (**Figure 15**). The Image dialog box will open (**Figure 16**).

5. Move to the Other Location tab page and place the insertion marker in the From Location text box (**Figure 24**).

6. Press Ctrl+V on the keyboard to paste the absolute URL into the text box (**Figure 32**).

7. Click OK. It will take a few seconds before the image appears in your Web page (**Figure 25**).

Tip:

☉ If you are not connected to the Web when you open a Web page containing a graphic from another Web site, the broken image icon will appear in place of the graphic.

Find an Absolute URL

When you first save your Web page after adding images, a Save Image to FrontPage Web dialog box will appear (**Figure 33**). This box lets you decide whether you want to save the graphic with the currently open Web site. In most cases, you will want to click Yes. This will make the graphics available for loading onto the Web page when you publish your Web site to a server.

Figure 33. *The Save Image to FrontPage Web dialog box.*

With FrontPage Editor, you can add interlacing and transparency to your .gif images and convert .jpg files to the .gif format and vice versa. (For details about these image formats, take a look at the "Graphic File Formats and the Web" sidebar on page 135 .)

Figure 34. *Choose Image Properties from the pop-up menu.*

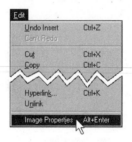

Figure 35. *Choose Image Properties from the Edit menu.*

To convert a JPEG file to a GIF (and vice versa):

1. Right click on the image you want to convert and choose Image Properties from the pop-up menu (**Figure 34**) or select the image and choose Image Properties from the Edit menu (**Figure 35**) or press Alt+Enter on the keyboard. The Image Properties dialog box will open with the General tab page in front (**Figure 36**). In the Type area, if the image is a .gif file, the GIF radio button will be selected. If the image is a .jpg file, the JPEG radio button will be selected (**Figure 37**).

Figure 36. *Use the Type area of the Image Properties dialog box.*

Figure 37. *In the Type area, select the GIF or JPEG radio button to convert the image to that file format.*

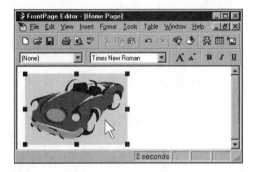

Figure 38. *Select the image with the mouse pointer.*

Figure 39. *Click the Make Transparent button on the Image toolbar.*

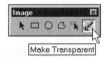

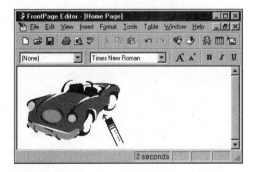

Figure 40. *When you click on a color with the eraser pointer (in this case the gray background seen in Figure 38) the color disappears.*

2. Select the radio button for the type of file you want to convert the graphic to. If you choose JPEG, the Quality text box will become available. The number in this box controls the *file compression*. File compression removes tiny details from an image, squashing the size of the file down. The higher the number in the Quality text box, the lower the amount of compression will be. Hence, the image quality will be better, though, the file size will be larger. If you would like to, type a new number in the Quality text box, but keep in mind that smaller file sizes are best. You can always adjust the Quality again later if the image size is so large that it slows down load time.

3. Click OK. FrontPage will convert the graphic.

To make a GIF transparent:

1. Select the Image with the mouse (**Figure 38**). The Image toolbar will appear.

2. On the Image toolbar, click the Make Transparent button (**Figure 39**). As you pass the mouse over the image, the pointer will change to a pencil eraser with a little arrow attached to it.

3. Position the pointer over the color you want to make transparent.

4. Click the mouse. The color will disappear (**Figure 40**).

Make a GIF Transparent

To create an interlaced GIF:

1. Right click on the graphic and choose Image Properties from the pop-up menu (**Figure 41**). The Image Properties dialog box will appear (**Figure 42**).

2. In the Type area on the General tab page, put a check mark in the Interlaced check box near the GIF radio button.

3. Click OK. The dialog will close. Next time you view your Web page in a browser, the image will load in chunks as it appears.

Once you've added an image to your Web page, you can set its alignment in relation to surrounding text, the amount of empty space surrounding the graphic, and the size of the image.

To align an image with the surrounding text:

1. Open the Image Properties dialog box by right clicking on the image and selecting Image Properties from the pop-up menu (**Figure 41**) or selecting the image and choosing Image Properties from the Edit menu.

2. Click the Appearance tab to bring that tab page to the front (**Figure 43**).

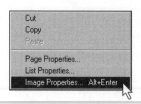

Figure 41.
Choose Image Properties from the pop-up menu.

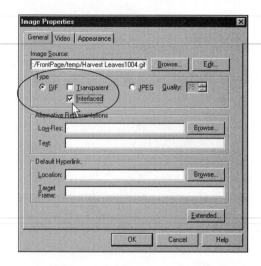

Figure 42. *Put a check mark in the Interlaced check box.*

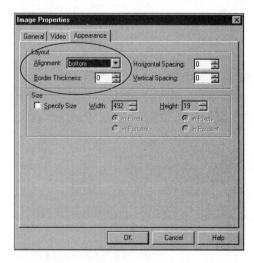

Figure 43. *Use the Alignment drop-down list in the Layout area to select an alignment.*

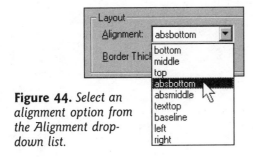

Figure 44. *Select an alignment option from the Alignment drop-down list.*

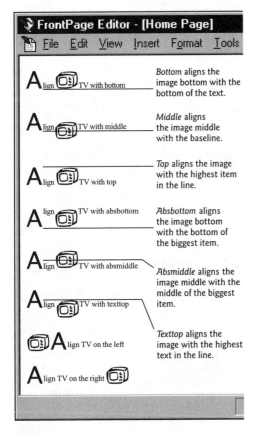

Figure 45. *There are 4 items on each line: a graphic of the letter A, some text, a graphic of a TV, and more text. The alignment positions are illustrated in relation to the TV.*

3. In the Layout area, use the Alignment drop-down list to select an option (**Figure 44**). Here are the alignments you can choose from (**Figure 45**):

- *Bottom* aligns the bottom of the image with the bottom of the text.

- *Middle* aligns the middle of the image with the baseline of the text.

- *Top* aligns the image with the highest element in the line.

- *Absbottom* aligns the bottom of the image with the bottom of the largest item.

- *Absmiddle* aligns the middle of the image with the middle of the largest item.

- *Texttop* aligns the image with the highest text in the line.

- *Baseline* works the same as bottom.

- *Left* places the image in the left margin and wraps the text around the right side of the image.

- *Right* places the image in the right margin and wraps the text around the left side of the image.

4. Click OK. The image's alignment changes to what you selected.

Set Text and Image Alignment

To set an empty space around the image:

1. Open the Image Properties dialog box by right clicking on the image and selecting Image Properties from the pop-up menu or selecting the image and choosing Image Properties from the Edit menu.

2. Click the Appearance tab to bring that tab page to the front (**Figure 46**).

3. In the Layout area, use the Horizontal Spacing text box to set the number of pixels of blank space between the image and what is to the right or left of the image (**Figure 47**).

4. Use the Vertical Spacing text box to set the number of pixels of blank space you want between the image and what is above and below it.

5. Click OK. The spacing around the image will change to the new settings (**Figure 48**).

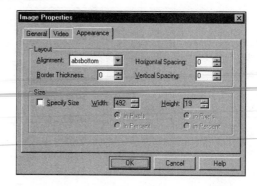

Figure 46. *Use the Appearance tab page to set the empty space around an image.*

Figure 47. *In the Layout area, set the alignment and horizontal and vertical spacing.*

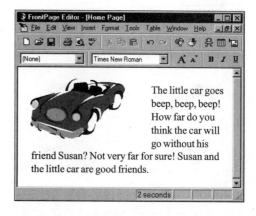

Figure 48. *When you click OK, the empty spacing appears around the image.*

Figure 49. *When you select the image, eight handles appear around it.*

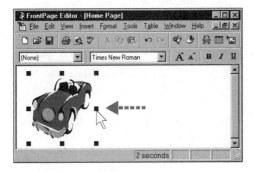

Figure 50. *Drag the handle to resize the image.*

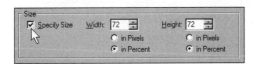

Figure 51. *In the Size area, put a check in the Specify Size check box, then use the Width and Height text boxes to set the new size for the image.*

To change the size of an image:

1. Select the image. Eight black *handles* appear around it (**Figure 49**).

2. Position the mouse pointer over a handle, press the mouse button and drag. The image will resize (**Figure 50**).

or

1. Open the Image Properties dialog box by right clicking on the image and selecting Image Properties from the pop-up menu or selecting the image and choosing Image Properties from the Edit menu.

2. Click the Appearance tab to bring that tab page to the front (**Figure 46**).

3. In the Size area, put a check in the Specify Size check box (**Figure 51**).

4. Use the Width and Height text boxes to specify a number of pixels or a percentage of the original size.

5. Click OK. The image will resize (**Figure 50**).

Tip:

⊚ Before you use the Width and Height text boxes the first time, the image's size is shown in pixels.

*A*s you add images to your Web pages, it's a good idea to give them *alternate text*. When someone is browsing your Web site, alternate text appears inside the placeholder where your graphic will appear once it loads. If the person is using a text-only browser, alternate text will give them an idea of what they are not seeing.

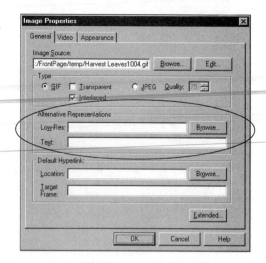

Figure 52. *To set the alternate text, use the Alternative Representations area of the Image Properties dialog box.*

To set alternate text for an image:

1. Open the Image Properties dialog box (**Figure 52**) by right clicking on the image and selecting Image Properties from the pop-up menu or selecting the image and choosing Image Properties from the Edit menu.

2. On the General tab page in the Alternative Representations area, type the alternate text in the Text text box. (**Figure 53**).

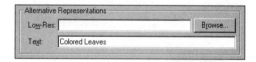

Figure 53. *Type the alternate text in the Text text box.*

3. Click OK. The next time you view your Web page in a browser, you will see the alternate text in the image placeholder while it loads (**Figure 54**).

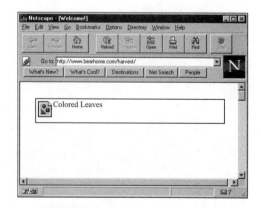

Figure 54. *As the Web page loads in a browser, the alternate text tells the user what's coming.*

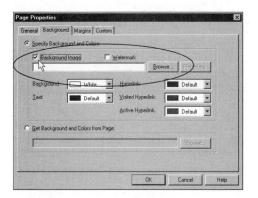

Figure 55. *Use the Background tab page to set a background image.*

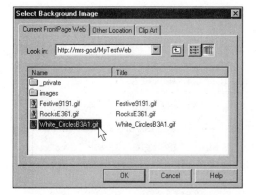

Figure 56. *Use the Current FrontPage Web tab page to select a graphic saved with the Web site.*

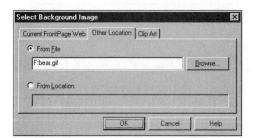

Figure 57. *Use the Other Location tab page to select a background image from your computer or the World Wide Web.*

When you add a graphic as a background image, most browsers will *tile* the image automatically. This means that the image will be duplicated across and down, completely filling the background with the image.

To add an image as the page background:

1. Open the Web page to which you want to add the background.

2. Open the Page Properties dialog box by selecting Page Properties from the File menu or right clicking on the page area and selecting Page Properties from the pop-up menu.

3. Click the Background tab to move to that tab page (**Figure 55**).

4. Put a check mark in the Background Image check box, then click the Browse button. The Select Background Image dialog box will open (**Figure 56**).

5. There are three ways to choose a graphic:

   ⦿ Use the Current Front Page Web tab page to select a graphic currently saved with the Web site (**Figure 56**).

   ⦿ Use the Other Location tab page to select a graphic file located on your computer or the World Wide Web (**Figure 57**).

⑨ Use the Clip Art tab to select a background from the FrontPage clip art collection (**Figure 58**).

6. Click OK. The Select Background Image dialog box will close.

7. Click OK again to close the Page Properties dialog box. The background will appear on your Web page.

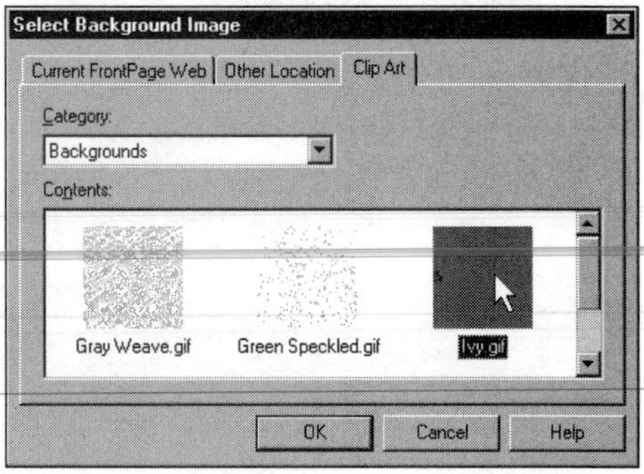

Figure 58. *Use the Clip Art tab page to select a background.*

Tip:

⑨ When you use a tiled background image, make sure the text is still easy to read.

GRAPHICS FOR DOWNLOADING FROM THE WEB

There are thousands of images to choose from on the Web, but not all of them are appropriate as background images. If an image is very dark or has a lot of "motion," most likely any text on this kind of background will be very hard to read. High contrast between your background image and text is good.

Yahoo contains an extensive list of sites that you can browse for images, animations, and backgrounds for your Web pages. Visit:

http://www.yahoo.com/computers_and_internet/internet/
world_wide_web/page_design_and_layout/graphics/

SUMMARY

In this chapter you learned how to:

⑨ Insert a horizontal line

⑨ Change background color

⑨ Insert graphics

⑨ Align images

⑨ Convert a JPEG to a GIF

⑨ Make a GIF transparent

⑨ Make a GIF interlaced

⑨ Set alternate text

Add a Background Image

Adding Sounds and Videos

Now that you know how to add attention getting images to your Web pages, it's time to add the multimedia elements—sounds and videos—that will make your site really snappy and interesting. Music, movies, and words can be combined to create an impressive Web-page presentation for your viewers.

FrontPage supports several different sound file formats, including Wave files (.wav), Midi sequences (.mid), AIFF files (.aif, .aifc, .aiff), and AU files (.au, .snd).

There is only one kind of video file format that FrontPage supports. It is the Windows-based Audio-Visual file (.avi).

SOUNDS, VIDEOS, AND BROWSERS

When you use sounds and videos in your Web pages, the folks browsing your Web site must have computers equipped with sound cards and speakers. Microsoft Internet Explorer includes the ability to play sounds, but Netscape Navigator needs a special plug-in. To download the plug-in, visit:

http://home.netscape.com/comprod/mirror/navcomponents_download.html

Yahoo contains an extensive list of sites that you can browse for sounds and videos for your Web pages. To search for sounds, visit:

http://www.yahoo.com/computers_and_internet/multimedia/sound

To search for videos, visit:

http://www.yahoo.com/computers_and_internet/multimedia/video

Figure 1. *Choose Page Properties from the File menu.*

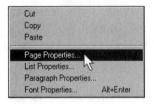

Figure 2. *Choose Page Properties from the pop-up menu.*

Background sounds and music add another dimension to your Web site, creating a mood and giving it a sophisticated multimedia feel.

To add a background sound to a Web page:

1. In the Editor, choose Page Properties from the File menu (**Figure 1**) or right click in the page area and choose Page Properties from the pop-up menu (**Figure 2**). The Page Properties dialog box will open with the General tab page in front (**Figure 3**).

2. In the Background Sound area (**Figure 4**), type the exact path and file name of the sound file or click the Browse button to open the Background Sound dialog box (**Figure 5**).

SOUNDS AND YOUR USERS

If you do choose to add sounds to your Web sites, remember that a sound playing over and over *can* get annoying. Usually a few iterations of a sound is enough.

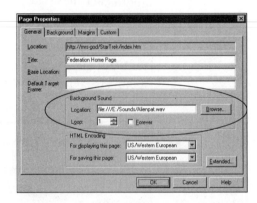

Figure 3. *Use the General tab page of the Page Properties dialog box to set a background sound for your Web page.*

Figure 4. *In the Background Sound area, type the name and path of the sound file or click the Browse button to locate the file.*

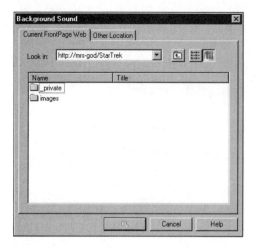

Figure 5. *Use the Current FrontPage Web tab to select a sound saved in the current Web site.*

Figure 6. *Use the Other Location tab page to select a file from your computer or from the World Wide Web.*

3. To select a sound file, use either of the two tab pages in the Background Sound dialog box:

   ◉ Use the Current FrontPage Web tab page to select a sound file from the open Web site (**Figure 5**).

   ◉ Use the Other Location tab page to select a sound file from a folder on your computer or from the World Wide Web (**Figure 6**). (If you want to use a sound file from the World Wide Web, you must have the absolute URL for that file.)

4. When you have located the sound file, click OK to close the dialog box and return to the Page Properties dialog box.

5. Use the Loop text box to set how many times the sound will loop or put a check in the Forever check box to make the sound repeat forever (**Figure 7**).

6. Click OK. When you view the Web page with a browser, the sound will play.

Figure 7. *In the Background Sound area of the Page Properties dialog box, use the Loop text box to set how many times the sound will play or put a check in the Forever check box.*

Add a Background Sound

Yet another way to make your Web site really hot is to add a video. Video files are usually large, so transferring a video file to someone browsing your site can take a long time.

Figure 8. *Choose Video from the Insert menu.*

To add a video to your Web page:

1. Position the insertion marker where you want to place the video.

2. Choose Video from the Insert menu (**Figure 8**). The Video dialog box will open (**Figure 9**).

3. Use this dialog box to load a video file from the existing Web site, another location on your computer, or from the World Wide Web.

4. Click OK. The opening frame of the video file will appear on your Web page as a placeholder (**Figure 10**).

5. Right click on the video file placeholder and choose Image Properties from the pop-up menu (**Figure 11**). The Image Properties dialog box will open with the Video tab page in the front (**Figure 12**).

6. If you want a set of controls, Play and Stop, to appear on your Web page when the video plays, put a check in the Show Controls in Browser check box.

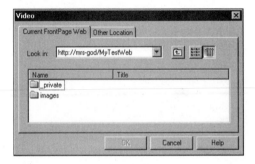

Figure 9. *Use the Video dialog box to select a video saved with the Web site, on your computer, or from the World Wide Web.*

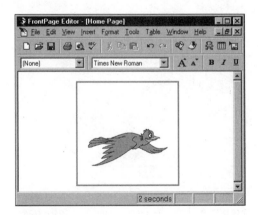

Figure 10. *The opening frame of the video appears as a placeholder.*

Figure 11.
*Choose Image
Properties from
the pop-up
menu.*

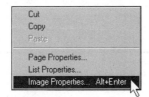

7. Use the Repeat area to set how
many times the video will play,
and the delay (in milliseconds)
between each time it plays. For
instance, if you wanted to set a
1 second delay, you would type
1000 in the Loop Delay text box.

8. Use the Start area to set whether
the Video will play immediately
when the page opens or when
the user passes the mouse over
the video placeholder.

9. Click OK. View your Web page
in a browser to watch the
video play (**Figure 13**).

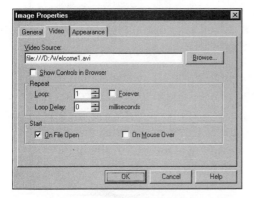

Figure 12. *Use the Video tab page to set
how many times the video will play.*

Figure 13. *When you view the Web page
in a browser, the video plays.*

Add a Video to Your Web Page

VIDEO FILE SIZE

Video files can be *huge*. Before
you decide to add a video to a
Web page, consider who will
be using your Web site. If
your site will be used over the
Internet, you may want to
reconsider, because it can take
several minutes to download
a video. (Some folks won't
wait that long!) If you are
working with a corporate site
on an intranet, download
times will be much quicker.

HOW LONG WILL MY PAGE TAKE TO LOAD?

When you have browsed the World Wide Web, you have probably come across Web pages that have many images with large file sizes that take forever to load.

If you aren't careful when you design your Web pages, graphic, sound, and video file sizes can add up, making for a long load time. Try to keep the size of your Web pages under 30k. It will take users with 14.4 kbps modems about 30 seconds to load a 30k Web page.

FrontPage includes a handy loading time counter at the bottom of the Editor window. In the Status Bar is the estimated number of seconds it will take your Web page to load in a user's browser with a computer equipped with a 28.8 kbps modem (**Figure 14**). As you add elements to your Web page, the estimated download time will automatically update.

Figure 14. *The bottom of the FrontPage Editor window shows the estimated number of seconds it will take your Web page to load.*

SUMMARY

In this chapter you learned how to:

- Add a background sound from the open Web site
- Add a background sound from your computer or the World Wide Web
- Add a video from the open Web site
- Add a video from your computer or the World Wide Web

Tables Made Easy

reating tables directly with HTML code is not much fun! FrontPage 97 takes the drudgery out of creating tables. All that is left for you to do is add the table content you need.

Tables are used to present information in an organized way. Tables let you position information accurately within *cells*. This means that you won't have to manually format text and image placement in an attempt to get it to line up. Tables do this for you.

Tables are made up of columns and rows of cells. These cells can contain text, images, forms, background images, and even another table. If you create a table and discover that you need to add or delete cells or change cell size, FrontPage Editor makes it easy to customize an existing table. **Figure 1** shows a Web page organized using an invisible table.

Figure 1. *The elements on this Web page are arranged with an invisible table. Invisible tables are often used as a way to precisely place Web page elements.*

To create a table:

1. In the Editor, position the insertion marker on your Web page where you would like the table to begin.

2. Choose Insert Table from the Table menu (**Figure 2**). The Insert Table dialog box will appear (**Figure 3**).

3. In the Size area, enter the number of rows and columns that you will need in your table. (If you find you need to, you can add and delete rows and columns later.)

4. In the Layout area, use the Alignment drop-down list to set whether the table will appear on the left side of the page, in the center, or on the right side of the page (**Figure 4**).

5. If you would like a border around the table, enter the border's width in pixels in the Border Size text box.

6. Use the Cell Padding text box to enter the number of pixels you would like between a cell's contents and each of its borders.

7. In the Cell Spacing text box, enter the number of pixels you would like between each cell in the table. The default setting is 2.

8. You can use the Width area to specify the exact width of the table. (This is optional. If you don't specify an exact width, FrontPage will automatically

Figure 2. *Choose Insert Table from the Table menu.*

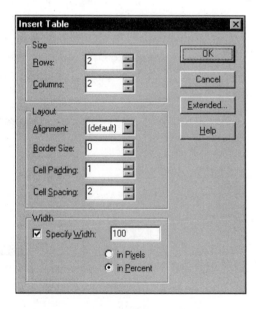

Figure 3. *Use the Insert Table dialog box to set up the table.*

Create a Table

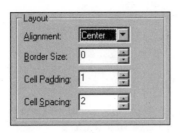

Figure 4. *Use the Layout area to set the table's alignment, border size, and cell padding and spacing.*

Figure 5. *The table appears in the Editor.*

Figure 6. *Position the mouse over the Insert Table button, then press the left button. A table grid appears.*

Figure 7. *Drag the mouse to select the number of rows and columns.*

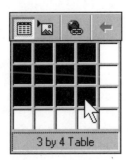

create a table that spans the entire width of the Web page.) To set an exact Width, put a check in the Specify Width check box, then either enter the number of pixels or a percentage of the Web page's width. For instance, a table width of 50 percent will span half the width of the page.

9. Click OK. The table will appear in the Web page (**Figure 5**).

or

1. Position the insertion marker where you would like the table to appear.

2. Click and hold down the left mouse button on the Insert Table button on the Standard toolbar (**Figure 6**). An empty grid appears below the button and your mouse.

3. Drag the mouse down and to the right to select the number of rows and columns that you want the table to contain (**Figure 7**). As you highlight grid boxes, table dimensions appear at the bottom of the grid. If you drag past the last grid box in a column or row, the grid will expand.

4. Release the mouse button. The table will appear on the page (**Figure 5**).

To add text to a table:

1. Place the insertion marker within a cell (**Figure 8**).

2. Type your text. The cell will automatically expand to accommodate the text.

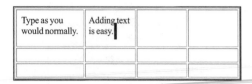

Figure 8. *Place the insertion marker in the cell, then type your text.*

Tips:

- ⊚ You can quickly move from one cell to the next in a table by pressing the Tab key.

- ⊚ To quickly add another row to a table, position the insertion marker in the lower-right cell and press the Tab key.

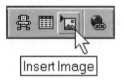

Figure 9. *Click the Insert Image button on the Standard toolbar.*

To add an image to a table:

1. Place the insertion marker in the cell where you want the image to appear.

2. Click the Insert Image button on the Standard toolbar (**Figure 9**).

3. Select an image using the Image dialog box (**Figure 10**), then click OK. The image will appear in the cell (**Figure 11**).

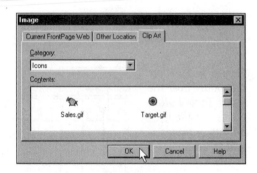

Figure 10. *Use the Image dialog box to select a graphic.*

Tip:

- ⊚ Inserting images into Web pages is discussed in detail in Chapter 10.

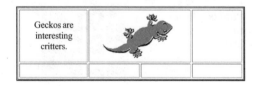

Figure 11. *When you click OK, the image appears in the cell.*

Figure 12.
*Choose Insert
Caption from
the Table menu.*

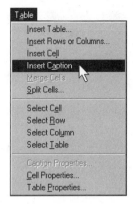

𝓐 table caption can help describe the information presented in a table. A caption can be placed above or below a table.

To add a table caption:

1. Place the insertion marker anywhere within the table.

2. Choose Insert Caption from the Table menu (**Figure 12**). The table will move down one line and the insertion marker will automatically appear centered above the table (**Figure 13**).

3. Type in the caption. You can now format the caption like any other Web page text, making it larger, smaller, bold, left aligned, etc.

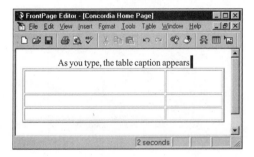

Figure 13. *When the insertion marker appears above the table, type the caption.*

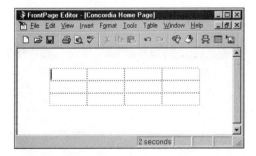

Figure 14. *A table with no borders is displayed with dashed lines so you can see it in the Editor.*

TABLES WITHOUT BORDERS

If you create a table with no borders, FrontPage Editor automatically shows dashed lines surrounding each table cell (**Figure 14**). These dashed lines will not appear on the page when it is viewed in a browser. If you want to view the table without these lines in the Editor, click the Show/Hide Paragraph button.

Add a Table Caption

To move a table caption below the table:

1. Place the insertion marker anywhere within the table caption text.

2. Choose Caption Properties from the Table menu (**Figure 15**) or right click on the caption and choose Caption Properties from the pop-up menu (**Figure 16**). The Caption Properties dialog box will open (**Figure 17**).

3. Select the Bottom of Table radio button, then click OK. The caption will move below the table (**Figure 18**).

Tip:

⑨ To move a caption from below to above a table, follow steps 1 and 2, then select the Top of Table radio button in the Caption Properties dialog box.

Figure 15. *Choose Caption Properties from the Table menu.*

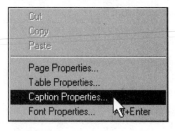

Figure 16. *Choose Caption Properties from the pop-up menu.*

Figure 18. *The table caption moves below the table.*

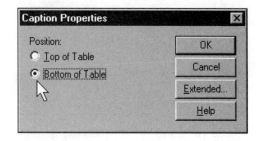

Figure 17. *Select the Bottom of Table radio button, then click OK.*

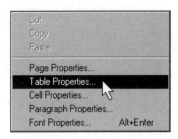

Figure 19. *Choose Table Properties from the pop-up menu.*

Figure 20.
Choose Table Properties from the Table menu.

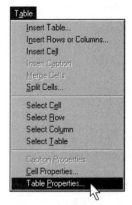

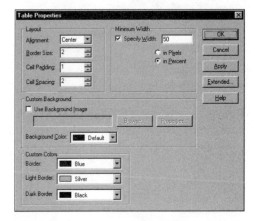

Figure 21. *Use the Table Properties dialog box to change the settings for your table.*

𝒴ou can change the settings for a table at any time by using the Table Properties command. In addition, you can add a background image or color, and if your table has borders, use custom colors to create a three-dimensional look.

To change table settings:

1. Place the insertion marker anywhere in the table.

2. Right click and select Table Properties from the pop-up menu (**Figure 19**) or choose Table Properties from the Table menu (**Figure 20**). The Table Properties dialog box will open (**Figure 21**).

3. Use the Layout area to select table alignment, set the border width in pixels, and add cell padding and cell spacing.

4. If you want to specify a minimum width for the table, put a check mark in the Specify Width check box in the Minimum Width area. Then set the table width in pixels or percent of the screen width.

5. While you are working with this dialog box, you can click Apply to add the changes you have made to the table. The Table Properties dialog box will remain open so you can continue to select new settings.

6. When you are finished changing the settings, click OK. The table will assume the new settings.

Change Table Settings

To add a background color or image to a table:

1. Place the insertion marker anywhere in the table.

2. Right click and select Table Properties from the pop-up menu or choose Table Properties from the Table menu. The Table Properties dialog box will open (**Figure 21**).

3. In the Custom Background area, use the Background Color drop-down list to select a background color for the table (**Figure 22**).

   or

   In the Custom Background area, put a check in the Use Background Image check box, then click the Browse button (**Figure 23**). Use the Select Background Image dialog box to choose an image already saved with the Web site, from your computer, from the World Wide Web, or from the FrontPage Clip Art collection (**Figure 24**). (Using the Select Background Image dialog box is discussed in detail in Chapter 10.)

4. Click OK. The background image will appear in the table (**Figure 25**).

Tip:

⊚ If the table has a caption, the background image will extend up (or down) to include the caption.

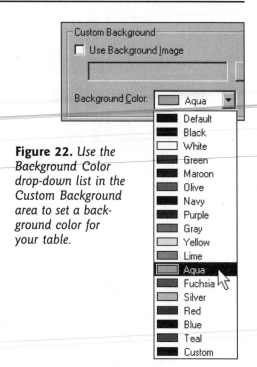

Figure 22. *Use the Background Color drop-down list in the Custom Background area to set a background color for your table.*

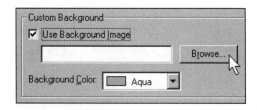

Figure 23. *Put a check in the Use Background Image check box, then click the Browse button.*

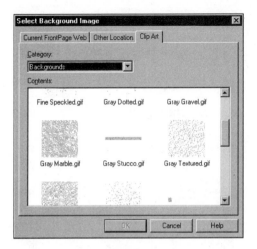

Figure 24. *Use the Select Background Image dialog box to choose an image from the current Web site, your computer, the World Wide Web, or the FrontPage 97 Clip Art collection.*

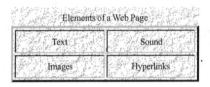

Figure 25. *When you click OK, the background image appears in the table.*

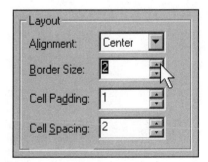

Figure 26. *Make sure the Border Size is set to at least 1.*

To give table borders a 3D look:

1. Place the insertion marker anywhere in the table.

2. Right click and select Table Properties from the pop-up menu or choose Table Properties from the Table menu. The Table Properties dialog box will open (**Figure 21**).

3. In the Layout area, make sure the Border Size is set to at least 1 (**Figure 26**). (This means that the table has a 1-pixel width border.)

4. In the Custom Colors area, use the Border drop-down list to select the main border color (**Figure 27**).

5. Use the Light Border drop-down list to select the highlight color and the Dark Border drop-down list to select the shadow color.

6. Click OK. The table's border will assume the custom colors you have chosen.

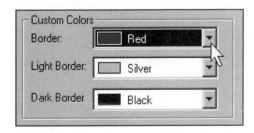

Figure 27. *Use the Custom Colors area to set the border color, highlight, and shadow.*

Cells also have special properties of their own, such as text alignment within a cell, background color or image, the number of rows or columns a cell spans, and the minimum width. To change any of these properties you first need to know how to select a cell, row, column, or the entire table.

To select a cell:

1. Position the insertion marker in the cell you want to select.

2. Choose Select Cell from the Table menu (**Figure 28**). The cell will be highlighted (**Figure 29**).

Tip:

⊚ To select more than one cell, you can also hold down the Shift key while clicking in the cells you want to select.

To select a row:

1. Position the insertion marker in one of the cells in the row you want to select.

2. Choose Select Row from the Table menu (**Figure 30**). The row will be highlighted (**Figure 31**).

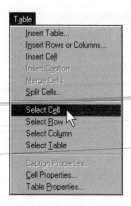

Figure 28. *Choose Select Cell from the Table menu.*

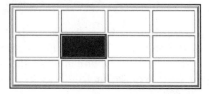

Figure 29. *When the cell is selected, it is highlighted.*

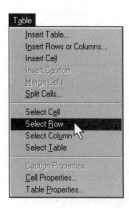

Figure 30. *Choose Select Row from the Table menu.*

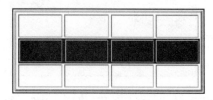

Figure 31. *The selected row is highlighted.*

Select a Cell; Select a Row

Figure 32.
Choose Select Column from the Table menu.

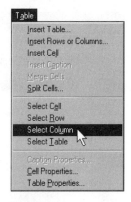

To select a column:

1. Position the insertion marker in one of the cells in the column you want to select.

2. Choose Select Column from the Table menu (**Figure 32**). The column will be highlighted (**Figure 33**).

To select the entire table:

1. Place the insertion marker anywhere in the table.

2. Choose Select Table from the Table menu (**Figure 34**). The table will be highlighted (**Figure 35**).

Figure 33. *The selected column is highlighted.*

Figure 34.
Choose Select Table from the Table menu.

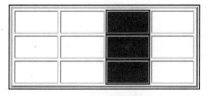

TABLE ALIGNMENT

You can quickly change a table's alignment on a Web page by selecting the entire table and then clicking the Align Left, Center, or Align Right buttons on the Format toolbar.

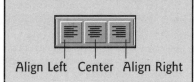

Align Left   Center   Align Right

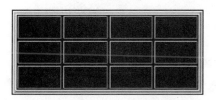

Figure 35. *The entire table is highlighted.*

Select a Column; Select a Table

To change cell settings:

1. Select the cells whose settings you want to change.

2. Right click on the selected cells and choose Cell Properties from the pop-up menu (**Figure 36**) or choose Cell Properties from the Table menu (**Figure 37**). The Cell Properties dialog box will appear (**Figure 38**).

3. In the Layout area, use the Horizontal Alignment and Vertical Alignment drop-down lists to set the alignment for the contents of a cell (**Figure 39**). For instance, if you want to align text in the center of the cell, select Center from the Horizontal Alignment drop-down list and Middle from the Vertical Alignment drop-down list.

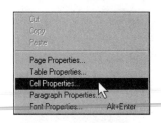

Figure 36. *Choose Cell Properties from the pop-up menu.*

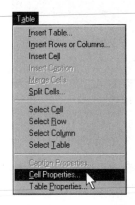

Figure 37. *Choose Cell Properties from the Table menu.*

Figure 38. *The Cell Properties dialog box.*

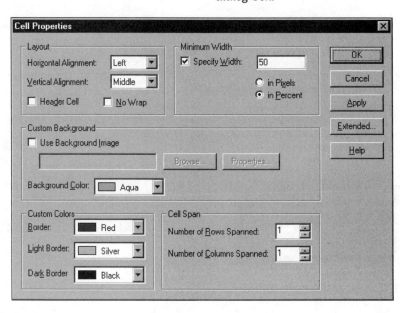

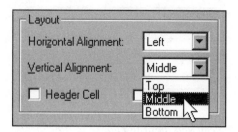

Figure 39. *Use the Layout area to set the horizontal and vertical alignment for the cell's contents.*

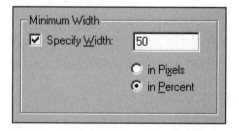

Figure 40. *You can use the Minimum Width area to set the minimum width for a cell.*

Figure 41. *Use the Custom Background area to set a background color or image for the cell.*

4. Use the Minimum Width area to specify a width for the selected cells (**Figure 40**). Put a check in the Specify Width check box, then either enter the number of pixels or a percentage of the table's width. For instance, a cell width of 50 percent will span half the width of the table.

5. Use the Custom Background area to set a special background image or color for the selected cells (**Figure 41**).

6. Use the Custom Colors area to set a special 3D border for the selected cells (**Figure 42**).

7. When you are happy with your selections, click OK. The cells you selected will assume the changes you picked.

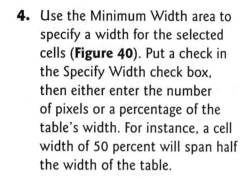

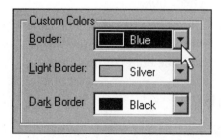

Figure 42. *To set a special 3D look for the cell's borders, use the Border, Light Border, and Dark Border drop-down lists.*

Change Cell Settings

Many times, a table will have a descriptive title in bold at the head of a column or to the left of a row. Also, any cell whose contents should be prominent could also be emphasized using bold text. To quickly create these special cells, change a regular cell into a *header cell*.

Figure 43. *Place the insertion marker in the cell you want to change to a header cell.*

To change a cell into a header cell:

1. Place the insertion marker in the cell you want to change (**Figure 43**).

2. Choose Cell Properties from the Table menu or right click on the cell and choose Cell Properties from the pop-up menu. The Cell Properties dialog box will open (**Figure 38**).

3. In the Layout area, put a check mark in the Header Cell check box (**Figure 44**).

4. If you don't want the text to automatically wrap in the cell into two or more lines, put a check mark in the No Wrap check box.

5. Click OK. The cell will become a header cell and the text will become bold (**Figure 45**).

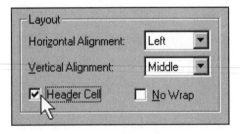

Figure 44. *In the Layout area of the Cell Properties dialog box, put a check in the Header Cell check box, then click OK.*

Tip:

- ✪ You can also format text in individual cells using the Bold, Italic, and Underline buttons on the Format toolbar.

Figure 45. *The text in the header cell becomes bold.*

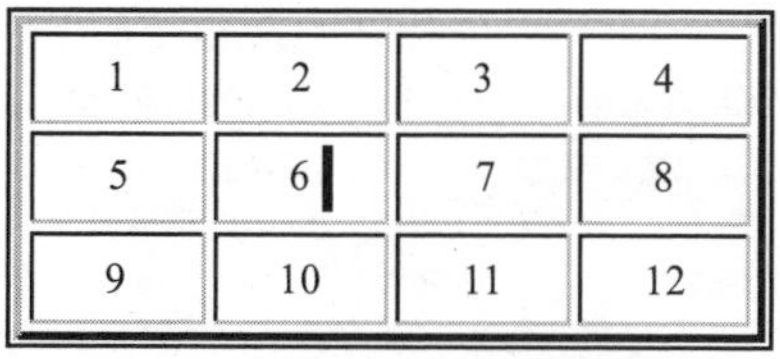

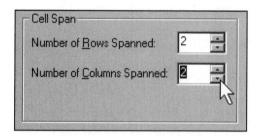

Figure 46. *Place the insertion marker in the cell whose span you want to change.*

Figure 47. *Use the Cell Span area of the Cell Properties dialog box to set how many rows and columns the cell will span.*

Figure 48. *Depending on the columns and rows the cell is spanning, the shape of the table can change and become irregular.*

*U*sing FrontPage Editor, you can easily set a cell to span more than one row or column. One reason you would want to do this is to include a large image in a cell below two cells of text.

To change the cell span:

1. Place the insertion marker in the cell whose span you want to change (**Figure 46**).

2. Open the Cell Properties dialog box (**Figure 38**) by choosing Cell Properties from the Table menu or right clicking on the cell and choosing Cell Properties from the pop-up menu.

3. In the Cell Span area, use the Number of Rows Spanned and the Number of Columns Spanned text boxes to set the cell's vertical and horizontal span (**Figure 47**).

4. Click OK. The cell span will change to the setting you chose (**Figure 48**).

I WANT A SYMMETRICAL TABLE!

If you change the cell span of a cell and the table becomes irregularly shaped, you may want to make the table symmetrical again. To do so, select the empty cells creating the irregular shape (for instance, the cells numbered 8, 11, and 12 in Figure 48) and delete them. If some of the cells contain data that you want to keep, add new cells to even out the irregular rows (for instance, two cells could be added next to cell 4 and one cell could be added next to cell 8 in Figure 48).

Change the Cell Span

What if you decide your table is not large enough? Don't worry—it's easy to add cells, rows, and columns.

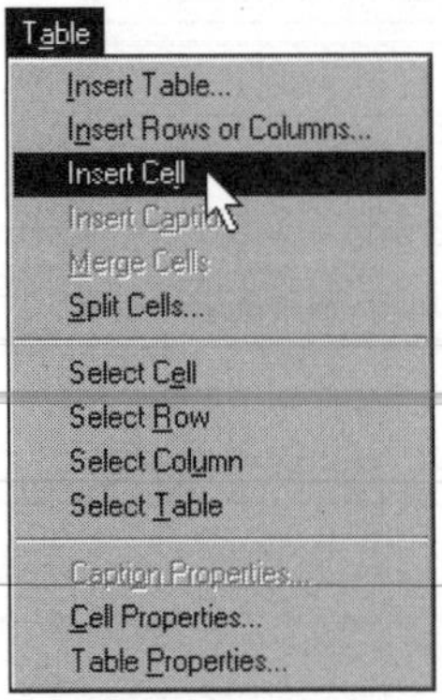

To add a cell:

1. Place the insertion marker in the cell to the left of where you want the new cell to appear.

2. Choose Insert Cell from the Table menu (**Figure 49**). The new cell will appear in the table.

To add new rows:

1. Place the insertion marker in a cell below or above where you want the new row to appear.

2. Choose Insert Rows or Columns from the Table menu (**Figure 50**). The Insert Rows or Columns dialog box will appear (**Figure 51**).

3. Select the Rows radio button.

4. Type in how many rows you want to add in the Number of Rows text box, then select whether the rows will appear above or below the insertion marker.

5. Click OK. The number of rows you entered will appear in the table.

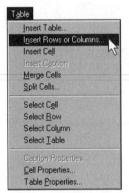

Figure 49.
Choose Insert Cell from the Table menu.

Figure 50.
Choose Insert Rows or Columns from the Table menu.

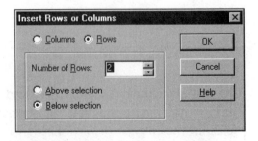

Figure 51. *Select the Rows radio button, then set the number of rows to be added and whether they will appear above or below the insertion marker.*

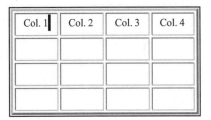

Figure 52. *Place the insertion marker in a cell next to where you want the new column to appear.*

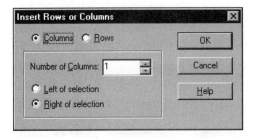

Figure 53. *Select the Columns radio button, then set how many columns will be added to the table and whether they will appear to the right or left of the insertion marker.*

New column

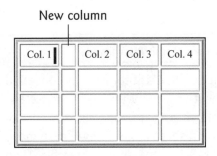

Figure 54. *When you click OK, the new column appears in the table.*

To add new columns:

1. Position the insertion marker to the right or left of where you want the new column to appear (**Figure 52**).

2. Choose Insert Rows or Columns from the Table menu (**Figure 50**). The Insert Rows or Columns dialog box will appear (**Figure 53**).

3. Select the Columns radio button.

4. Type in how many columns you want to add in the Number of Columns text box, then select whether the columns will appear to the left or the right of the insertion marker.

5. Click OK. The number of columns you entered will appear in the table (**Figure 54**). You can now enter text or images in the new cells or change the new cells' settings using the Cell Properties dialog box.

To delete a row or column:

Select the row you want to delete, then press the Delete or Backspace key on the keyboard.

Add Columns; Delete a Row or Column

Sometimes information in a cell can be quite complex and is more easily explained if it is in table format. With FrontPage, it's simple to insert a table into an individual cell. Some folks refer to this as "a table in a table."

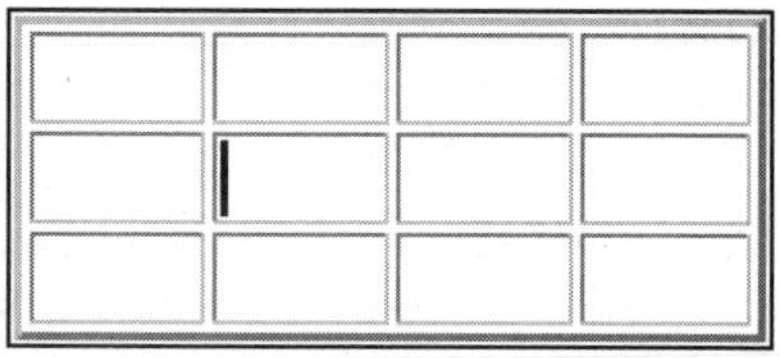

Figure 55. *Place the insertion marker in the cell where you would like to add the new table.*

To insert a table in a table:

1. Position the insertion marker in the cell where you want to add the new table (**Figure 55**).

2. Use the Insert Table button on the Standard toolbar (**Figure 6**) to add the table or choose Insert Table from the Table menu (**Figure 2**) and use the Insert Table dialog box (**Figure 3**) to set up the new table. The new table will appear in the cell (**Figure 56**).

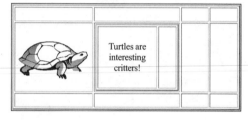

Figure 56. *The table within the cell can be used like any other table.*

Tips:

- Inserting a table into a cell can substantially change a table's shape and/or size.

- A complete discussion of inserting a table can be found on page 158.

INSERTING EXCEL SPREADSHEETS INTO YOUR WEB PAGES

When you insert an Excel spreadsheet into the Editor, it's automatically converted into table format. To add an Excel spreadsheet to your Web page, choose File from the Insert menu. In the Select a File dialog box that opens, use the Files of Type drop-down list to find Microsoft Excel Worksheet (*.xls, *.xlw), then move to the folder where the spreadsheet is saved. Select the spreadsheet file, then click Open. The spreadsheet will appear in your Web page.

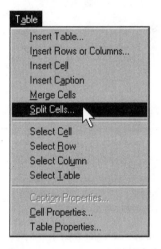

1	2	3	4
5	6	7	8
9	10	11	12

Figure 57. *Place the insertion marker in the cell you want to split.*

Besides adding cells and changing the span of a cell to adjust how a table presents information, you can also split and merge cells. Splitting cells can let you give more detailed information or, if you're using an invisible table to line up the contents of a page, help clean up formatting. Merging cells is handy when you want to combine the contents of several adjoining cells into one cell.

To split a cell:

1. Place the insertion marker in the cell you want to split (**Figure 57**).

2. Choose Split Cells from the Table menu (**Figure 58**). The Split Cells dialog box will appear (**Figure 59**).

3. Select either the Split into Columns radio button or the Split into Rows radio button, then enter the number of new columns or rows you want to appear in that cell.

4. Click OK. The cell will split as you specified (**Figure 60**).

Figure 58. *Choose Split Cells from the Table menu.*

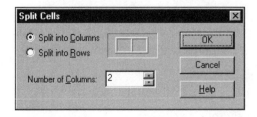

Figure 59. *Select whether you want to split the cell into columns or rows.*

Split cell

1	2	3	4
5	6		7	8
9	10	11	12

Figure 60. *When you click OK, the cell splits as you specified.*

Split a Cell

Merging cells combines several neighboring cells into one cell. While it may look similar to changing the cell span, cell span does not join cells together, it spreads one cell across any number of rows and/or columns. In addition, changing cell span will alter the size and shape of a table, whereas merging cells will not.

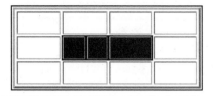

Figure 61. *Select the cells you want to merge.*

To merge cells:

1. Select the cells you want to merge (**Figure 61**). (The cells selected must make up a rectangular area.)

2. Choose Merge Cells from the Table menu (**Figure 62**). Any borders shared by the selected cells disappear and a single larger cell remains (**Figure 63**).

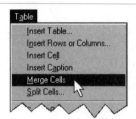

Figure 62. *Choose Merge Cells from the Table menu.*

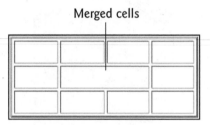

Figure 63. *The cells that you selected merge together.*

SUMMARY

In this chapter you learned how to:

- Create tables
- Add text, images, and backgrounds to tables
- Add a table caption
- Select cells, rows, and columns, and tables
- Create a header cell

- Change how many rows and colums a cell spans
- Add cells, rows, and columns
- Insert a table in a table
- Split a cell
- Merge cells together

The To Do List

K eeping track of tasks can be hard to do. When building a Web site, by yourself or as part of a team, there are many small details that need to get done. Unfortunately, sometimes things fall through the cracks. Luckily, Front-Page Explorer creates a To Do List every time a new Web site is created. This To Do List is shared across a Web site by all the folks helping to build it.

The To Do List is a roster of tasks that need to be completed for a particular site. It lists each task with a description and priority, and to whom the task is assigned. You can completely customize the To Do List by adding, deleting, changing, and reassigning tasks. **Figure 1** shows the To Do List window.

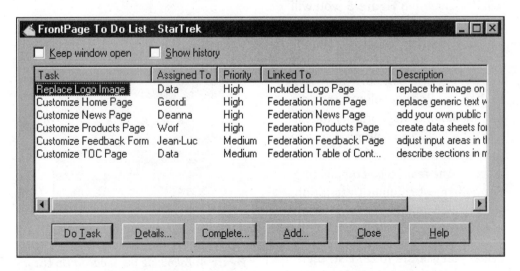

Figure 1. *The FrontPage To Do List window is used to assign tasks, show what needs to be done, and help you stay organized while you create your Web site.*

The To Do List can be opened from either the Editor or Explorer. To open it in the Editor, you must first have the Web site opened in Explorer.

To open the To Do List:

In either the Editor or Explorer, choose Show To Do List from the Tools menu (**Figure 2**) or click the Show To Do list button on the toolbar (**Figure 3**). The To Do List window will open (**Figure 1**).

Tip:

⑨ In FrontPage Explorer, the Show To Do list item on the Tools menu is followed by the number of tasks left undone on the list (**Figure 4**).

To Do List Features

If you take a look at the To Do List window shown in **Figure 5**, you will see that the tasks are listed in the left-most column. The next column, Assigned To, lists who is responsible for completing a particular task. Next to that, the Priority column shows a low, medium, or high priority for each task. The Linked To column displays the page that needs to be edited in order for the task to be completed. The right-most column, Description, gives a brief summary of what needs to be done.

Before you use the To Do List, there are some other features listed on the next page you should know about.

Figure 2. *Choose Show To Do List from the Editor's or Explorer's Tools menu.*

Figure 3. *Click the Show To Do List button on the Editor's or Explorer's toolbar.*

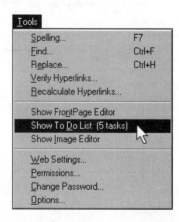

Figure 4. *Following the Show To Do List item on the Explorer's Tools menu is the number of tasks that need to be completed.*

1 Keep window open check box   **2** Show history check box   **3** Column headers   **4** Column dividers

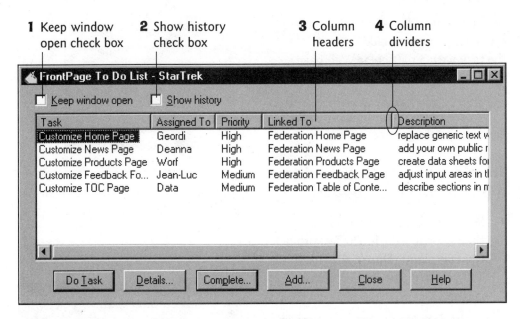

Figure 5. *The FrontPage To Do List window contains check boxes that let you keep the window open and show completed tasks, as well as let you sort the tasks by column type and resize the columns themselves.*

1 *Keep window open check box*

Ordinarily, when you click the Do Task button to start working on a specific task, the To Do List window closes. To keep the To Do List open, put a check in this check box.

2 *Show history check box*

To see a list of all tasks, including the ones marked as completed, put a check in this check box. A new column, labeled Completed, will appear, showing the date the task was completed. When the check box is unchecked, the To Do List only displays those tasks yet to be completed.

3 *Column headers*

Column headers are handy because you can use them to sort your list. To sort by a particular column type, click that column header. For instance, if you want to find all the tasks assigned to you, click the Assigned To column header. The list will sort alphabetically by name.

4 *Column dividers*

You can use the column dividers to make any column wider or narrower. Position the mouse pointer on a column divider. The pointer will change to a double-headed black arrow. Press the left mouse button and drag the column divider to resize the column.

When you add a task to the To Do List, you can decide to associate the task with a particular Web page or not. Tasks don't have to be linked to a particular page. For instance, you could add a task reminding yourself to create a certain graphic.

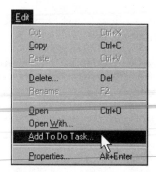

Figure 6. *Choose Add To Do Task from the Explorer's Edit menu.*

To add a new task linked to a particular Web page:

1. Select the page in the Explorer, then choose Add To Do Task from the Edit menu (**Figure 6**). The Add To Do Task dialog box will open (**Figure 7**).

2. In the Task Name text box, type in a name for the task (**Figure 8**). (This item will appear in the Task column in the To Do List window.)

3. Use the Assign To text box to assign the task to a particular person.

4. Use the Priority area to select a High, Medium, or Low priority for the task (**Figure 9**).

5. Add a brief description for the task in the Description text box (**Figure 10**).

6. Click OK. The task will be added to the To Do List.

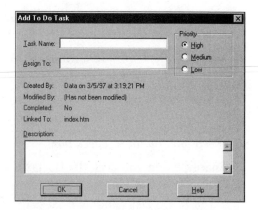

Figure 7. *The Add To Do Task dialog box is used to set a task name and priority, assign the task, and give it a description.*

Tip:

⑨ Notice that there is a specific page listed after Linked To in the Add To Do Task dialog box in Figure 7.

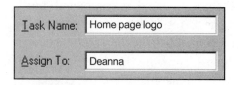

Figure 8. *Use the Task Name and Assign To text boxes to give the task a name and assign it to a particular person.*

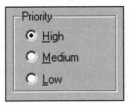

Figure 9. *Use the Priority area to select a High, Medium, or Low priority for the task.*

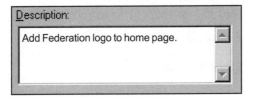

Figure 10. *Type a brief description of the task in the Description text box.*

To add a new task not linked to a specific page:

1. Open the To Do List window by clicking the Show To Do List button on the Editor's or Explorer's toolbar or choosing Show To Do List from the Editor's or Explorer's Tools menu.

2. Click the Add button. The Add To Do Task dialog box will appear (**Figure 11**).

3. Use the dialog box as described from steps 2 through 6 on the previous page.

Tip:

- Notice that there is no page listed after Linked To in the Add To Do Task dialog box in Figure 11.

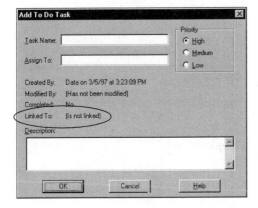

Figure 11. *When you add a task to the To Do List that is not linked to a specific page, the Linked To area will state just that.*

WHICH WEB PAGES NEED THE MOST WORK?

To see which pages on the To Do List have the most tasks assigned to them, click the Linked To column header to sort the tasks by page.

When you work on a Web site, the information in the To Do List will need to be kept up-to-date. For instance, once a task is finished, you can mark it as completed, or you can change the description of a task if it changes.

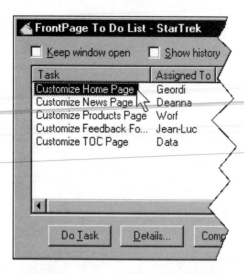

Figure 12. *Click on the task you want to work on in the Task column, then click the Do Task button.*

To work on a task:

1. Click on a task in the Task column (**Figure 12**).

2. Click the Do Task button. The Editor will open to the page where the task needs to be done.

3. Work on the task until it's finished or until you have to stop.

4. Save the page containing the task. FrontPage will ask you whether you want to mark the task as completed (**Figure 13**).

5. If you finished the task, click Yes. The task will be marked as completed and removed from the To Do List. (If you want to see what items have been completed on the To Do List, check the Show history check box.) If you left the task unfinished, click No. The task will not be marked as completed and you can continue working in the Editor later.

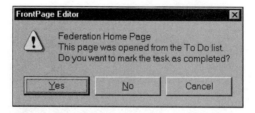

Figure 13. *When you save the page you've been working on, FrontPage Editor asks you whether you want to mark the task as completed.*

Tip:

☺ If a task is not associated with a specific Web page, the Do Task button will be grayed out.

(sidebar) **Work on a Task**

Figure 14.
Select the task you want to change, then click the Details button.

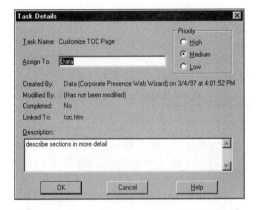

Figure 15. *Use the Task Details dialog box to make any changes you need.*

Figure 16. *When you click OK, the task's details change. In Figure 14, the Customize TOC Page task was assigned to Data. Here it has been reassigned to Jake.*

You may find that you will need to change the details for a particular task after it has been worked on or not completed or if you want to assign the task to a different person.

To change task details:

1. Open the To Do List window and select the task whose details you want to change (**Figure 14**).

2. Click the Details button. The Task Details dialog box will open (**Figure 15**).

3. Use the Assign To text box to reassign the task to another person.

4. Use the Priority area to change the task's priority by selecting the High, Medium, or Low radio buttons.

5. Change the task's description using the Description text box.

6. Click OK. The task's details will change in the To Do List window (**Figure 16**).

Tip:

◉ You may have noticed that the Task Details dialog box shown in Figure 15 looks familiar. That's because it is exactly the same as the Add To Do Task dialog box shown in Figure 7.

Change Task Details

To mark a task as completed or to delete a task:

1. Open the To Do List window and select the task you want to mark as completed.

2. Click the Complete button. The Complete Task dialog box will open (**Figure 17**).

3. To mark the task as completed, select the Mark this task as completed radio button.

   or

   To delete the task, select the Delete this task (do not save in the To Do List history) radio button.

4. Click OK.

Tip:

☺ When you select the radio button that will delete the task and click OK, FrontPage *does not* open a dialog box asking you to confirm the deletion. So be sure you want to delete the task before you click OK.

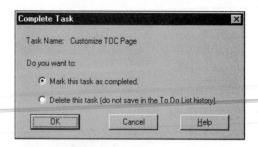

Figure 17. *The Complete Task dialog box is used to mark a task as completed or to delete the task from the To Do List altogether.*

THE TO DO LIST AND YOUR TEAM'S WORK LOAD

If you are heading up a team working on a Web site, check the To Do List periodically to see if your team's work load is evenly distributed. If there's one person with much more work than the rest of the team, even up the work load by reassigning some of that person's tasks.

SUMMARY

In this chapter you learned how to:

☺ Open the To Do List window

☺ Add tasks to the To Do List

☺ Work on a To Do List task

☺ Change task details

☺ Mark a task as completed

☺ Delete a task

Complete or Delete a Task

Hyperlinks and Hotspots

*H*yperlinks and image *hotspots* are connections from one Web page to another. If you've surfed the Web, there's little doubt that you've used them to move from one page to another within a site or from one Web site to another.

Hyperlinks, also called *links*, are the underlined text and bordered images that a user can click to jump to another location. Links work by including the URL of the destination Web page within the HTML codes associated with the text or image clicked by the user. The text or image is usually descriptive of where the hyperlink will take the user. For instance, a text link that says "Home" will take the user to the site's home page. A comparable image could be one of a little house.

Another type of hyperlink, a *bookmark* or *anchor*, moves the user around a Web page. When the user clicks a bookmark, the Web page moves to a specific location in the browser. For instance, suppose you had a Web page with a large article divided into sections. You could have a mini table of contents at the top of the article with bookmark links that would jump the user to the various sections.

Hot spots are specific areas of an image that a user clicks to jump to another location. Hot spots are contained within an *image map*. An image map is automatically created by FrontPage when you add hot spots to an image. The image map tells a Web browser the precise location of each hotspot, using coordinates in pixels.

When you create a hyperlink, there are several places you can link to: any Web page currently open in the Editor, any page in the open Web site, a site or page on the World Wide Web, or a new Web page that will be added to the open Web site.

Figure 1. *When you select a graphic, eight black handles appear around the image.*

To create a hyperlink to a page open in the Editor:

1. In the Editor, select the text or image that will become the link to another place (**Figure 1**). If you are using an image, click on it to select it. Eight black handles will appear around the image.

2. Choose Hyperlink from the Insert menu (**Figure 2**) or click the Create or Edit Hyperlink button on the Standard toolbar (**Figure 3**) or press Ctrl+K on the keyboard. The Create Hyperlink dialog box will open (**Figure 4**).

3. Click the Open Pages tab to bring that tab page to the front.

4. Select the name of a Web page from the Open Pages list box.

5. Click OK. The link will be embedded in the HTML code underlying the Web page. If you selected text for the hyperlink, it will be underlined. If you selected an image, a blue border will appear around it (**Figure 5**).

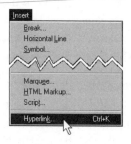

Figure 2. *Choose Hyperlink from the Insert menu.*

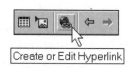

Figure 3. *Click the Create or Edit Hyperlink button on the Standard toolbar.*

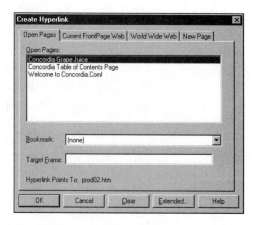

Figure 4. *Use the Open Pages tab page to select a target Web page to link to.*

Figure 5. *A border appears around the hyperlinked image.*

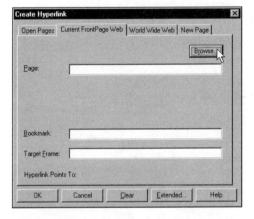

Figure 6. *Use the Current FrontPage Web tab page to select a page from the open Web site.*

Figure 7. *Select a Web page from the list box in the Current Web dialog box.*

To create a hyperlink to a page in the open Web site:

1. In the Editor, select the text or image that will become the link to another place. If you are using an image, click on it to select it. Eight black handles will appear around the image.

2. Choose Hyperlink from the Insert menu (**Figure 2**) or click the Create or Edit Hyperlink button on the Standard toolbar (**Figure 3**) or press Ctrl+K on the keyboard. The Create Hyperlink dialog box will open (**Figure 4**).

3. Click the Current FrontPage Web tab to bring that tab page to the front (**Figure 6**).

4. Click the Browse button above the Page text box. The Current Web dialog box will open (**Figure 7**).

5. Select a Web page that you want to link to, then click OK. The Current Web dialog box will close and the name of the page you selected will appear in the Page text box.

6. Click OK. The link will be embedded in the HTML code underlying the Web page. If you selected text for the hyperlink, it will be underlined. If you selected an image, a blue border will appear around it.

Create a Link to a Page in the Site

Create a Link to a Page on the Web

To create a hyperlink to a World Wide Web site:

1. In the Editor, select the text or image that will become the link to the World Wide Web site.

2. Choose Hyperlink from the Insert menu or click the Create or Edit Hyperlink button on the Standard toolbar. The Create Hyperlink dialog box will open.

3. Click the World Wide Web tab to bring that tab page to the front (**Figure 8**).

4. Select the type of protocol you want to use from the Hyperlink Type drop-down list (**Figure 9**). The default for this item is the http: protocol (see page 12 for more about protocols).

5. In the URL text box, enter the URL of the Web page or site you want to link to (**Figure 10**).

6. Click OK. The link will be embedded in the HTML code underlying the Web page. If you selected text for the hyperlink, it will be underlined. If you selected an image, a blue border will appear around it.

Tip:

⊚ You may have noticed that the protocol (for example, http://) is entered automatically in the URL text box when you select a protocol using the Hyperlink Type drop-down list.

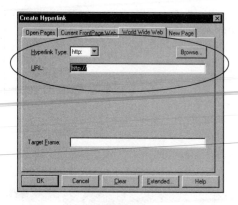

Figure 8. *Use the World Wide Web tab page to create a hyperlink to another Web site.*

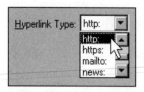

Figure 9. *Select http: from the Hyperlink Type drop-down list.*

Figure 10. *Type the address for the Web site or page in the URL text box.*

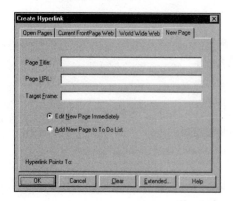

Figure 11. *Use the New Page tab page to create a hyperlink to a page not yet created.*

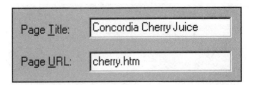

Figure 12. *Use the Page Title and Page URL text boxes to enter a title and filename.*

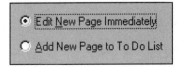

Figure 13. *To work on the new page right away, select the Edit New Page Immediately radio button.*

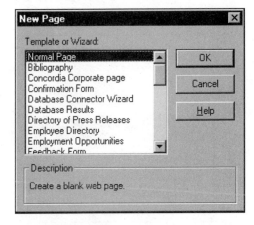

Figure 14. *Select a page template or wizard using the list box in the New Page dialog box.*

To create a hyperlink to a Web page that has not been created yet:

1. In the Editor, select the text or image that will become the link to the page not yet created.

2. Choose Hyperlink from the Insert menu or click the Create or Edit Hyperlink button on the Standard toolbar. The Create Hyperlink dialog box will open.

3. Click the New Page tab to bring that tab page to the front (**Figure 11**).

4. Type in a title for the new Web page in the Page Title text box (**Figure 12**).

5. Add a filename for the new page in the Page URL text box. This filename should have the .Htm extension. For instance, Home.Htm.

6. Set whether you want to work on the new page now or later by selecting either the Edit New Page Immediately radio button or the Add New Page to To Do List radio button (**Figure 13**).

7. Click OK. The New Page dialog box will appear (**Figure 14**).

8. Select the type of page you want to create, then click OK. Depending on the radio button you selected on the New Page tab, the new page will appear in the Editor or a task will be added to the To Do List.

To create a link that sends e-mail:

1. In the Editor, select the text or image that will become the link that will send e-mail.

2. Choose Hyperlink from the Insert menu or click the Create or Edit Hyperlink button on the Standard toolbar. The Create Hyperlink dialog box will open.

3. Click the World Wide Web tab to bring that tab page to the front (**Figure 15**).

4. Select the mailto: protocol from the Hyperlink Type drop-down list (**Figure 16**).

5. In the URL text box, enter the e-mail address after the mailto: protocol (**Figure 17**).

6. Click OK. The e-mail link will be embedded in the HTML code underlying the Web page.

Tip:

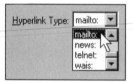 The FrontPage Editor will automatically create hyperlinks for you if you type in a specific protocol or Web address. For instance, if you type mailto:info@bearhome.com, the Editor will create an e-mail hyperlink, underlining that text. The hyperlinks shown in **Figure 18** were all created automatically just by typing them in the Editor window. The Create Hyperlink dialog box didn't even open!

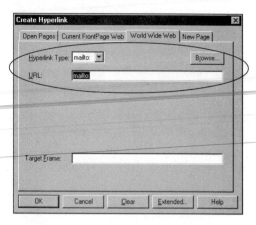

Figure 15. *Use the World Wide Web tab page to create an e-mail hyperlink.*

Figure 16. *Select mailto: from the Hyperlink Type drop-down list.*

Figure 17. *Type the e-mail address in the URL text box.*

Figure 18. *These hyperlinks were created automatically.*

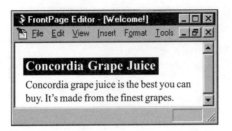

Figure 19. *Select the text that the user will jump to when a hyperlink is clicked.*

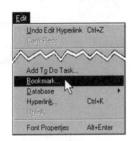

Figure 20. *Choose Bookmark from the Edit menu.*

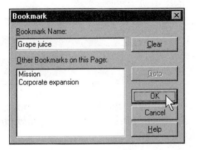

Figure 21. *Type a descriptive name for the bookmark in the Bookmark Name text box.*

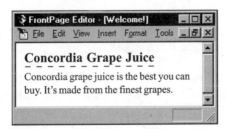

Figure 22. *A dashed line appears under the text that was selected as a bookmark.*

ookmarks, also known as *anchors*, are a set of text characters that you select in the Editor window. These characters become the target of a hyperlink. Using hyperlinks to bookmarks lets the user jump to any point within a Web page.

To create a bookmark:

1. Use the mouse to select the text that will become the bookmark. This is the text that you want the user to jump to when she clicks a hyperlink (**Figure 19**).

2. Choose Bookmark from the Edit menu (**Figure 20**). The Bookmark dialog box will open (**Figure 21**).

3. Type a name for the bookmark in the Bookmark Name text box. This name should be something distinctive because later you will have to select it from a list when you create the hyperlink to the bookmark.

4. Click OK. The text that you selected will become underlined with a blue-dashed line indicating that it is a bookmark (**Figure 22**).

Create a Bookmark

To create a hyperlink using a bookmark:

1. Select the text or image that will become the link to the bookmark. If you are using an image, click on it to select it. Eight black handles will appear around the image.

2. Choose Hyperlink from the Insert menu (**Figure 2**) or click the Create or Edit Hyperlink button on the Standard toolbar (**Figure 3**) or press Ctrl+K on the keyboard. The Create Hyperlink dialog box will open (**Figure 4**).

3. Click the Current FrontPage Web tab to bring that tab page to the front (**Figure 23**).

4. In the Bookmark text box, type the name of the bookmark *exactly* as you created it in the Bookmark dialog box (**Figure 24**). The bookmark must have the same capitalization, spelling, and spaces.

5. Click OK. The hyperlink will be set up. The next time you preview the page in a browser, you'll be able to use the hyperlink to jump to the bookmark.

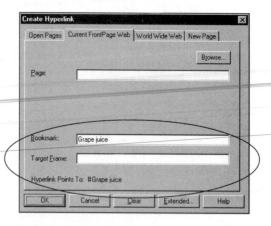

Figure 23. *Use the Current FrontPage Web tab to create a hyperlink to the bookmark.*

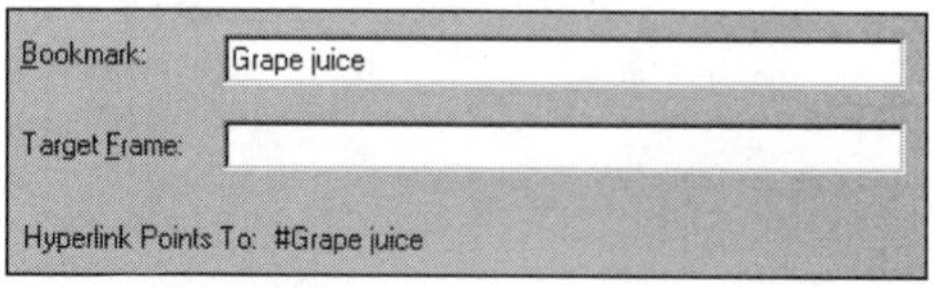

Bookmark: Grape juice
Target Frame:
Hyperlink Points To: #Grape juice

Figure 24. *Type the name of the bookmark exactly as you created it in the Bookmark dialog box.*

WRITE DOWN THE NAMES YOU GIVE BOOKMARKS

When you are ready to create the links using the bookmarks, open the Bookmark dialog box. On a piece of paper, write down the bookmarks *exactly* as they appear in the Other Bookmarks on this Page list box, including exact spelling, capitalization, and spaces. This is important because when you create the hyperlink, you will have to enter the exact bookmark name or the hyperlink won't work.

Create a Link using a Bookmark

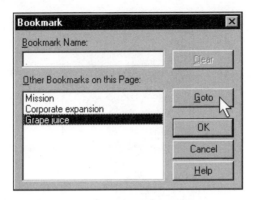

Figure 25. *Select the bookmark, then click the Goto button.*

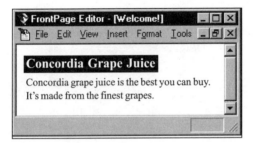

Figure 26. *FrontPage Editor will scroll to the bookmark and select it.*

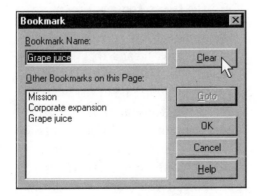

Figure 27. *Click the Clear button to delete the bookmark.*

You can use bookmarks to easily move around a Web page. Or if you forget where a bookmark is, the Bookmark dialog box will take you right to it.

To go to a bookmark:

1. Choose Bookmark from the Edit menu (**Figure 20**). The Bookmark dialog box will open (**Figure 25**).

2. Select the bookmark you want to go to from the Other Bookmarks on this Page list box.

3. Click Goto. The Web page will move to the bookmark location and the bookmark will be selected (**Figure 26**).

To delete a bookmark:

1. Choose Bookmark from the Edit menu (**Figure 20**). The Bookmark dialog box will appear (**Figure 25**).

2. Select the bookmark you want to delete.

3. Click the Goto button. This will move you to the bookmark and select it. The Clear button in the Bookmark dialog box will become enabled (**Figure 27**).

4. Click the Clear button. The text will remain and the bookmark will be removed.

Go to a Bookmark

In order to create hotspots on an image, you will need to use the Image toolbar. Usually, when you select an image with the mouse, the Image toolbar will appear on the Editor screen. If it doesn't appear, it's easy to open.

To view the Image toolbar:

Choose Image Toolbar from the View menu (**Figure 28**). The Image toolbar will appear (**Figure 29**). If an image is not selected, the Image toolbar will be grayed out and unusable.

Tip:

◉ To remove the Image toolbar from view, just choose Image Toolbar from the View menu.

You can make all or part of an image into a hotspot that links to other locations. For instance, suppose you were creating a Web page for Concordia Corp., a maker of fine fruit juices. You could use an image of different kinds of fruits as the link to other juice pages. You could add a hotspot on an apple that would link to an apple juice page, a hotspot on a pear that would link to a pear juice page, and a hotspot on some cherries for a link to a cherry juice page.

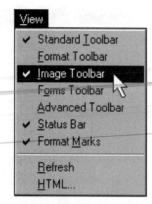

Figure 28. *Choose Image Toolbar from the View menu.*

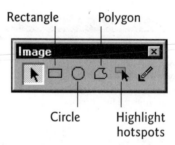

Figure 29. *The Image toolbar is used to create and view hotspots.*

THE IMAGE TOOLBAR FLOATS

The Image toolbar is a floating toolbar. This means that you can move it around the screen and place it where it won't be in the way. To move the toolbar, position the mouse pointer over the toolbar's title bar, press the left mouse button, and drag it to its new position. If you want to dock the toolbar, just drag it to the top of the Editor window.

View the Image Toolbar

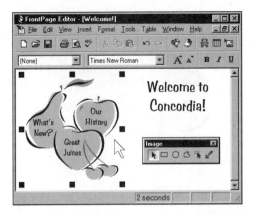

Figure 30. *Select the image you want to add the hotspot to.*

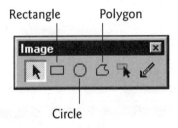

Figure 31. *Click the Rectangle, Circle, or Polygon button on the Image toolbar.*

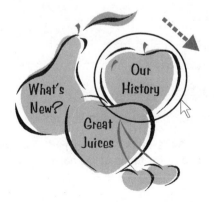

Figure 32. *After you select the Rectangle or Circle button, press the left mouse button and drag diagonally to create the hotspot.*

To create a hotspot:

1. Select the image to which you'll be adding the hotspot (**Figure 30**). The Image toolbar will appear, if it is not already visible, and it will become enabled with the Select button depressed.

2. Figure out what shape you want the hotspot to be. Will it be square, round, or irregularly shaped?

3. Click the Rectangle, Circle, or Polygon toolbar button, depending upon the shape of the area you want to define as the hotspot (**Figure 31**). The Rectangle button will create a rectangular hotspot, the Circle button a circular hotspot, and the Polygon button an irregularly shaped hotspot.

4. Draw the hotspot around the part of the image you want to become the link to another location.

   ☞ If you are using the Rectangle or Circle toolbar button to create a rectangular or circular hotspot, position the mouse pointer at the upper left of the area you want to select as the hotspot. Press the left mouse button and drag diagonally towards the lower-right to create the hotspot (**Figure 32**).

Create a Hotspot

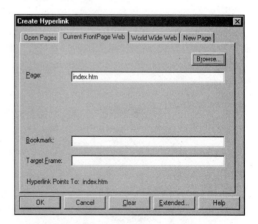

🌀 If you are using the Polygon toolbar button to create an irregularly shaped hotspot, position the mouse pointer where you want the hotspot to start and click the left mouse button. The first point of the polygon will appear. Move the mouse to the next place where you want to insert a point of the polygon and click the mouse. Continue moving the mouse and clicking until you have encompassed the entire irregularly shaped area. To complete the hotspot, click on the original place where you created the first point of the polygon (**Figure 33**).

Figure 33. *After you click the Polygon button, position the mouse pointer where you want to start the polygonal hotspot and click. Continue moving the mouse and clicking until the desired shape of the hotspot is complete.*

5. When you have completed drawing the hotspot on the image, the Create Hyperlink dialog box will appear (**Figure 34**). Use this dialog box to set the target for your hyperlink. Using the different tab pages, you can link to Web pages currently open in the Editor, Web pages available in the Web site currently open in the Explorer, Web pages on the World Wide Web, or a new page that hasn't been created yet.

Figure 34. *Use the Create Hyperlink dialog box to add the link that the hotspot will jump the user to.*

Tip:

🌀 If your hotspot is not in the exact location you intended, don't worry! You can move and resize it.

Figure 35. *Select the image containing the hotspot you want to move or resize.*

Figure 36. *Press the left mouse button and drag the hotspot to its new position.*

Figure 37. *Position the mouse over one of the hotspot points and drag it to its new location.*

To move or resize a hotspot:

1. Select the image containing the hotspot you want to move or resize. The different hotspots will become apparent (**Figure 35**) and the Image toolbar will appear enabled.

2. Select the hotspot you want to move or resize.

3. To move a hotspot:

    a. Position the mouse pointer in the center of the hotspot.

    b. Press the left mouse button and drag it to its new location (**Figure 36**). (You can also use the arrow keys on the keyboard to nudge the hotspot around.)

    To resize a hotspot:

    a. Position the mouse pointer over the hotspot point you want to move to change the size.

    b. Press the left mouse button and drag the point to its new position (**Figure 37**).

Tip:

⊚ What if you move or resize a hotspot and decide you don't like the change you have made? *Before you release the left mouse button you've been dragging* press the Esc key on the keyboard. This will return the hotspot to its original position and/or shape.

Move or Resize a Hotspot

Once you've created a hotspot link, you can change the target of the hotspot if you need to.

To edit a hotspot link:

1. Select the image containing the hotspot.

2. Open the Edit Hyperlink dialog box:

   Double-click on the hotspot.

   or

   Right click on the hotspot and choose Image Hotspot Properties from the pop-up menu (**Figure 38**).

   or

   Choose Image Hotspot Properties from the bottom of the Edit menu (**Figure 39**).

   or

   Press Alt+Enter on the keyboard.

   The Edit Hyperlink dialog box will appear (**Figure 40**). (Notice that this dialog box is exactly the same as the Create Hyperlink dialog box shown in Figure 4.)

Figure 38. *Choose Image Hotspot Properties from the pop-up menu.*

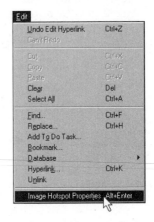

Figure 39. *Choose Image Hotspot Properties from the Edit menu.*

Figure 40. *Use the Open Pages tab page of the Edit Hyperlink dialog box to select a new link to an open Web page.*

Figure 41. *Use the Current FrontPage Web tab to create a new link to a page in the open Web site.*

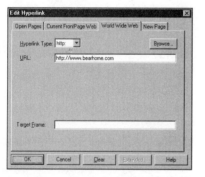

Figure 42. *Use the World Wide Web tab page to create a new link to a Web site or page.*

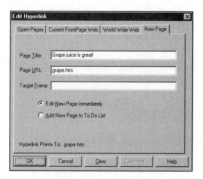

Figure 43. *Use the New Page tab page to create a new link to a page that hasn't been created yet.*

3. Use the tab pages of the Edit Hyperlink dialog box to change the target for your hyperlink. Use the:

- ⊚ Open Pages tab page to create links to Web pages currently open in the Editor (**Figure 40**).

- ⊚ Current FrontPage Web tab page to create links to Web pages in the site currently open in the Explorer (**Figure 41**).

- ⊚ World Wide Web tab page to create links to sites or pages on the World Wide Web (**Figure 42**).

- ⊚ New Page tab page to create links to a new page that hasn't been created yet (**Figure 43**).

4. When you are finished editing the hyperlink, click OK to close the Edit Hyperlink dialog box.

THE TARGET FRAME TEXT BOX

You've probably noticed the Target Frame text box on the Open Pages tab and Current FrontPage Web tab of the Edit Hyperlink and Create Hyperlink dialog boxes. This text box is used to create hyperlinks to Web pages that contain *frames*. Frames will be discussed in detail in Chapter 15.

Edit a Hotspot Link

Sometimes it can be hard to see all the hotspots you've added to an image, especially if the image is complex.

Figure 44. *Select the image containing the hotspots you want to see.*

To show all hotspots on an image:

1. Select the image (**Figure 44**). The Image toolbar will appear.

2. Click the Highlight Hotspots button on the Image toolbar (**Figure 45**). The image will become invisible and the hotspot borders will appear in aqua (**Figure 46**).

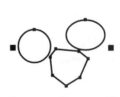

Figure 45. *Click the Highlight Hotspots button on the Image toolbar.*

Tip:

◎ To make the image visible, click the Highlight Hotspots button again.

To delete a hotspot:

1. Select the image containing the hotspot you want to delete.

2. Select the hotspot, then press the Delete or Backspace key on the keyboard.

Figure 46. *When the image becomes invisible, the hotspots are easy to see.*

SUMMARY

In this chapter you learned how to:

◎ Create hyperlinks

◎ Make an e-mail hyperlink

◎ Create bookmarks and link them to target locations

◎ View the Image toolbar

◎ Create hotspots

◎ Move and resize hotspots

◎ Delete a hotspot

Using Frames

Frames split the browser window into separate rectangular regions. Each region can display a Web page. You can have as many frames on a page as you want. The frames that make up a Web page are called a *frameset*.

When someone is browsing a page made up of frames, the content of one frame can change while the others remain the same or hyperlinks in one frame can make the page shown in another page change. A typical use for frames is to have a Web page divided into three frames. A frame across the top of the Web page displays a company name or topic. A left frame displays a table of contents page that contains hyperlinks to every page on the site. When the user clicks one of these hyperlinks, the right frame displays the Web page. The Web page shown in the right frame depends on what the user clicks in the left frame (**Figure 1**). **Figure 2** shows a Web page using this table of contents plan.

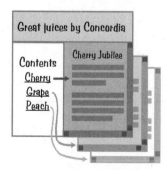

Figure 1. *When a user clicks a hyperlink in the left frame, the right page displays the Web page that it links to.*

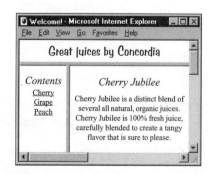

Figure 2. *A Web page displaying a table of contents frame on the left with hyperlinks to pages that display in the right frame.*

How Frames Work

The Web page displayed in Figure 2 actually shows four Web pages. Each of the three frames shows a Web page—the upper frame shows a page that says "Great juices by Concordia," the left frame shows a page that contains the table of contents with hyperlinks, and the right frame shows a page that tells about Cherry Jubilee juice. The fourth Web page contains the frames that display the three Web pages.

This chapter will take you through creating a Web page with frames set up in this arrangement.

To get started, launch FrontPage Explorer and create a new Normal Web site with a blank Home Page. (The home page will be used later in a browser to link to the page containing the frames and display it.)

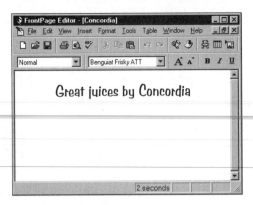

Figure 3. *The concordia.htm Web page will eventually become the banner across the frame Web page.*

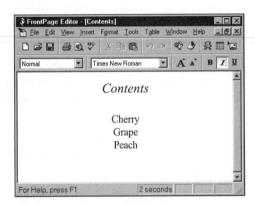

Figure 4. *The contents.htm Web page will eventually fill the left table of contents frame on the frame Web page.*

LEARNING MORE ABOUT FRAMES ON THE WEB

If you want to learn more about what frames can do for your Web site, visit:

http://www.microsoft.com/workshop/design/

http://www.netscape.com/comprod/products/navigator/version_3.0/layout/

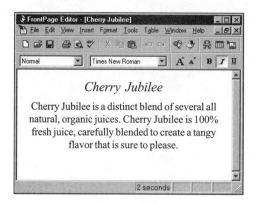

Figure 5. *The cherry.htm Web page will become the default Web page filling the right frame in the frame Web page. In addition, a hyperlink in the table of contents frame will link to this page.*

Figure 6. *The alternate.htm Web page will appear if the browser used to surf the Web site does not support frames.*

Use the Editor to create the Web pages that will become the frame contents. For this example, the Web page that says "Great juices by Concordia" will be named concordia.htm (**Figure 3**), and the page containing the table of contents and hyperlinks will be named contents.htm (**Figure 4**). The Web pages that appear in the right frame when a hyperlink is clicked in the left table of contents frame will be named cherry.htm (**Figure 5**), grape.htm, and peach.htm.

In addition to the Web pages that will be displayed in the frames, it's a good idea to create an alternate page that can be displayed if the user's browser does not support frames. That way, the user will still be able to navigate through the site without frames. For this example, the alternate Web page will be named alternate.htm (**Figure 6**).

Create the Pages for the Frames

DON'T OVERUSE FRAMES

As a Web design element, frames tend to be overused. If more than three or four frames are used on a Web page, the page can have a crowded feeling. In addition, frames can be a cause of browser crashes. Frames are a powerful design tool, but they should be used sparingly in Web sites.

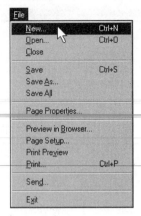

O nce you've created the Web pages that will become the contents for the frames, it's time to create the Web page that will contain the frames. To do this, you will use the Frames Wizard.

Figure 7. *Choose New from the Editor's File menu.*

To create a frameset Web page:

1. Launch the FrontPage Explorer and open the Web site containing the Web pages that will become the frame contents.

2. Start the Editor by double-clicking on a Web page in the Explorer or clicking the Show FrontPage Editor button on the toolbar.

3. In the Editor, choose New from the File menu (**Figure 7**). The New Page dialog box will appear (**Figure 8**).

4. Select Frames Wizard from the list box, then click OK. The first panel of the wizard, Frames Wizard – Choose Technique, will appear (**Figure 9**).

5. Select the Make a custom grid radio button.

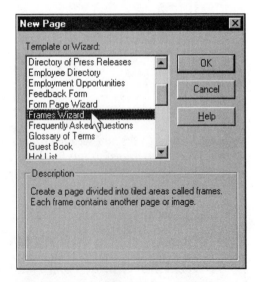

Figure 8. *In the New Page dialog box, scroll down the Template or Wizard list box until you find Frames Wizard. Select it, then click OK.*

Create a Frameset Web Page

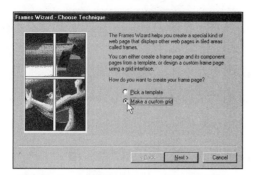

Figure 9. *In the first panel of the Frames Wizard, select the Make a custom grid radio button then click Next.*

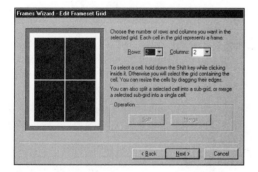

Figure 10. *Use the Frames Wizard – Edit Frameset Grid to set the number of frames and their size.*

6. Click Next. The wizard will move to the next panel, Frames Wizard – Edit Frameset Grid (**Figure 10**). This window is used to set the number and size of the frames on the frame Web page. The number of rows and columns is set using the Rows and Columns drop-down lists. The frameset you are creating is shown in the view pane to the left of the panel. Each frame is separated by a white line. You can move these lines to change the size of the frames.

7. To achieve the number of frames and the layout for this table of contents example, use the Columns drop-down list to change the number of columns to 1. The frameset in the view pane will look something like **Figure 11**.

Figure 11. When *1* is selected in the Columns drop-down list, upper and lower frames remain in the view pane.

8. To create the thin frame across the top of the page, you will need to change the size of the upper frame in the view pane.

   a. Position the mouse over the white line dividing the two frames. The mouse pointer will change to a double-headed arrow.

   b. Press the left mouse button and drag the white line up to make the upper frame thinner (**Figure 12**).

   c. When you are finished sizing the upper frame, release the mouse button.

9. To create the left table of contents frame and right juice description frame, you will need to select the large lower frame and split it.

   a. To select the large lower frame, press the shift key and click on the lower frame. It will become highlighted (**Figure 13**).

   b. In the Operation area of the Frames Wizard – Edit Frameset Grid panel, click Split (**Figure 14**). The selected frame will split into four frames (**Figure 15**).

   c. Using the Rows drop-down list select 1 (**Figure 16**). The two extra frames will disappear and left and right frames will remain (**Figure 17**).

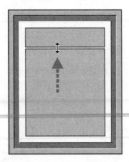

Figure 12. *Press the left mouse button and drag the white line up to resize the frame.*

Figure 13. *Press the shift key and click on the lower frame to select it.*

Figure 14. *In the Operation area, click the Split button to split the selected frame.*

Figure 15. *When the Split button is clicked, the selected frame splits into four frames.*

Figure 16. *Select 1 from the Rows drop-down list.*

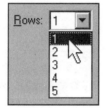

10. Position the mouse pointer over the white line dividing the two new frames, press the left mouse button and drag to the left. This will make the left frame thinner than the right frame (**Figure 18**).

11. When you are finished sizing the left and right frames, release the mouse button. *Congratulations!* You've just finished setting the number of frames and their size for the special frame Web page.

Figure 17. *Left and right frames remain after the Rows drop-down list is set to 1.*

Figure 18. *Press the left mouse button and drag the white frame divider to the left to resize the left and right frames.*

Set the Frame Layout; Resize Frames

SETTING THE NUMBER OF FRAMES

If you need to create a set of frames with a different layout, use the techniques described above to set the number of columns and rows and to size the frames. FrontPage lets you create a frame grid with up to 5 rows and 5 columns.

---

12. Click Next. The wizard will move to the next panel, Frames Wizard – Edit Frames Attributes (**Figure 19**). This panel is used to set a name for each frame and to choose the Web page that will be shown in each specific frame. Notice that nothing is selected in the view pane and that all the text boxes and buttons are grayed out.

13. For this example, start with the top frame that will say, "Great juices by Concordia." Select the upper frame by clicking on it in the view pane. The text boxes and buttons on the panel will become enabled (**Figure 20**).

14. Type a name for the frame in the Name text box. For the example, this frame will be named Banner (**Figure 21**).

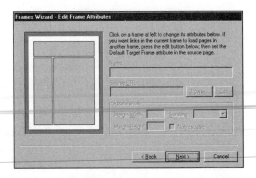

Figure 19. *The Frames Wizard – Edit Frames Attributes panel is used to set a name and associated Web page for each frame.*

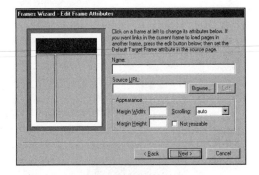

Figure 20. *Click the upper frame to activate the text boxes and buttons on the panel and start naming frames.*

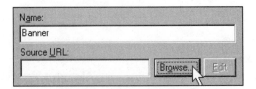

Figure 21. *In the Name text box, type in the name for the frame, then click Browse. For this example, the frame's name is Banner.*

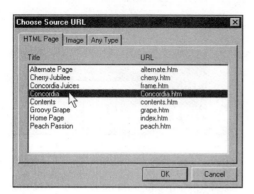

Figure 22. *Select a Web page from the list box in the Choose Source URL dialog box. For the example concordia.htm is selected.*

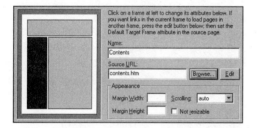

Figure 23. *Click the left frame, then name it and associate a Web page with the frame. For the example, the frame's name is Contents and the associated Web page is contents.htm.*

15. Click the Browse button next to the Source URL text box. The Choose Source URL dialog box will appear (**Figure 22**).

16. Select the Web page that you want to appear in this frame. In this case, concordia.htm is selected.

17. Click OK to close the dialog box and return to the wizard. Use these same techniques to assign names and Web pages to the other two frames.

18. Click the left frame that will become the table of contents frame (**Figure 23**). Give it a name using the Name text box. In this case it is named Contents. Click the Browse button to assign a Web page to the frame using the Choose Source URL dialog box. For this example, contents.htm is selected.

Set Frame Names and Web Pages

REMEMBER THE NAMES YOU GIVE TO FRAMES!

It's very important to remember the name you assign to each frame. Write them down on a piece of paper exactly as they appear, including spelling, capitalization, and any spaces between words. When you add hyperlinks to Web pages that will be included in a particular frame, you will need to know the name of the frame.

19. Click the right frame that will hold the Web pages describing the Concordia juices. This frame will change depending on the hyperlink clicked in the table of contents frame, but a default Web page should be set for this frame to start with. For this example, Juices is typed into the Name text box (**Figure 24**). When the Browse button is clicked, cherry.htm is selected from the Choose Source URL dialog box.

20. When you are finished assigning names and Web pages to the frames, click Next. The wizard will move to the next panel, Frames Wizard – Choose Alternate Content (**Figure 25**). This panel is used to assign a Web page that will appear in place of the frame page if someone with a browser that does not support frames surfs your Web site.

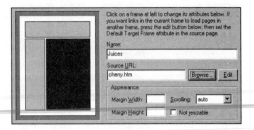

Figure 24. *Click the right pane, then name and associate a Web page with it. For the example, the frame's name is Juices and the associated Web page is cherry.htm.*

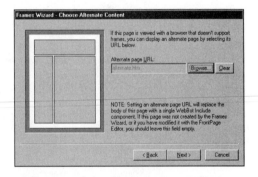

Figure 25. *Use the Frames Wizard – Choose Alternate Content panel to select an alternate Web page (this is optional).*

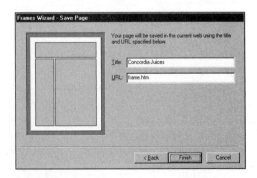

Figure 26. *Use the Frames Wizard – Save Page panel to set a title and file name for the new frame Web page.*

21. Click the Browse button. The Choose Source URL dialog box will appear (**Figure 22**).

22. Select the Web page that will be the alternate. In this case alternate.htm is selected.

23. Click OK to close the dialog box and return to the wizard.

24. Click Next. The wizard will move to the next panel, Frames Wizard – Save Page (**Figure 26**). This page is used to give a title to and name the new Web page containing the frames.

25. Type a title for the new frame Web page in the Title text box and enter a filename for the page in the URL text box. For the example, the title is Concordia Juices and the page filename is frame.htm.

26. Click Finish. The Frames Wizard takes all the information you've entered and creates the new frame Web page. The new frame Web page, named Concordia Juices, and the Web pages you associated with the various frames appear linked in FrontPage Explorer (**Figure 27**). Good job!

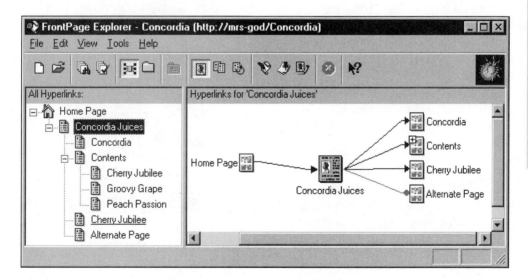

Figure 27. *The new frame Web page (for the example it is Concordia Juices) and the Web pages associated with each frame are shown linked in FrontPage Explorer.*

Name the Frameset Web Page

The next thing you need to do is create the hyperlinks in the table of contents that will make the juice descriptions appear in the right frame. To continue the example, the table of contents page will contain the hyperlinks.

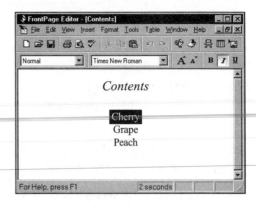

Figure 28. *Open the Web page in the Editor that will contain the hyperlinks the user will click.*

To create a hyperlink to a frame:

1. In the Editor, open the Web page that will contain the hyperlinks the user will click. In this example, contents.htm is open (**Figure 28**).

2. Select the text or image that will become the hyperlink. "Cherry" is selected in Figure 28.

3. Choose Hyperlink from the Insert menu (**Figure 29**). The Create Hyperlink dialog box will open with the Current FrontPage Web tab page in front (**Figure 30**).

4. Click the Browse button in the upper right of the tab page. The Current Web dialog box will open (**Figure 31**).

5. Select the Web page that will appear when the hyperlink is clicked by the user. In Figure 31, cherry.htm is selected.

6. Click OK to close the dialog box and return to the Create Hyperlink dialog box.

Figure 29. *Choose Hyperlink from the Insert menu.*

(left margin) **Create a Hyperlink to a Frame**

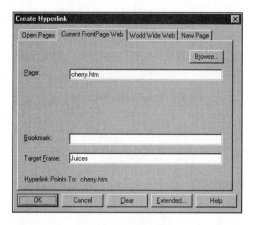

Figure 30. *Use the Create Hyperlink dialog box to link a Web page to a frame.*

Figure 31. *In the Current Web dialog box, select the Web page that will appear in the frame when the user clicks the hyperlink. In this example, cherry.htm is selected.*

Figure 32. *In the Target Frame text box, type the name of the frame that the hyperlinked Web page will appear in.*

7. Move down the tab page to the Target Frame text box. In the Target Frame text box, type the name of the frame that you want the Web page to appear in when the hyperlink is clicked (**Figure 32**). In this case, the target frame is the right frame, named Juices. (Remember to type the exact name you gave the frame in the Frames Wizard.)

8. Click OK to close the dialog box. The hyperlink will be created and the text underlined. If you selected an image, a border will appear around the image.

For the frame example, create the other two hyperlinks, one to the Grape Juice page and one to the Peach Juice page. When you are finished creating hyperlinks, save the Web page by choosing Save from the File menu or by pressing Ctrl+S on the keyboard.

> ### MAKING LINKS JUMP INTO THE SAME FRAME
>
> In the Concordia Juice example, when the user clicks a hyperlink in the left frame, the linked Web page appears in the right frame. If you want a linked Web page to replace the Web page containing the hyperlink, name the frame **_self**.

Create a Hyperlink to a Frame

The last thing you need to do before viewing what you've done in a browser is to add the hyperlink that will display the Web page containing the frames. Since the frame Web page is a special page, you can't just open it in the Editor and then view it in a browser. If you try to do this, the Frames Wizard will appear, ready to let you edit the frameset itself. (You'll discover how to edit the frame Web page on the next page.)

In this example, the hyperlink is placed in the home page that you created way back at the beginning of the chapter. Type in the text that will become the hyperlink, select it, then use the Create Hyperlink dialog box to associate the frame Web page, frame.htm, with the link.

When the home page is viewed in a browser (choose View in Browser from the File menu) and the hyperlink to the frame Web page is clicked, you'll see that you have created a great frame Web page (**Figure 33**).

After you've created a frame Web page, you may need to edit it to change the number of frames on the page or to change a Web page that is associated with a particular frame.

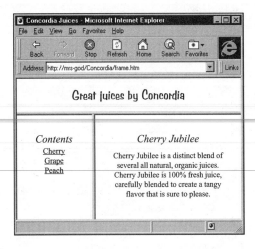

Figure 33. *When you check out the frame Web page you created, you'll discover a sophisticated, professional Web page.*

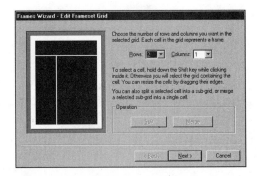

Figure 34. *Use the Frames Wizard – Edit Frameset Grid panel to change the number and size of frames on the frame Web page.*

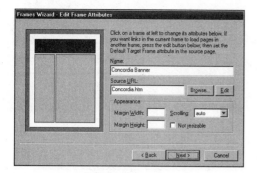

Figure 35. *Use the Frames Wizard – Edit Frame Attributes panel to change the name of a frame or the Web page associated with a frame.*

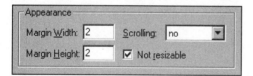

Figure 36. *In the Appearance area on the Frames Wizard – Frame Attributes panel, you can set a frame's margin width and height, whether a frame will include scroll bars, and whether it will be resizable.*

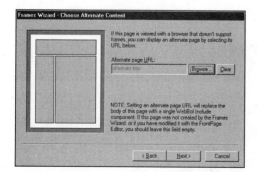

Figure 37. *Use the Frames Wizard – Choose Alternate Content panel to set a new alternate Web page.*

To edit a frameset Web page:

1. Double-click on the frame Web page in the Explorer.

   or

   Open the frame Web page in the Editor.

   The Frames Wizard – Edit Frameset Grid panel will appear (**Figure 34**). Use this panel to change the size of any frame or change the number of frames appearing on the Web page.

2. Click Next to move to the Frames Wizard – Edit Frame Attributes panel (**Figure 35**).Use this panel to change the name of a frame or the Web page associated with the frame.

   In the Appearance area (**Figure 36**), you can also set:

   - ⑨ Margin Width and Margin Height: use these text boxes to set the amount (in pixels) that should be left around the edges of the frame.

   - ⑨ Scrolling: use this drop-down list to specify whether scroll bars will appear in the frame when the frame's contents are too big to fit.

   - ⑨ Not resizable: use this check box to set whether a frame will resize within a browser when the browser window is resized.

3. Click Next to move to the Frames Wizard – Choose Alternate Content panel (**Figure 37**). Use this panel to set a new alternate Web page, if you wish.

4. Click Next to move to the Frames Wizard – Save Page panel (**Figure 38**). Use this panel to change the frame Web page's title or change its filename.

5. Click Finish to save the frame Web page. If you did not change the page's filename, the Frames Wizard will ask you whether you want to replace the existing frame Web page (**Figure 39**). If you click Yes, the frame Web page will be saved over the previous version. If you click No, the Frames Wizard – Save Page panel will reappear, giving you the chance to change the file-name for the frame Web page.

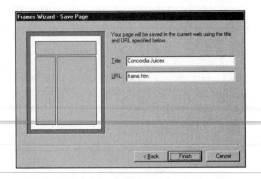

Figure 38. *Use the Frames Wizard – Save Page panel to save the frame Web page with a new Title or filename, if you wish.*

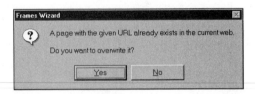

Figure 39. *If you are saving the frameset Web page with the same name that it had before you edited it, the Frames Wizard will ask if you're sure.*

SUMMARY

In this chapter you learned how to:

- Create a frameset
- Set the number of frames a frameset will have
- Size the frames
- Associate Web pages with specific frames
- Set an alternate Web page
- Create hyperlinks to a frame
- Edit a frameset
- Change a frameset's filename

Web Site Administration

Many Web sites are built by one person, others by a team. Even if you are "flying solo," you may want to know about administration. If you are working with a team, it's important to understand Web site administration.

Members of a Web site design team have different jobs. One person might write the text for a page while another might lay it out. These people would need different types of access to the Web site—one person would only be able to look at a site while another would be able to create, edit and delete pages.

If you are the administrator for a Web site team, it's your job to decide what kind of access each person on your team should have. FrontPage 97 calls these different levels of Web site access *permissions*.

There are three permissions levels that can be designated:

- ◉ *Administrator*—an administrator can set who has access to a Web site, and can also create and delete Web sites, and create, edit, and delete Web pages.
- ◉ *Author*—an author can create, edit, and delete Web pages.
- ◉ *Browse*—someone with browse access can only look at the Web page in a browser.

Every Web site must have at least one administrator. If you installed FrontPage 97, as described in Chapter 4, you used the FrontPage Server Administrator to set an administrator name and password, making you the administrator. Using FrontPage Explorer, an administrator can designate other administrators for a Web site, as well as authors and browsers.

FrontPage Root Webs

The default Web page that will show up in a browser when a FrontPage Web site is posted to a server is located in the Web server's *Root Web*. The Root Web contains the main Web site. You can create other Web sites that are sub-sites of this Root Web. These sub-Web sites can link to the main Web site or be separate, unconnected sites. **Figure 1** shows a diagram of this structure.

Permissions can be set using the Root Web, meaning that all Web sites contained within the Root Web, the main site and the sub-Web sites, will use the same permissions. Or, permissions can be set on a site-by-site basis. In addition, you can set up access rights for individual users, using separate passwords, or groups of users, using an Internet Protocol (IP) *address mask*. (For more about Internet Protocols, see page 20.)

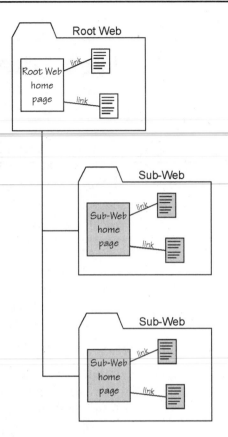

Figure 1. *A Root Web contains the main Web site and can have as many sub-Web sites as you want.*

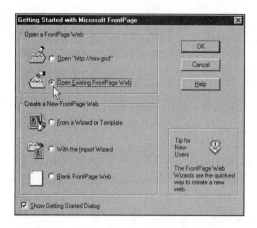

Figure 2. *Select the Open Existing Front-Page Web radio button, then click OK.*

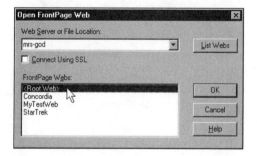

Figure 3. *Select <Root Web> from the FrontPage Webs list box, then click OK.*

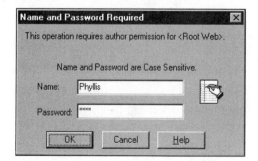

Figure 4. *Enter your name and password in the appropriate text boxes. You must be an administrator to change permissions.*

To set permissions for an individual user with the Root Web:

1. Launch FrontPage Explorer. The Getting Started with Microsoft FrontPage dialog box will appear (**Figure 2**).

2. In the Getting Started with Microsoft FrontPage dialog box, select the Open Existing FrontPage Web radio button.

3. Click OK. The Open FrontPage Web dialog box will open (**Figure 3**).

4. Click the List Webs button. All of the Web sites you've created, including the Root Web will appear in the FrontPage Webs list box.

5. Select <Root Web>, then click OK. The Name and Password Required dialog box will open (**Figure 4**).

6. Use the Name and Password text boxes to enter the administrator's name and password. (If you've forgotten your password, see page 50). Click OK. The Root Web will open in Explorer.

Set Individual Root Web Permissions

7. Choose Permissions from the Tools menu (**Figure 5**). The Permissions dialog box will appear with the Users tab page in front (**Figure 6**). With this tab page, you can add new users, edit user's access rights, and remove users.

To add a new user:

a. Click the Add button. The Add Users dialog box will open (**Figure 7**).

b. Type the name of the new user in the Name text box.

c. Type the password for the new user in the Password and Confirm Password text boxes. (The new user can change her password to something she likes later.)

d. In the User Can area, select the radio button for the access you want to give the person: Browse this web, Author and browse this web, or Administer, author, and browse this web.

e. Click OK to close the dialog box and return to the Permissions dialog box. The new user's name will appear in the Name list box.

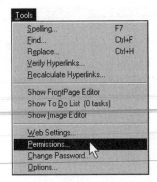

Figure 5. *Choose Permissions from the Explorer's Tools menu.*

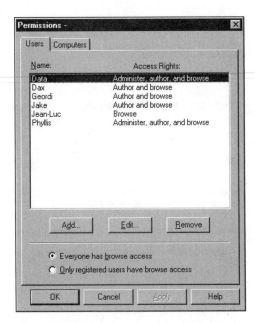

Figure 6. *The Permissions dialog box is used to add users, edit their rights, and remove users.*

Add a New User

Figure 7. *In the Add Users dialog box, enter the user's name and a password. Then select the type of access for the user.*

Figure 8. *In the Edit Users dialog box, select the new access rights for the user.*

To edit a user's access rights:

a. Click the Edit button in the Permissions dialog box. The Edit Users dialog box will appear (**Figure 8**).

b. In the User Can area, select the radio button for the access you want to give the person: Browse this web, Author and browse this web, or Administer, author, and browse this web.

c. Click OK to close the dialog box and return to the Permissions dialog box. The user's changed access rights will appear in the Access Rights column.

To remove a user:

a. Select the user's name in the list box on the Users tab page of the Permissions dialog box.

b. Click the Remove button. The user will disappear from the list.

8. When you are finished adding users, editing their access rights, and removing users, click OK to close the Permissions dialog box and return to Explorer.

PERMISSIONS AND FRONTPAGE

FrontPage permissions only work if you are working on a Web site located on the FrontPage Personal Web Server. If your Web site is saved in a folder on a computer, for instance C:\MyWeb, the Permissions item on the Tools menu will be grayed out and unavailable.

Edit a User's Rights; Remove a User

To set up permissions for a group of computers, you'll need to use the common IP address mask for the group. An IP address consists of four numbers separated by periods, such as 207.71.18.55. An IP address mask is made up of a combination of these numbers and asterisks. This mask is then used to ascertain whether a computer has access to a particular location on the Internet, such as a FrontPage Web site. Examples of IP address masks that would allow connection to the IP address above are 207.*.*.* or 207.71.*.*.

To set permissions for a group with the Root Web:

1. Launch FrontPage Explorer. The Getting Started with Microsoft FrontPage dialog box will appear (**Figure 2**).

2. In the Getting Started with Microsoft FrontPage dialog box, select the Open Existing FrontPage Web radio button.

3. Click OK. The Open FrontPage Web dialog box will open (**Figure 3**).

4. Click the List Webs button. All of the Web sites you've created, including the Root Web will appear in the FrontPage Webs list box.

5. Select <Root Web>, then click OK. The Name and Password Required dialog box will open (**Figure 4**).

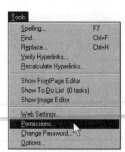

Figure 9. *Choose Permissions from the Explorer's Tools menu.*

Figure 10. *The Permissions dialog box opens with the Users tab page in front.*

Figure 11. *Click the Computers tab to bring that tab page to the front.*

Set Group Root Web Permissions

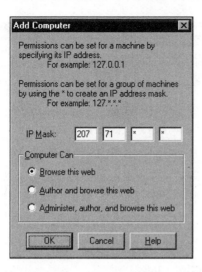

Figure 12. *In the Add Computer dialog box, enter the numbers and asterisks in the IP Mask text boxes, then select the access rights for that group.*

Figure 13. *The new group, identified by the IP Mask you entered in the Add Computer dialog box, appears in the list box on the Computers tab page.*

6. Use the Name and Password text boxes to enter the administrator's name and password. (If you've forgotten your password, see page 50). Click OK. The Root Web will open in Explorer.

7. Choose Permissions from the Tools menu (**Figure 9**). The Permissions dialog box will appear with the Users tab page in front (**Figure 10**).

8. Click the Computers tab to bring that tab page to the front (**Figure 11**). Use this tab page to set IP address masks and the access rights for the computers designated by those masks.

To add a group of computers:

a. Click the Add button. The Add Computer dialog box will open (**Figure 12**).

b. In the four IP Mask text boxes enter the combination of numbers and asterisks that make up the IP address mask.

c. In the Computer Can area, select the radio button for the access you want to give the group: Browse this web, Author and browse this web, or Administer, author, and browse this web.

d. Click OK to close the dialog box. The group's mask will appear in the list box on the Computers tab page (**Figure 13**).

Add a Group

To edit a group's access rights:

a. Select the group's IP mask from the list box on the Computers tab page, then click the Edit button. The Edit Computer dialog box will appear **(Figure 14)**.

b. In the Computer Can area, select the radio button for the access you want to give the group: Browse this web, Author and browse this web, or Administer, author, and browse this web.

c. Click OK to close the dialog box and return to the Permissions dialog box. The group's changed access rights will appear in the Access Rights column **(Figure 15)**.

To remove a group:

a. Select the group's IP mask from the list box on the Computers tab page.

b. Click the Remove button. The group will disappear from the list.

9. When you are finished adding groups of computers, editing their access rights, and removing groups, click OK to close the Permissions dialog box and return to Explorer.

Figure 14. In the Edit Computer dialog box, select the new access rights for the selected group.

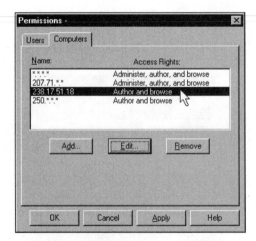

Figure 15. After you click OK in the Edit Computer dialog box, the selected group's new access rights appear in the list box on the Computers tab page.

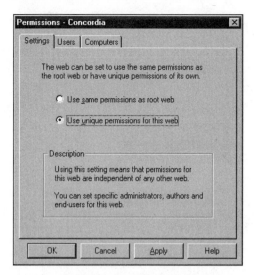

Figure 16. *With the Settings tab page, you can set whether an individual site uses the same permissions as the Root Web or has unique permissions.*

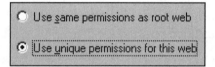

Figure 17. *Select the Use unique permissions for this web radio button, then click Apply.*

To set permissions for a single Web site:

1. Open the Web site you want to set access rights for in Explorer.

2. Choose Permissions from the Tools menu (**Figure 9**). The Permissions dialog box will open with the Settings tab page in front (**Figure 16**).

3. Select the Use unique permissions for this web radio button (**Figure 17**).

4. Click Apply. The new setting will take affect.

5. You can now set individual access rights with the Users tab page (see step 7 on page 220) or access rights for an entire group with the Computers tab page (see step 8 on page 223).

6. When you are finished setting permissions for the Web site, click OK to close the Permissions dialog box and return to Explorer.

Set Permissions for a Web Site

THE SETTINGS TAB PAGE

The Settings tab page is only used for assigning rights to individual Web sites. You may have already noticed that this tab page did not exist in the Permissions dialog box when the Root Web was used to assign global Web site permissions.

Whether you are a Web site administrator or a designated user, you may want to change your password from time-to-time for security reasons.

Figure 18.
*Choose Change
Password from
the Explorer's
Tools menu.*

To change your password:

1. In Explorer, choose Change Password from the Tools menu (**Figure 18**). The Change Password dialog box will appear (**Figure 19**). Notice that the name you used to log on is listed in the dialog box's title bar.

2. Enter the password you are currently using in the Old Password text box.

3. Type the new password twice, once in the New Password text box and once in the Confirm Password text box.

4. Click OK. FrontPage will register your new password.

Tip:

◉ Passwords are case sensitive, so be sure you type yours the same every time!

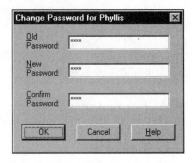

Figure 19. *Type in the old password, then enter the new password and confirm it.*

I FORGOT MY PASSWORD!

If you are an administrator and you've forgotten your password, turn to page 50 for directions on setting a new one. Otherwise, see your project administrator.

SUMMARY

In this chapter you learned how to:

◉ Set access for individual users with the Root Web

◉ Set access for groups with the Root Web

◉ Set access for individual Web sites

◉ Use Explorer to change passwords

(side text) **Change Your Password**

Adding WebBots to Your Pages

WebBots, or *Bots* for short, are programs you can add to Web pages using the FrontPage Editor. WebBots work with the FrontPage Server Extensions and the FrontPage Personal Web Server (for more about the Server Extensions, see page 38). When a WebBot is inserted into a Web page, it is actually creating a reference that tells the FrontPage-enabled servers to activate the WebBot program.

There are several WebBots that ship with Front-Page. Some of them, such as the Confirmation Field, Save Results Search, and Substitution WebBots, are meant to work with forms and will be discussed in Chapter 18. The following WebBots are covered in this chapter:

- *Include* WebBot lets you quickly insert the same information from one Web page, such as copyright notices and logos, onto as many pages as you want in your Web site.

- *Scheduled Include* WebBot works like the Include WebBot, but inserts its information during a specified time period.

- *Scheduled Image* WebBot also works like the Include Bot, but inserts a graphic during a specified time period.

- *Table of Contents* WebBot creates a table of contents for a Web site with hyperlinks to each Web page.

- *Timestamp* WebBot shows the time and date a Web page was last updated.

Types of WebBots

227

The Include WebBot

The Include WebBot works in a similar fashion to the *master pages* of a page layout program. Whatever one places on the master pages appears on the regular pages of a document.

The Include WebBot uses a Web page as the master page. The WebBot itself is placed on the page where you want the text and/or images to appear. For instance, if you want a copyright notice to appear on all your Web pages, create a master page with the copyright notice on it, then insert the Include WebBot on all the pages where you want the copyright to appear, referencing the master page. If you want to update the copyright notice, all you need to do is change the master page. The Web pages with the Include WebBot on them will update automatically.

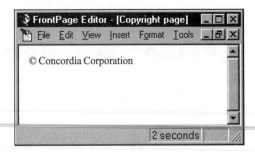

Figure 1. *Create a master Web page that contains the information you want to add to other Web pages.*

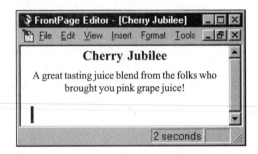

Figure 2. *Position the insertion marker where you want the WebBot inserted.*

Figure 3. *Choose WebBot Component from the Insert menu.*

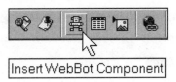

Figure 4. *Click the Insert WebBot Component button on the Standard toolbar.*

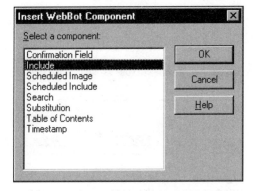

Figure 5. *In the Insert WebBot Component dialog box, select Include, then click OK.*

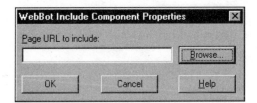

Figure 6. *Click the Browse button in the WebBot Include Component Properties dialog box.*

To insert the Include WebBot on a Web page:

1. In the Editor, create the master page with the information you want to include on other pages (**Figure 1**).

2. Open a Web page to which you want to add the contents of the master page.

3. Position the insertion marker on the Web page where you want the WebBot to appear (**Figure 2**).

4. Choose WebBot Component from the Insert menu (**Figure 3**) or click the Insert WebBot Component button on the Standard toolbar (**Figure 4**). The Insert WebBot Component dialog box will appear (**Figure 5**).

5. Select Include from the Select a component list box, then click OK. The Insert WebBot Component dialog box will close and the WebBot Include Component Properties dialog box will appear (**Figure 6**).

Insert an Include WebBot

6. Click the Browse button. The Current Web dialog box will appear (**Figure 7**). Select the master page from the list box.

7. Click OK. The Current Web dialog box will close and the Web page's filename will appear in the Page URL to include text box in the WebBot Component Properties dialog box (**Figure 8**).

8. Click OK to close the WebBot Include Component Properties dialog box. The text from the master Web page will appear where the insertion marker was positioned (**Figure 9**).

Tips:

◉ You can use text and images in the master Web page, but be sure to save the images in the same place as the master Web page. Otherwise, a broken image icon will appear when the page loads.

◉ When you pass the mouse over an inserted WebBot, a little robot appears next to the pointer. This robot is there to remind you that the text or image you're seeing on the Web page is there because of a WebBot.

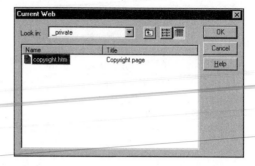

Figure 7. *Select the master Web page from the list box in the Current Web dialog box, then click OK.*

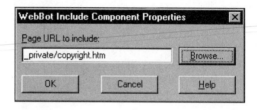

Figure 8. *The filename for the master Web page appears in the Page URL to include text box.*

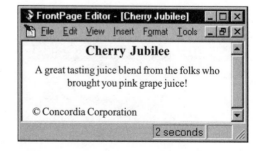

Figure 9. *The text and/or images from the master Web page appear where you positioned the insertion marker.*

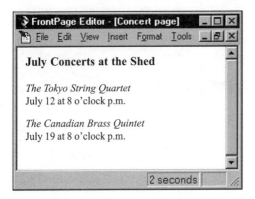

Figure 10. *Create the master page containing the information that will appear during a specific time frame.*

Figure 11. *Position the insertion marker where you want the WebBot to appear.*

The Scheduled Include WebBot

The Scheduled Include Bot works just like the Include WebBot except that the information that appears on the Web pages happens only during a specific period of time.

This WebBot is handy if you need to announce upcoming events. Instead of having to manually update a Web page to make sure the next event is shown, you can get the Scheduled Include WebBot to do it for you automatically. To have a schedule change, you would need to create a master Web page for each schedule change, then insert several Scheduled Include WebBots onto the target Web page, one for each change of schedule.

To insert the Scheduled Include WebBot:

1. In the Editor, create the master page with the information you want to include on other pages (**Figure 10**).

2. Open a Web page to which you want to add the contents of the master page.

3. Position the insertion marker on the Web page where you want the WebBot to appear (**Figure 11**).

Insert a Scheduled Include WebBot

4. Choose WebBot Component from the Insert menu **(Figure 3)** or click the Insert WebBot Component button on the Standard toolbar **(Figure 4)**. The Insert WebBot Component dialog box will appear **(Figure 12)**.

5. Select Scheduled Include from the Select a component list box, then click OK. The Insert WebBot Component dialog box will close and the WebBot Scheduled Include Component Properties dialog box will appear **(Figure 13)**.

6. Click the Browse button next to the Page URL to include text box near the top of the dialog box. The Current Web dialog box will appear **(Figure 14)**.

7. Select the master Web page from the list box. This is the information that will appear on the Web page during the scheduled period.

8. Click OK to close the dialog box and return to the WebBot Scheduled Include Component Properties dialog box.

9. In the Starting date and time area, use the drop-down list boxes to select the year, month, day, and time that the information from the master Web page will appear **(Figure 15)**.

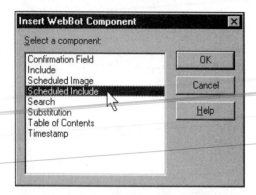

Figure 12. *Select Scheduled Include from the list box, then click OK.*

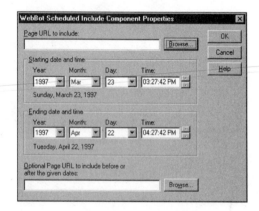

Figure 13. *Click the Browse button near the top of the dialog box.*

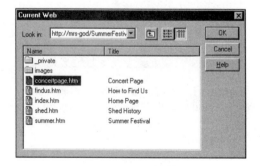

Figure 14. *Select the master Web page from the list box, then click OK.*

Insert a Scheduled Include WebBot

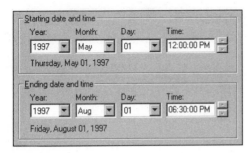

Figure 15. *Use the Starting and Ending date and time areas to set when the information will appear and disappear.*

Figure 16. *If the scheduled date and time has not arrived or has gone by, a message appears in the Editor. Otherwise, the information appears in the Web page.*

IMAGES AND THE SCHEDULED INCLUDE WEBBOT

You can use text and images in the master Web page, but be sure to save the images in the same place as the master Web page. Otherwise, a broken image icon will appear when the page loads.

---

10. In the Ending date and time area, use the drop-down list boxes to select the year, month, day, and time that the information from the master Web page will no longer be valid and disappear.

11. As an optional item, you can add another master page that will be shown before and after the scheduled one, by clicking the Browse button next to the Optional Page URL to include before or after the given dates text box. If you do click the Browse button, the Current Web dialog box will appear (**Figure 14**). Select the master page from the list box, then click OK.

12. When you are finished setting the properties for the Scheduled Include WebBot, click OK to close the dialog box. The message *[Expired Scheduled Include]* will appear in the Web page if the date and time you scheduled has not arrived yet or has gone by (**Figure 16**). If you added the optional master page, the information from that page will appear instead of the message.

Tip:

⊚ Even though the *[Expired Scheduled Include]* message appears on your Web page in the FrontPage Editor, this message will be invisible to anyone browsing your site.

The Scheduled Image WebBot

The Scheduled Image Bot works the same as the Scheduled Include WebBot, but instead of inserting the contents of a master Web page onto a Web page, the Scheduled Image WebBot inserts an image for a specified period of time.

To insert a Scheduled Image WebBot:

1. Create the image you want to appear at the scheduled time and save it in the Web site where you want it to appear.

2. Position the insertion marker on the Web page where you want the WebBot to appear (**Figure 17**).

3. Choose WebBot Component from the Insert menu (**Figure 3**) or click the Insert WebBot Component button on the Standard toolbar (**Figure 4**). The Insert WebBot Component dialog box will appear (**Figure 18**).

4. Select Scheduled Image from the Select a component list box, then click OK. The Insert WebBot Component dialog box will close and the WebBot Scheduled Image Component Properties dialog box will appear (**Figure 19**).

Figure 17. *Position the insertion marker where you want the WebBot to appear.*

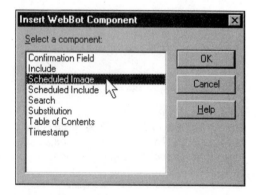

Figure 18. *In the Insert WebBot Component dialog box, select Scheduled Image, then click OK.*

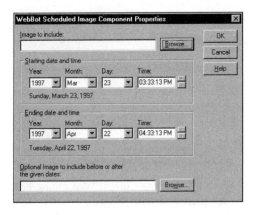

Figure 19. *Click the Browse button near the top of the dialog box.*

Figure 20. *Select the image using the Current Web dialog box, then click OK.*

5. Click the Browse button near the top of the dialog box that is next to the Image to include text box. The Current Web dialog box will appear (**Figure 20**).

6. Select the image from the list box. (If you don't see the image, you may have saved it in the Images folder. To open the Images folder, double-click on it).

7. Click OK to close the dialog box and return to the WebBot Scheduled Image Component Properties dialog box.

8. In the Starting date and time area, use the drop-down list boxes to select the year, month, day, and time that the image will appear (**Figure 21**).

9. In the Ending date and time area, use the drop-down list boxes to select the year, month, day, and time that the image will no longer be valid and disappear (**Figure 22**).

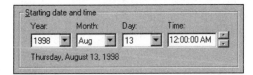

Figure 21. *In the Starting date and time area, use the drop-down list boxes to set the year, month, day, and time.*

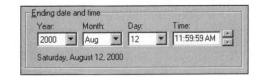

Figure 22. *In the Ending date and time area, use the drop-down list boxes to set the year, month, day, and time.*

Insert a Scheduled Image WebBot

10. As an optional item, you can add another image that will be shown before and after the scheduled one, by clicking the Browse button next to the Optional Image to include before or after the given dates text box. If you do click the Browse button, the Current Web dialog box will appear (**Figure 23**). Select the image from the list box, then click OK.

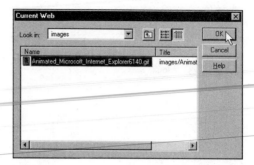

Figure 23. *Use the Current Web dialog box to select an alternate image.*

11. When you are finished setting the properties for the Scheduled Image WebBot, click OK to close the dialog box. The message *[Expired Scheduled Image]* will appear in the Web page if the date and time you scheduled has not arrived yet or has gone by (**Figure 24**). If you added the optional image, that image will appear instead of the *[Expired Scheduled Image]* message.

Tip:

⑨ Even though the *[Expired Scheduled Image]* message appears on your Web page in the FrontPage Editor, this message will be invisible to anyone browsing your site.

Figure 24. *If the scheduled date and time has not arrived yet or has passed by the message [Expired Scheduled Image] appears in the Editor. Otherwise, the image appears in the Web page.*

Insert a Scheduled Image WebBot

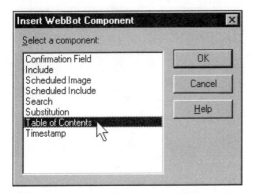

Figure 25. *In the Insert WebBot Component dialog box, select Table of Contents, then click OK.*

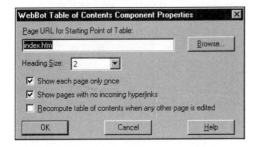

Figure 26. *Use the WebBot Table of Contents Component Properties dialog box to set which page to use as a starting point for the table of contents, set heading size, and set Web page options.*

The Table of Contents WebBot

A great way to help folks browsing your site find their way around is to include a table of contents. A good table of contents shows the titles for the entire site's Web pages with links to each page. If you have a large site, the enormity of this task can be overwhelming. This is where the Table of Contents WebBot comes in. This WebBot will create a full hierarchical table of contents with links *and* it will automatically update the table of contents if any pages change.

To insert a Table of Contents WebBot:

1. Position the insertion marker on the Web page where you would like the table of contents to appear.

2. Choose WebBot Component from the Insert menu (**Figure 3**) or click the Insert WebBot Component button on the Standard toolbar (**Figure 4**). The Insert WebBot Component dialog box will appear (**Figure 25**).

3. Select Table of Contents from the Select a component list box, then click OK. The Insert WebBot Component dialog box will close and the WebBot Table of Contents Component Properties dialog box will appear (**Figure 26**).

4. The Page URL for Starting Point of Table text box automatically displays the home page for the Web site. This is the page that will appear at the top of the Table of Contents. If you want a different page to appear in this position in the Table of Contents:

a. Click the Browse button next to the text box. The Current Web dialog box will appear (**Figure 27**).

Figure 27. *If you want to select a different starting point for the table of contents, use the list box in the Current Web dialog box to select a Web page.*

b. Select a Web page from the list box, then click OK to return to the WebBot Table of Contents Component Properties dialog box.

5. Use the Heading Size drop-down list to select the type size for the first item in the table of contents (**Figure 28**). (Heading sizes are discussed in detail on page 121). If you want the first item in the list to look like the other items in the list, select none.

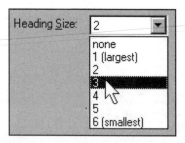

Figure 28. *Use the Heading Size drop-down list to select type size of the first item in the table of contents.*

6. Put a check mark in the Show each page only once check box, if you want each page to appear only once in the table of contents (**Figure 29**). If you don't select this option, Web pages with links to more than one page in the Web site will appear more than once in the table of contents.

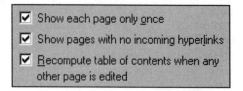

Figure 29. *Use the check boxes to set how many times a page is shown, to show pages with no links to them, and to automatically update if any Web pages change.*

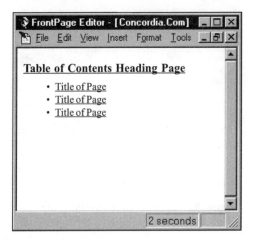

Figure 30. *No matter how large the table of contents will actually be, a four-line placeholder appears in the Web page in the Editor.*

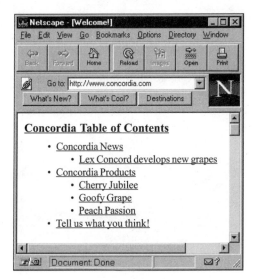

Figure 31. *To see the actual table of contents, view the Web page in a browser.*

7. Put a check mark in the Show pages with no incoming hyperlinks check box, if you want pages without any hyperlinks to appear in the table of contents. If you select this option, the only access the user will have to these pages will be through the table of contents.

8. Put a check mark in the Recompute table of contents when any other page is edited check box, if you want the WebBot to automatically update the table of contents when a Web page changes. If you don't select this option and a Web page changes, you will have to recalculate the site's hyperlinks manually. (Recalculating hyperlinks is discussed in Chapter 19 on page 273).

9. When you are finished setting options, click OK. A table of contents placeholder appears in the Editor (**Figure 30**). To see the actual table of contents with all its topics, view the Web page in a browser (**Figure 31**).

Insert a Table of Contents WebBot

The Timestamp WebBot

The Timestamp Bot is used to insert the time and/or date a Web page was last modified. This can be a handy way to help you keep track of updated pages on your Web site. It can also let users who browse your site frequently know that there's something new on a particular Web page.

To insert a Timestamp WebBot:

1. Position the insertion marker on the Web page where you would like the timestamp to appear.

2. Choose WebBot Component from the Insert menu (**Figure 3**) or click the Insert WebBot Component button on the Standard toolbar (**Figure 4**). The Insert WebBot Component dialog box will appear (**Figure 32**).

3. Select Timestamp from the Select a component list box, then click OK. The Insert WebBot Component dialog box will close and the WebBot Timestamp Component Properties dialog box will appear (**Figure 33**).

4. Depending on what you want displayed, select either the Date this page was last edited radio button or the Date this page was last automatically updated radio button.

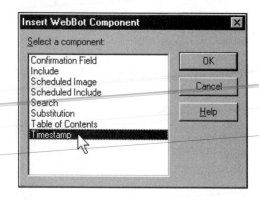

Figure 32. *Select Timestamp from the Select a component list box, then click OK.*

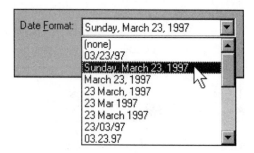

Figure 33. *Use the WebBot Timestamp Component Properties dialog box to set when the timestamp updates and whether it displays the date and/or time.*

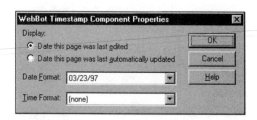

Figure 34. *Use the Date Format drop-down list to select the way the date is displayed.*

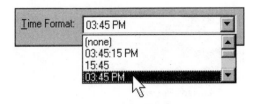

Figure 35. *Use the Time Format drop-down list to select how the time will be displayed.*

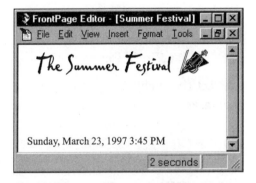

Figure 36. *The timestamp appears where the insertion marker was placed.*

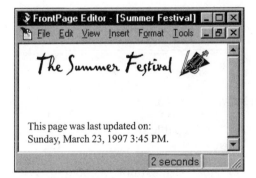

Figure 37. *You can add text before and after a timestamp to indicate the purpose of the timestamp.*

5. Use the Date Format drop-down list to select the way the date will be displayed (**Figure 34**). If you don't want to display the date, select (none).

6. Use the Time Format drop-down list to select the way the time will be displayed (**Figure 35**). If you don't want to display the time, select (none).

7. When you are finished selecting date and time options, click OK. The date and/or time the Web page was last modified will appear where you positioned the insertion marker (**Figure 36**).

Tip:

- You can add text before and after the Timestamp WebBot, indicating what the timestamp is for (**Figure 37**).

> ### WHAT'S MY TIME ZONE?
>
> If you want to set a timestamp showing your time zone after the time, select one of the time formats with the letters "TZ" after it from the Time Format dialog box (**Figure 35**).

*A*fter you've inserted a WebBot, you may need to edit its properties. This is easy to do.

To edit a WebBot's properties:

1. Select the WebBot whose properties you want to edit.

2. Right click on the WebBot and choose WebBot Component Properties from the pop-up menu (**Figure 38**). The appropriate properties dialog box for that WebBot will appear. (If you need help with the properties dialog box for a WebBot, take a look at the directions for inserting that particular WebBot in this chapter.)

3. Edit the WebBot's properties, then click OK to return to the Editor.

Cut
Copy
Paste
Page Properties...
Paragraph Properties...
Font Properties...
WebBot Component Properties... Alt+Enter

Figure 38. *Choose WebBot Components Properties from the pop-up menu.*

ANOTHER WAY TO ACCESS A WEBBOT'S PROPERTIES

Select the WebBot with the mouse pointer, then press Alt+Enter on the keyboard. The appropriate properties dialog box for that WebBot will open.

SUMMARY

In this chapter you learned how to:

- Add an Include WebBot
- Insert a Scheduled Include WebBot
- Insert a Scheduled Image WebBot
- Add a Table of Contents WebBot
- Add a Timestamp WebBot
- Edit the properties of a WebBot

Edit a WebBot's Properties

Forms and User Input

Forms add user interactivity to Web pages. Instead of just browsing a page, a user can input information, letting her search your Web site, register for events, complete surveys, order items, and so on.

Forms work by collecting information from users who enter it into text boxes or select specific items using radio buttons and drop-down lists. These places, where users enter information, are called *form fields*. After entering information into the form fields, users click a button, submitting the information.

When submitted, this information is organized into *name* and *value* pairs. A name is a unique label assigned to a field. This field name is invisible to users; it only appears in the HTML code. A value is the information submitted by the users in a particular field.

After the information is submitted, a *form handler* (a program on a Web server) takes the form data and processes it, perhaps responding to the user by displaying a confirmation page, while saving the information or formatting the results as a Web page and sending it back to the browser.

FrontPage forms use special form WebBots (see Chapter 17). In order for these WebBots to work, your Web site must be loaded on a server that supports the FrontPage Server Extensions. (For more about finding Internet Service Providers who support the FrontPage Server Extensions, see page 22.)

Form Fields; Form Handlers

Form Templates Make Life Incredibly Easy

FrontPage ships with a number of page templates and wizards that quickly create forms. You can get started with a templates or wizard and, if you need to, modify them to suit your needs.

Figure 1. *Click the Show FrontPage Editor button on the Explorer's toolbar.*

- ⑨ Feedback Form: this form is used to collect comments and suggestions from folks using your site.

- ⑨ Form Page Wizard: this wizard lets you design a custom form.

- ⑨ Guest Book: this form collects a person's information, and saves the submissions on a public Web page.

- ⑨ Product or Event Registration: this form lets customers register products or register for events.

- ⑨ Search Page: this form uses the Search WebBot to create an index of your Web pages, letting users perform word searches of your site.

- ⑨ Survey Form: this form is great for collecting customer information about popular opinions, marketing, and specific products.

- ⑨ User Registration: this form lets users create a Web site log on name and password for access to a members-only Web site.

This chapter takes you through adding forms using the FrontPage templates, inserting new form fields, editing existing fields, and selecting and setting up a form handler.

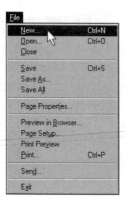

Figure 2. *Choose New from the Editor's File menu.*

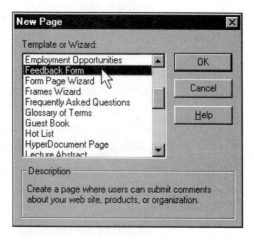

Figure 3. *Select a form template or wizard from the list box, then click OK.*

FrontPage Form Templates

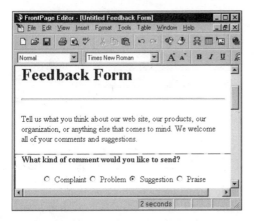

Figure 4. *The new form Web page appears in the Editor.*

Figure 5. *Choose Save from the File menu.*

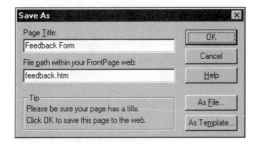

Figure 6. *Use the Save As dialog box to give the page a title and file name.*

To create a Web page using one of the form templates:

1. Using the Explorer, open the Web site to which you want to add the page.

2. Launch the Editor by double-clicking on one of the Web pages in the Explorer or clicking the Show FrontPage Editor button on the toolbar (**Figure 1**).

3. In the Editor, choose New from the File menu (**Figure 2**). The New Page dialog box will appear (**Figure 3**).

4. Select one of the form templates from the list box, then click OK. The new Web page will appear in the Editor (**Figure 4**). (For this example, the Feedback Form has been selected.)

5. Save the new page by choosing Save from the File menu (**Figure 5**). The Save As dialog box will appear (**Figure 6**).

6. Use the text boxes to set the page's title and its file name. (For the example feedback form, the title is set as Feedback Form and the file name as feedback.htm.)

7. Click OK to save the Web page and close the Save As dialog box.

Form Field Types

If you take a look at the feedback form just created in the previous section, you'll see that it includes several kinds of form fields. Actually, the Feedback Form contains at least one of every form field type, including two push buttons.

- ⑨ *Radio buttons*—Beneath the line, "What kind of comment would you like to send?" you'll see a group of radio buttons (**Figure 7**). Radio buttons work together as a group. They are used when you want the user to select a specific option from a group of options.

- ⑨ *Drop-down menu*—Beneath the line, "What about us do you want to comment on?" is what FrontPage calls a drop-down menu (**Figure 8**). (Some folks call this form field a drop-down list.) The choices on the menu can be customized when you set the form field's properties.

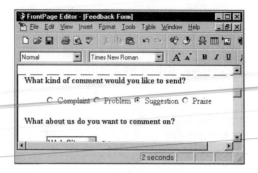

Figure 7. *Radio buttons are used in groups, letting the user select an item from a number of options.*

Figure 8. *Drop-down menus let the user select from a list or menu of items.*

Figure 9. *One-line text boxes let users enter a line of text.*

Figure 10. *A scrolling text box lets users enter several lines of text.*

Figure 11. *A check box lets a user decide between a yes or no choice. Push buttons make something happen when the user clicks them.*

- *One-line text box*—Right next to the drop-down list is what FrontPage calls a one-line text box (**Figure 9**). Users of your site can type text into this form field.

- *Scrolling text box*—Below "Enter your comments in the space provided" is a scrolling text box (**Figure 10**). (This is sometimes called a multiline text box.) This text box lets users enter long descriptions or comments.

- *Check box*—Near the bottom of the form, next to "Please contact me as soon as possible regarding this matter" is a check box (**Figure 11**). Check boxes let users decide between a yes or no choice.

- *Push button*—Below the check box are two push buttons (**Figure 11**). This type of button usually has a few words on it, describing what will happen if users click it. There are three types of push buttons to choose from: Submit, Reset, and Normal.

Types of Form Fields

CREATING FORMS USING TABLES

If you decide to design your own form or modify an existing one, you can use tables to line up the form fields. To make the table invisible, use the Table Properties dialog box to set the border width to 0 (see page 163).

Inserting form fields

The next sections show you how to add each of the form fields described on pages 246–247 and how to set their properties.

To make adding form fields easy, you should use the Form Fields toolbar (**Figure 12**).

One-line text box   Check Box   Drop-down menu

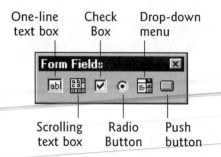

Scrolling text box   Radio Button   Push button

Figure 12. *The Form Fields toolbar lets you quickly add fields to a form.*

To view the Form Fields toolbar:

Choose Forms Toolbar from the View menu (**Figure 13**). The Form Fields toolbar will appear.

Figure 13. *Choose Forms Toolbar from the View menu.*

Radio Buttons

Radio buttons work together in a group. They present a group of options that the user must decide between, letting her pick only one. Each option button needs a *Group Name* and a *Value*. The Group Name must be the same for all the option buttons in the group and the Value is what that particular button represents. For instance, suppose you wanted to find out someone's favorite ice cream flavor. You could set up a group of radio buttons. The Group Name for the entire group of radio buttons could be Favorite Flavor and the Value for one radio button could be Vanilla while the Value for another radio button could be Chocolate.

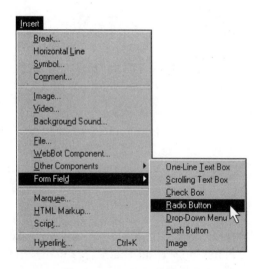

Figure 14. *Choose Radio Button from the Form Field fly-out found on the Insert menu.*

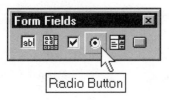

Figure 15. *Click Radio Button on the Form Fields toolbar.*

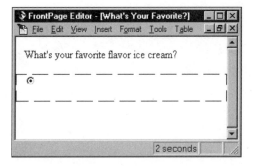

Figure 16. *The radio button appears where the cursor was positioned and a dashed rectangle appears around the form area.*

To insert a group of radio buttons:

1. Position the insertion marker where you want to add the radio button group.

2. Choose Radio Button from the Form Field fly-out on the Insert menu (**Figure 14**) or click Radio Button on the Form Fields toolbar (**Figure 15**). A radio button will appear on the Web page (**Figure 16**).

3. Right click on the radio button and select Form Field Properties from the pop-up menu (**Figure 17**) or double-click on the radio button. The Radio Button Properties dialog box will appear (**Figure 18**).

Insert a Group of Radio Buttons

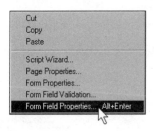

Figure 17. *Choose Form Field Properties from the pop-up menu.*

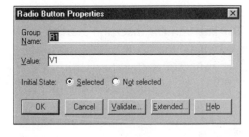

Figure 18. *The Radio Button Properties dialog box opens with default values in the Group Name and Value text boxes.*

4. Enter the name for the group of radio buttons in the Group Name text box (**Figure 19**). For the ice cream flavor example, the Group Name is Favorite Flavor.

5. Type in the value for the radio button in the Value text box. For the ice cream flavor example, this radio button's Value is Vanilla.

6. Use the Initial State radio buttons to set whether this radio button will be the one that is selected when the Web page first opens.

7. Click OK to close the Radio Button Properties dialog box and return to the Editor window.

8. Click the mouse to the right of the radio button. The insertion marker will appear there, blinking. Type in the value for that radio button (**Figure 20**). Even though you gave the button a value in the Radio Button Properites dialog box, you still need to give the button a descriptive label in the Web page itself. For the ice cream flavor example, you would type Vanilla.

9. Position the insertion marker where you want to add the next radio button for the group. This may be to the right of the first radio button or below it.

Figure 19. *Use the text boxes to enter a group name and value for the radio button.*

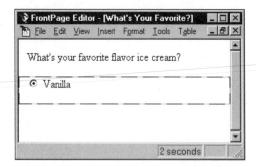

Figure 20. *Type a descriptive label next to the radio button, indicating what the choice is to the user.*

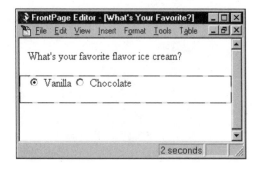

Figure 21. *Add a second radio button to give the user something to choose between.*

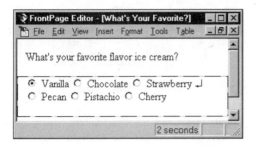

Figure 22. *Continue adding radio buttons to the group until you have added all the items you want the user to choose from.*

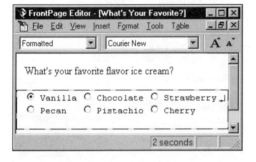

Figure 23. *Use the Formatted text style to quickly line up the radio buttons.*

WHERE'S MY FORM?

A form on a FrontPage Web page is shown in the Editor contained within a dashed rectangle that surrounds the form fields. This rectangle is not visible to the user in a browser.

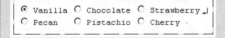

10. Create a second radio button and set its Group Name and Value properties by repeating steps 2 through 8. For the ice cream flavor example, the Group Name would be Favorite Flavor (just like the first radio button) and the Value would be Chocolate.

11. Click the mouse to the right of the second radio button and type in the value for that radio button (**Figure 21**). For the ice cream flavor example, you would type Chocolate.

12. Continue following steps 2 through 9 until you have created all the options you want the user to choose from (**Figure 22**).

Tips:

- An easy way to get radio buttons to line up is to use the Formatted text style or to use an invisible table (**Figure 23**).

- Don't forget to type a line of text above the radio buttons, telling the user what they are selecting. For instance, "What's your favorite flavor ice cream?"

Insert a Group of Radio Buttons

Drop-Down Menus

Another way to have users select one item from a group of choices is to use a drop-down menu. To continue the ice cream flavor example, you could have someone choose their favorite flavor from a drop-down menu.

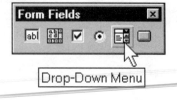

Figure 24. *Click the Drop-Down Menu button on the Form Fields toolbar.*

To insert a drop-down menu:

1. Position the insertion marker where you would like the drop-down menu to appear. (This could be next to some text describing what the user is supposed to select.)

2. Click the Drop-Down Menu button on the Form Fields toolbar (**Figure 24**) or choose Drop-Down Menu from the Form Field fly-out on the Insert menu (**Figure 25**). A drop-down menu will appear where the insertion marker was positioned (**Figure 26**).

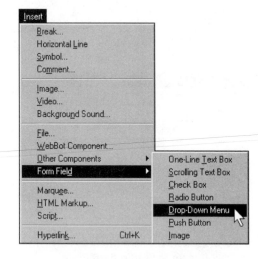

Figure 25. *Choose Drop-Down Menu from the Form Field fly-out on the Insert menu.*

Figure 26. *An empty drop-down menu appears where the insertion marker was positioned. The drop-down menu in this figure is positioned in a table.*

Figure 27. *Choose Form Field Properties from the pop-up menu.*

3. Right click on the drop-down menu and choose Form Field Properties from the pop-up menu (**Figure 27**) or double-click on the drop-down menu. The Drop-Down Menu Properties dialog box will open (**Figure 28**).

4. Type in a name to identify the drop-down menu in the Name text box. For the ice cream example, type in Favorite Flavor.

5. From this point there are several things you can do. You can add items that will appear in the drop-down menu, modify the properties of an item in the list, remove an item, and change the order of the menu by moving items up or down.

Figure 28. *The Drop-Down Menu Properties dialog box is used to add, modify, remove, and position the items on the portion of the form field that drops down.*

HIDING THE DASHED RECTANGLE SURROUNDING A FORM AREA

If you don't want to see the dashed rectangle while creating your form Web page, click the Show/Hide Paragraph button on the Editor's Standard toolbar.

Insert a Drop-Down Menu

To add an item to the drop-down menu:

a. Click the Add button. The Add Choice dialog box will appear (**Figure 29**). This dialog box is used to add the choices that will appear on the drop-down portion of the form field that the user can select from.

b. Type one item that the user could select in the Choice text box (**Figure 30**). For the ice cream example, you could type Vanilla.

c. The value of the item is the same as its Choice name by default. If you want the value to be different than the name (for instance, the flavor Vanilla could be equated to 1), put a check in the Specify Value check box, then type the value in the text box.

d. Use the radio buttons in the Initial State area to set whether the item will be the one that appears in the drop-down menu when the Web page first opens (**Figure 31**).

e. Click OK to close the Add Choice dialog box and return to the Drop-Down Menu Properties dialog box. You can continue adding items using these five steps.

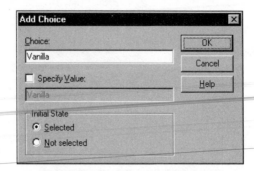

Figure 29. *Use the Add Choice dialog box to add items to the list.*

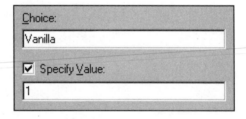

Figure 30. *In the Choice text box, enter an item that the user could select. If you want to use a value that is different than the Choice name, put a check in the Specify value check box and enter a value in the text box.*

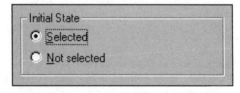

Figure 31. *Use the radio buttons in the Initial State area to set whether the item will be selected when the Web page first loads in a browser.*

Insert a Drop-Down Menu

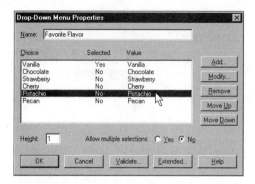

Figure 32. *Select the item that you want to modify in the list box, then click the Modify button.*

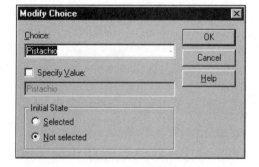

Figure 33. *Use the Modify Choice dialog box to change the item's Choice name, specify a value for the item, and change its initial state.*

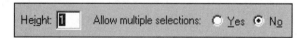

Figure 34. *Use the Height text box to set how many lines show at once and select whether the user can choose more than one item at a time.*

To modify the properties of an item:

a. Select the item from the list box in the Drop-Down Menu Properties dialog box (**Figure 32**).

b. Click the Modify button. The Modify Choice dialog box will open (**Figure 33**). Using this dialog box you can: change the choice the user will see in the drop-down menu by typing a new name in the Choice text box; use the Specify Value check box to set a value for the item that is different than the choice name; and set whether the item is selected or not using the radio buttons in the Initial State area.

c. When you are finished making changes, click OK to return to the Drop-Down Menu Properties dialog box.

To remove an item:

a. Select the item from the list box in the Drop-Down Menu Properties dialog box.

b. Click the Remove button.

Insert a Drop-Down Menu

To rearrange the order of items on the drop-down menu:

a. To move an item up the list, select it, then click the Move Up button.

b. To move an item down the list, select it, then click the Move Down button.

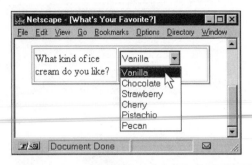

Figure 35a. *This drop-down list is set to a height of 1 and lets the user select from a list that drops down.*

6. Using the Height text box in the Drop-Down Menu Properties dialog box, you can set how many items the drop-down menu will show at one time (**Figure 34**). If this number is left at 1, the default, the drop-down menu will display one item and let the user access the rest by clicking a down arrow button (**Figure 35a**). If the number is set at 2 or more, the drop-down menu will appear with a scroll bar on the right side (**Figure 35b**).

7. If you want the user to be able to select more than one item at a time, click the Yes radio button next to Allow multiple selections near the bottom of the Drop-Down Menu Properties dialog box (**Figure 34**).

8. Click OK to close the dialog box. If you view the Web page in a browser, you'll see that the drop-down menu is ready to go (**Figures 35a–b**).

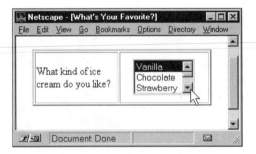

Figure 35b. *The drop-down list shown here is set to a height of 3 and lets the user choose from a scrolling list.*

Tip:

◎ The drop-down menu resizes its width automatically, stretching to fit the longest menu item.

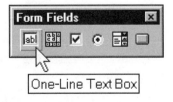

Figure 36. *Click the One-Line Text Box button on the Form Fields toolbar.*

Insert a Drop-Down Menu

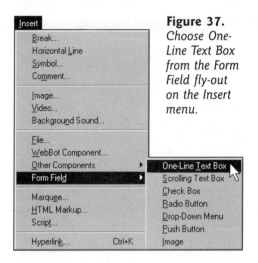

Figure 38. *The one-line text box appears where the insertion marker was positioned.*

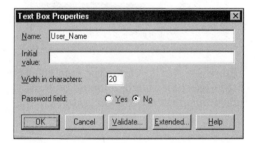

Figure 39. *Use the Text Box Properties dialog box to set a name for the one-line text box and whether there will be text in the box when it opens in a browser.*

One-Line Text Boxes

One-line text boxes let users enter a line of text. This text could be a name, address, comment, telephone number, e-mail address, etc.

To insert a one-line text box:

1. Position the insertion marker where you would like the one-line text box to appear. This could be next to some descriptive text that lets the user know what type of information should be entered in the text box.

2. Click the One-Line Text Box button on the Form Fields toolbar (**Figure 36**) or choose One-Line Text Box from the Form Field fly-out on the Insert menu (**Figure 37**). A one-line text box will appear where the insertion marker was positioned (**Figure 38**).

3. Right click on the one-line text box and choose Form Field Properties from the pop-up menu (**Figure 27**) or double-click on the text box. The Text Box Properties dialog box will open (**Figure 39**).

4. In the Name text box, type in a name that will identify the text box.

Insert a One-Line Text Box

5. If you want some text to appear in the text box when the Web page first opens, enter that text in the Initial value text box.

6. Use the text box next to Width in characters to set how wide the text box will be. If you're not sure how wide you want it to be, leave it at the default of 20. You can always resize the text box later by dragging its handles.

7. If this text box is going to be used for entering a password, select the Yes radio button next to Password field. Otherwise, leave the No radio button selected.

8. To set restrictions as to what can be entered in the text box, click Validate. The Text Box Validation dialog box will appear (**Figure 40**). Using the Data Type drop-down list, you can set whether the text box will accept any kind of entry, or text, integers or numbers only (**Figure 41**). Depending on what is selected in the Data Type drop-down list, a portion of the dialog box becomes active so you can select more specific items. When you are finished with this dialog box, click OK to close it.

9. When you are finished using the Text Box Properties dialog box, click OK to close it. Your one-line text box is ready to be used.

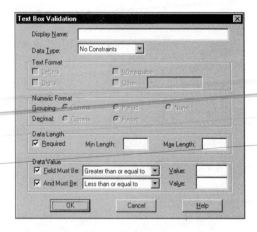

Figure 40. *Use the Text Box Validation dialog box to set what the user can enter in the one-line text box. This can come in handy if you want the user to enter a date in numeric form, for instance. If the user tries to enter text, the one-line text box won't let her.*

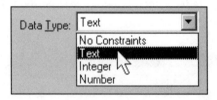

Figure 41. *Use the Data Type drop-down list to select the kind of information the user can type in the one-line text box.*

Insert a One-Line Text Box

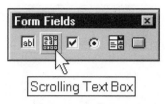

Figure 42. *Click the Scrolling Text Box button on the Form Fields toolbar.*

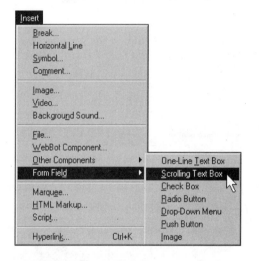

Figure 43. *Choose Scrolling Text Box from the Form Field fly-out on the Insert menu.*

Scrolling Text Boxes

A scrolling text box is similar to a one-line text box in that the user enters text in it. The difference is that the user can enter more than one line of text and use the scroll bars to see what they've typed.

To insert a scrolling text box:

1. Position the insertion marker where you want the scrolling text box to appear. This could be next to or below some text describing what the user is supposed to enter in the text box.

2. Click the Scrolling Text Box button on the Form Fields toolbar (**Figure 42**) or choose Scrolling Text Box from the Form Field fly-out found on the Insert menu (**Figure 43**). The scrolling text box will appear where the insertion marker was positioned (**Figure 44**).

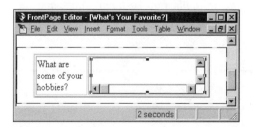

Figure 44. *The scrolling text box appears where the insertion marker was positioned. In this figure, the text box is located in a table.*

Insert a Scrolling Text Box

3. Right click on the text box and choose Form Field Properties from the pop-up menu (**Figure 45**) or double-click on the text box. The Scrolling Text Box Properties dialog box will open (**Figure 46**).

4. Enter a name to identify the scrolling text box in the Name text box (**Figure 47**).

5. If you want some text to appear in the scrolling text box when the page loads in a browser, enter that text in the Initial value text box.

6. Use the text box next to Width in characters to set how wide the text box will be (**Figure 48**).

7. Use the Number of lines text box to set the length of the scrolling text box. (If you aren't sure how big the text box should be, you can always resize it later by selecting it and dragging its handles.)

Figure 45. *Right click on the scrolling text box and choose Form Field Properties from the pop-up menu.*

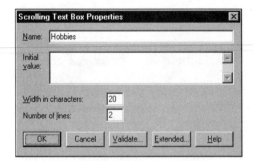

Figure 46. *Use the Scrolling Text Box Properties dialog box to set a name for the text box, whether there will already be text in it when the Web page loads in a browser, and its width and height.*

Insert a Scrolling Text Box

VIEW YOUR FORM WEB PAGE IN A BROWSER

After you have finished designing a form, you will need to view the Web page in a browser to see how the form will look and work when you publish your FrontPage Web site.

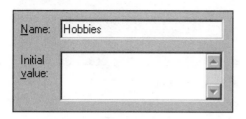

Figure 47. *Use the Name text box to enter a descriptive label for the text box.*

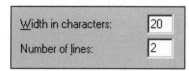

Figure 48. *Enter the width of the scrolling text box in the Width in characters text box and the height of the scrolling text box in the Number of lines text box.*

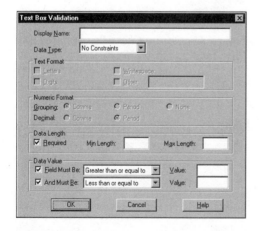

Figure 49. *If you want to restrict the type of information that can be entered in the scrolling text box, use the Text Box Validation dialog box.*

8. To set restrictions as to what can be entered in the text box, click Validate. The Text Box Validation dialog box will appear (**Figure 49**). Using the Data Type drop-down list, you can set whether the text box will accept any kind of entry, or text, integers or numbers only (**Figure 50**). Depending on what is selected in the Data Type drop-down list, a portion of the dialog box becomes active so you can select more specific items. When you are finished with this dialog box, click OK to close it.

9. When you are finished setting the properties for the scrolling text box, click OK. The Scrolling Text Box properties dialog box will close. To see the scrolling text box work, you will need to view the Web page in a browser.

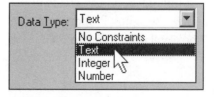

Figure 50. *Use the Data Type drop-down list to set what kind of information can be entered in the text box.*

Check Boxes

Check boxes can be used to let users choose between "Yes" (checked) or "No" (unchecked) and also to let them select many items from a pre-defined list. To use the favorite ice cream flavor example again, you could ask the user to put checks in the check boxes next to the various flavors she likes.

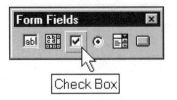

Figure 51. *Click Check Box on the Form Fields toolbar.*

To insert a check box:

1. Position the insertion marker where you want the check box to appear. (This could be next to or below a description of what the user is supposed to be selecting.)

2. Click Check Box on the Form Fields toolbar (**Figure 51**) or choose Check Box from the Form Field fly-out on the Insert menu (**Figure 52**). The check box will appear where the insertion marker was positioned (**Figure 53**).

3. Right click on the check box and select Form Field Properties from the pop-up menu (**Figure 45**) or double-click on the check box. The Check Box Properties dialog box will open (**Figure 54**).

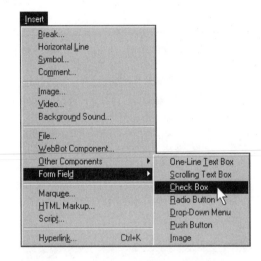

Figure 52. *Choose Check Box from the Form Field fly-out on the Insert menu.*

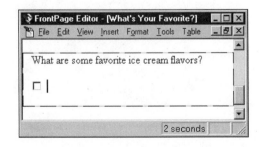

Figure 53. *A check box appears where the insertion marker was positioned.*

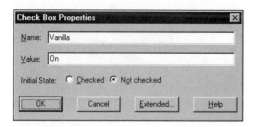

Figure 54. *Use the Check Box Properties dialog box to set a name and value for the check box and to set whether it is initially selected when the Web page loads in a browser.*

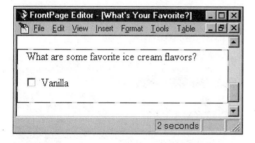

Figure 55. *Type a descriptive label next to the check box to let the user know what the box means.*

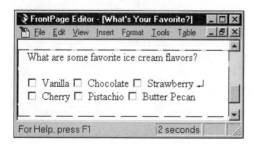

Figure 56. *Insert as many check boxes as you need to display all the items the user can choose.*

4. Use the Name text box to enter a name that will identify the check box. For the favorite ice cream flavor example, you could enter Vanilla.

5. In the text box next to Value, enter a word showing the value of the box if it is checked. You could use, for instance, On, Selected, or Checked.

6. Use the radio buttons next to Initial State to set whether the check box will have a check mark in it when the page loads in a browser.

7. When you are finished setting the properties for the check box, click OK to close the dialog box.

8. Click the mouse to the right of the check box and type the description of what this check box means if the user checks it (**Figure 55**). For the ice cream example, you could type Vanilla.

Tip:

◉ You can continue adding as many check boxes as you need using the steps outlined above (**Figure 56**).

Insert a Check Box

Push Buttons

The user clicks a push button when they want a specific action to occur, such as submitting a form, resetting a form so they can start again, or playing a sound. Push buttons come in three flavors: Normal, Submit, and Reset.

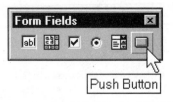

Figure 57. *Click Push Button on the Form Fields toolbar.*

To insert a push button:

1. Position the insertion marker where you want the push button to appear.

2. Click Push Button on the Form Fields toolbar (**Figure 57**) or choose Push Button from the Form Field fly-out on the Insert menu (**Figure 58**). The push button will appear where the insertion marker was positioned (**Figure 59**). By default, this is a Submit push button. You can change this in a minute if you want to.

3. Right click on the push button and choose Form Field Properties from the pop-up menu (**Figure 45**) or double-click on the push button. The Push Button Properties dialog box will appear (**Figure 60**).

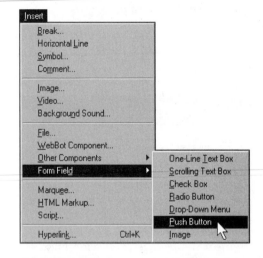

Figure 58. *Choose Push Button from the Form Field fly-out on the Insert menu.*

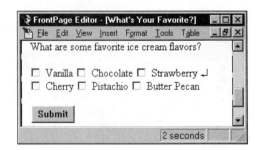

Figure 59. *A push button appears where the insertion marker was positioned. By default, the push button is a Submit button. You can change this using the Push Button Properties dialog box.*

(left margin) **Insert a Push Button**

Figure 60. *Use the Push Button Properties dialog box to set a Name for the button (this is optional), to enter the words that will appear on the button, and to choose the type of button it is: Submit, Reset, or Normal.*

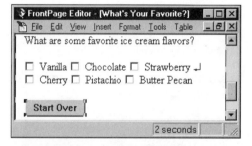

Figure 61. *When you close the Push Button Properties dialog box, the words you entered in the Value/Label text box appear on the push button.*

Figure 62. *Right click on the form field and choose Form Field Properties from the pop-up menu.*

4. Use the Name text box to set a name identifying the push button. This is optional.

5. Use the radio buttons next to Button type to set the type of button. The default setting is Submit.

6. In the Value/Label text box enter the words that will appear on the push button, letting the user know what the button's for.

7. When you are finished setting the push button's properties, click OK. The push button will appear with the text you entered in the Value/Label text box (**Figure 61**).

To edit a form field's properties:

Double-click on the form field or right click on the form field and choose Form Field Properties from the pop-up menu (**Figure 62**). The properties dialog box for that particular form field will appear. If you need help with this dialog box, take a look at the individual sections in this chapter for inserting that type of form field. The properties dialog box will be discussed there.

Edit a Form Field's Properties

Selecting a Form Handler

The form handler is used to process form results. The form handlers in FrontPage use WebBots to work. This means that your Web site must be published on a server that supports the FrontPage Server Extensions.

There are three WebBot form handlers: the WebBot Save Results Component, the WebBot Registration Component, and the WebBot Discussion Component. If you created a Web page using one of the FrontPage form templates discussed on page 244, then a form handler has already been selected and partially configured.

To select and set up a form handler:

1. Position the mouse pointer over the dashed form area and right click (**Figure 63**). Choose Form Properties from the pop-up menu (**Figure 64**). The Form Properties dialog box will appear (**Figure 65**).

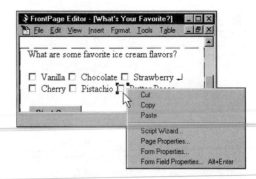

Figure 63. *Right click anywhere in the form area defined by the dashed rectangle to access the pop-up menu.*

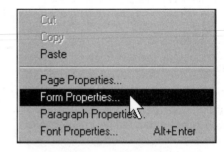

Figure 64. *Choose Form Properties from the pop-up menu.*

ADDING INITIAL TEXT TO YOUR TEXT BOXES

Setting initial text in some text boxes can be helpful to your users. For instance, if your form collects a country name as part of an address and most of your users are from the United States, you could set the text box's initial text to USA.

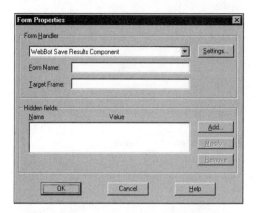

Figure 65. *Use the Form Properties dialog box to select a form hander, set up the form handler, and define the file the submitted information will be sent to.*

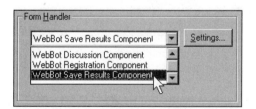

Figure 66. *In the Form Handler area, use the drop-down list to select the type of form handler you want to use: WebBot Save Results Component, WebBot Discussion Component, or WebBot Registration Component.*

2. In the Form Handler area, use the drop-down list to select a form handler (**Figure 66**). You can choose from:

🌀 WebBot Save Results Component: this WebBot collects the information from the form and saves it in a format that you select.

🌀 WebBot Discussion Component: this WebBot lets users partake in an online discussion group. The WebBot collects the information from a form, makes it into an HTML page, and saves the page on a Web server. Configuring this WebBot is quite complicated. If you want to create a discussion Web site, use the Discussion Web Wizard found in FrontPage Editor. The Wizard will set the discussion Web site up for you and configure the WebBot Discussion Component.

🌀 WebBot Registration Component: this WebBot lets users register for something offered in your Web site. If you use the Product or Event Registration or User Registration form template to create a Web page (see page 244), this handler will be selected and configured for you automatically.

Select and Set Up a Form Handler

3. To configure the form handler you've selected, click the Settings button to the right of the Form Handler drop-down list. The Settings dialog box for that handler will appear. For this example, since the WebBot Save Results Component was selected, the Settings for Saving Results of Form dialog box will open with the Results tab page in front (**Figure 67**).

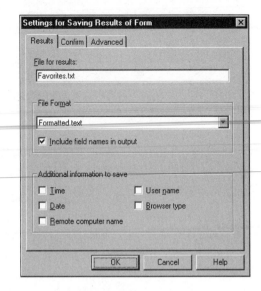

Figure 67. *Use the Settings for Saving Results of Form dialog box to configure the WebBot Save Results Component.*

4. In the File Format area, use the drop-down list to select how the submitted results will be formatted (**Figure 68**). You can choose from:

   ◉ HTML: this will format the file in HTML using Normal text style.

   ◉ HTML definition list: this will format the file in HTML using the Definition text style.

   ◉ HTML bulleted list: this will format the file in HTML using the Bulleted text style.

   ◉ Formatted text within HTML: this will format the file in HTML using the Formatted text style.

   ◉ Formatted text: this will format the file in a text format (readable in a text editing program such as Notepad).

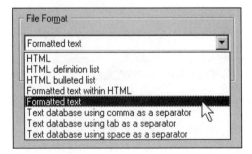

Figure 68. *In the File Format area, select a file format using the drop-down list.*

Select and Set Up a Form Handler

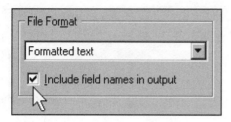

Figure 69. *If you want the names of the form fields included with the value data, put a check in the Include field names in output check box.*

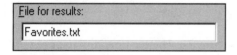

Figure 70. *Enter the name of the file where the submitted information will be saved in the File for results text box.*

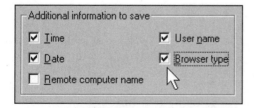

Figure 71. *In the Additional information to save area, put checks in the check boxes next to the type of information you would like saved with the submission.*

◉ Text database using comma as a separator: this will format the file in a text format with a comma separating each element.

◉ Text database using tab as a separator: this will format the file in a text format with a tab separating each element.

◉ Text database using space as a separator: this will format the file in a text format with a space separating each element.

5. To include field names with the values in the results file, put a check in the Include field names in output check box (**Figure 69**). (A field name is the name assigned to a form field using its properties dialog box.)

6. In the File for results text box, type in the name and folder location of the file where you want the results saved (**Figure 70**). This folder location can be within the Web site or in another location on the server. If the file does not exist when FrontPage goes to save the first results, it will automatically create the file.

7. In the Additional information to save area, use the check boxes to select the items that you want saved with the results (**Figure 71**).

Select and Set Up a Form Handler

8. Click the Confirm tab to bring that tab page to the front (**Figure 72**). Using this tab page, you can set an optional confirmation Web page and an optional page that will show a *validation error*. A validation error occurs when the user has not entered information in a particular field.

9. Click OK to close the Settings for Saving Results of Form dialog box and return to the Form Properties dialog box.

10. Click OK to close the Form Properties dialog box. The form handler is all set up.

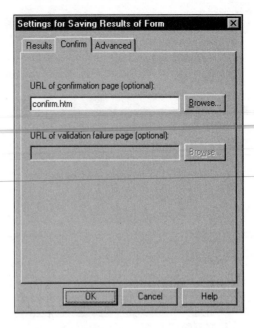

Figure 72. *Use the Confirm tab page of the Settings for Saving Results of Form dialog box to set a confirmation Web page and a validation error Web page. Setting both of these pages is optional.*

Select and Set Up a Form Handler

SUMMARY

In this chapter you learned how to:

- ◉ Use a form template to create a form Web page
- ◉ View the Form Fields toolbar
- ◉ Add radio buttons
- ◉ Insert drop-down menus
- ◉ Add one-line and scrolling text boxes
- ◉ Insert check boxes and push buttons
- ◉ Edit a form field's properties
- ◉ Set up a form handler

Publishing and Testing Your Site

Ready, set, go! Once you've finished creating your Web site, it's time to let the world see it. FrontPage calls this *publishing* your Web site. In order for your site to always be accessible to folks browsing the World Wide Web, you will need to store the site on a *dedicated* Web server—a server that is connected to the Internet 24 hours a day. For information on finding an Internet Service Provider that will be able to handle your FrontPage Web site, see page 22.

There are two stages to testing your Web site. The first comes when you've completed the site. You should use the Preview in Browser command found on the Editor's file menu to check your pages and all the hyperlinks on your pages. You can also use the Editor to move from hyperlink to hyperlink. In addition, you can use FrontPage Explorer to verify hyperlinks and fix broken links to images or URL addresses. The second stage of testing comes when you publish your site. You should run through the pages and links again, making sure everything works, all the images load correctly, and everything looks fine.

In addition to testing your site after you've published it to a dedicated Web server, you should check to see how long it takes for each Web page to load. If a page takes a long time, you might want to rework the page, using different graphics and/or multimedia files that are smaller in file size.

To follow hyperlinks using the Editor:

1. Open the Web site you want to check in Explorer.

2. Double-click on a Web page in the Explorer window to launch the Editor.

   or

   Click the Show FrontPage Editor button on the toolbar (**Figure 1**).

3. In the Editor, open the Web page you want to test (if it's not open already).

4. Hold down the Ctrl key and click on the linked image or text.

   or

   Select the linked image or position the insertion marker within the linked text and choose Follow Hyperlink from the Tools menu (**Figure 2**).

   The page that the text or image links to will open in the Editor.

Tip:

⊚ If you want to test a link to a site on the Web, make sure you are connected to the Web first, otherwise a message will appear, telling you the URL address is not valid (**Figure 3**). After you click OK, another message saying that FrontPage cannot open the site (**Figure 4**) will appear. Click OK.

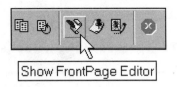

Figure 1. *Click the Show FrontPage Editor button on the Explorer's toolbar.*

Figure 2. *Choose Follow Hyperlink from the Tools menu.*

Figure 3. *If you try to follow a hyperlink to a Web URL and you aren't connected to the Web, FrontPage will tell you the address is not valid.*

Follow Hyperlinks using the Editor

Figure 4. *If you are not connected to the Web and try to verify a Web URL, Front-Page will not be able to open the page.*

If you have added new pages, hyper-links, or WebBots to your site, you should recalculate the hyperlinks for the entire site. It's a good idea to do this before verifying the links on your site. Recalculating hyperlinks will update your site and also update the table of contents WebBot if you've used one.

To recalculate hyperlinks using Explorer:

1. Open the Web site you want to recalculate in Explorer.

2. Choose Recalculate Hyperlinks from the Tools menu (**Figure 5**).

3. FrontPage will ask you whether you want to proceed (**Figure 6**). Click Yes. Depending on the size of your site, Explorer will work for a while resetting the hyperlinks.

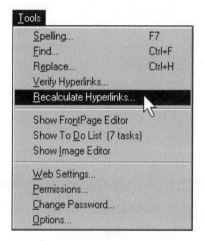

Figure 5. *Choose Recalculate Hyperlinks from the Tools menu.*

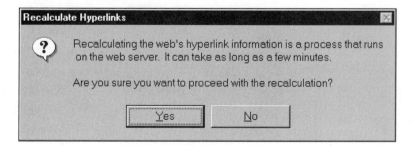

Figure 6. *FrontPage will ask you if you really want to recalculate hyperlinks. Click Yes.*

Recalculate Hyperlinks in Explorer

To verify links using Explorer:

1. Open the Web site you want to check in Explorer.

2. Choose Verify Hyperlinks from the Tools menu **(Figure 7)**. The Verify Hyperlinks dialog box will appear displaying any questionable links **(Figure 8)**. Before each link will be a colored circle:

   ⊚ A red circle with the word "Broken" next to it indicates a broken link. ● Broken

   ⊚ A yellow circle with a question mark next to it indicates that the link has not been verified. ○ ?

   ⊚ After the links are checked and fixed, the red and yellow circles will change to green ones with the word "OK" next to it, indicating that the links are good. If there are no links listed in the list box, then your site has no broken links. ● OK

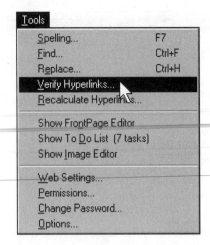

Figure 7. *Choose Verify Hyperlinks from the Explorer's Tools menu.*

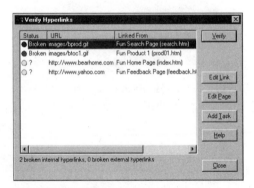

Figure 8. *The Verify Hyperlinks dialog box will display any questionable links and let you check and fix them.*

Verify Links Using Explorer

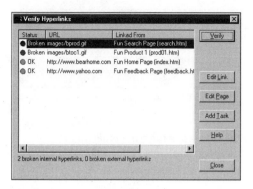

Figure 9. *After you click the Verify button, the status of questionable links may change to OK. Other links which are truly broken will remain so until you fix them.*

Broken image icon

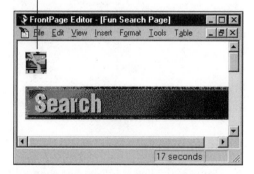

Figure 10. *When you select a broken link in the Verify Hyperlinks dialog box and click Edit Page, the page with the broken link appears in the Editor. In this case, the broken link is an image that is referenced incorrectly so the broken image icon appears on the page.*

3. To start the verification process, click the Verify button. FrontPage will verify all the links, then adjust the colored circles in the Status column as necessary (**Figure 9**). In Figure 9, the URL address checked out and the yellow circles changed to green ones, but the broken links, indicated by the red circles, remained red. (If you are checking external hyperlinks—links to URL addresses on the Web—you must be connected live to the Web.)

4. To repair a broken hyperlink, select the link in the list box, then click Edit Page. The Web page with the broken link will open in the Editor (**Figure 10**). In Figure 8, the broken link is an image that has been referenced incorrectly, so the broken image icon is displayed in Figure 10 instead of the image.

5. Fix the link by correcting a reference to an image that is wrong or a Web page that is incorrectly referenced. (For more about hyperlinks, turn to Chapter 14.)

Verify Links Using Explorer

6. When you are finished fixing the link, close the Web page in the Editor and save the changes you have made when the Editor asks you (**Figure 11**).

7. Minimize the Editor to view the Verify Hyperlinks dialog box again. Next to the link you just edited, the red circle will have changed to a yellow circle with the word "Edited" next to it (**Figure 12**).

8. Continue editing the broken links, following steps 4 through 7.

9. When all the circles in the Verify Hyperlinks dialog box are yellow or green, click the Verify button again. FrontPage will verify all the links and if you've fixed them correctly all circles will change to green.

10. Close the Verify Hyperlinks dialog box by clicking the Close button.

Tip:

⊚ If you discover that you have some broken hyperlinks, but don't want to fix them right away, you can add the task to the To Do List by selecting the broken link, then clicking Add Task.

Figure 11. *When you are finished editing the Web page with the broken link, close the page and save the changes you have made.*

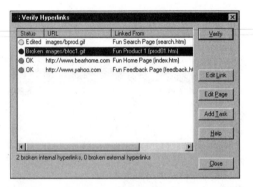

Figure 12. *When you return to the Verify Hyperlinks dialog box, you will notice that the status of the link you fixed has changed from a red circle to a yellow circle and the word "Edited" appears next to the circle.*

Figure 13. *Choose Publish FrontPage Web from the Explorer's File menu.*

*B*efore you publish your Web site, contact the Internet Service Provider you are going to use to get their directions about specific publishing procedures. If you are publishing your site to an intranet, talk with your system administrator.

To publish your Web site:

1. In the Explorer, open the Web site you want to publish.

2. If you are publishing your site to an Internet Service Provider on the Web, use your dial-up connection to connect to the Web.

3. Choose Publish FrontPage Web from the File menu (**Figure 13**). The Publish FrontPage Web dialog box will open (**Figure 14**).

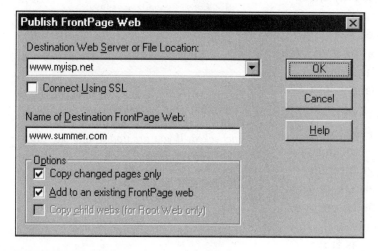

Figure 14. *Use the Publish FrontPage Web dialog box to set the server your Web site is going to and the name of your Web site at that destination.*

Publish Your Web Site

4. In the Destination Web Server or File Location text box, type the name of the ISP's dedicated Web server that you want to publish your site to (**Figure 15**). This server name will look something like www.yourserver.com or www.myisp.net. Your ISP or system administrator will be able to tell you the server name.

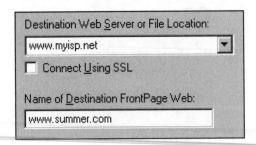

Figure 15. *In the Destination Web Server or File Location drop-down list, type in the name of the server where your Web site will be saved. Then, type the name of your Web site in the Name of Destination FrontPage Web text box.*

5. In the Name of Destination FrontPage Web text box, enter your Web site's domain name. This is the name that you selected or the ISP has assigned to you (to find out how to obtain an Internet domain, see page 21). This name will be something such as www.bearhome.com.

6. In the Options area, *uncheck* the Copy changed pages only check box if this is the first time you are publishing your Web site (**Figure 16**). If you are updating your Web site and want to only copy the pages that have changes, put a check in this check box.

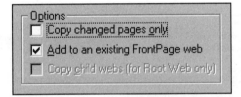

Figure 16. *If this is the first time you are publishing your Web site, make sure the Copy changed pages only check box is unchecked. If you are updating a site that is already published, put a check in the check box so only those files that have changed will be copied.*

7. Put a check in the Add to an existing FrontPage web check box. Most FrontPage Internet Service Providers will create a new account for you before you publish your Web site to it. Consequently, as far as FrontPage is concerned, you're adding to an existing Web site.

Publish Your Web Site

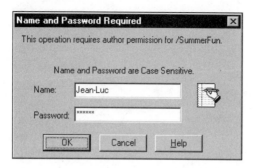

Figure 17. *Depending on the security procedures your ISP or system administrator uses, you may need to enter a user name and password.*

Figure 18. *When FrontPage has finished publishing your Web site to the destination server, it will tell you that the operation was successful.*

8. Click OK. The Publish FrontPage Web dialog box will close and FrontPage will contact the ISP's dedicated Web server. Depending on the security procedures that your ISP uses, you may need to enter a user name and password provided by the ISP (**Figure 17**). Once your Web site has been transferred, a dialog box will open telling you that the transfer was successful (**Figure 18**). *Your site is now published. Congratulations!*

Tips:

- If you update your site and want to publish the pages that have changed, just follow the directions above and make sure to put a check in the Copy changed pages only check box found in the Publish FrontPage Web dialog box (**Figure 16**).

- Once your Web site is published to the dedicated Web server, the Internet Service Provider or your system administrator will need to manually restart the Web server in order for your site to be recognized. Contact your ISP or system administrator for help with this.

Publish Your Web Site

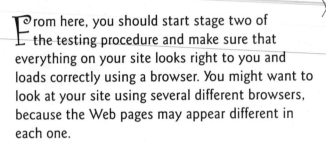

From here, you should start stage two of the testing procedure and make sure that everything on your site looks right to you and loads correctly using a browser. You might want to look at your site using several different browsers, because the Web pages may appear different in each one.

In addition, if you have included hyperlinks on your site to other sites on the World Wide Web, you should test these links periodically. Web sites change and Web pages are removed. So a page you've set up a link to may disappear.

You've come a long way from the first time you launched FrontPage Explorer and started a Web site. You've created a fully functional, professional Web site that is available to folks browsing the Web or an intranet. Congratulations!

SUMMARY

In this chapter you learned how to:

- Follow hyperlinks in the Editor
- Recalculate hyperlinks in Explorer
- Verify links using Explorer
- Publish your Web site and go "live"

Good Books

L isted below are a few good books to get you started and help you along with any special Web-related interests you may have.

Two good books for getting started on the road to the World Wide Web are:

- *The Little Web Book* by Alfred Glossbrenner and Emily Glossbrenner (Peachpit Press)
- *Web Wambooli* by Dan Gookin (Peachpit Press)

For those who want to learn more about HTML code and tags:

- *HTML for the World Wide Web: Visual QuickStart Guide*, 2nd ed., by Elizabeth Castro (Peachpit Press)
- *HTML: The Definitive Guide* by Chuck Musciano and Bill Kennedy (O'Reilly & Associates)

To find out more about creating Web graphics:

- *<designing web graphics>* by Lynda Weinman (New Riders)

For learning how to create amazing graphical effects using Photoshop:

- *The Photoshop Wow! Book* by Linnea Dayton and Jack Davis (Peachpit Press)

Good Books

A few books with interesting and provocative ideas about Web site and page design:

- *Creating Killer Web Sites* by David Siegel (Hayden Books)

- *Creating Web Pages for Dummies* by Bud Smith and Arthur Bebak (IDG Books)

- *Elements of Web Design* by Darcy DiNucci, Maria Giudice, and Lynne Stiles (Peachpit Press)

- *Home Sweet Home Page* by Robin Williams (Peachpit Press)

To find Web sites with topics that interest you, take a look at:

- *What's on the Internet*, 3rd ed., by Eric Gagnon with Edwinna von Baeyer (Peachpit Press)

A useful guide of computer terms:

- *Jargon* by Robin Williams with Steve Cummings (Peachpit Press)

For those of you who are interested in advanced topics, such as working with the FrontPage Software Developer's Kit, Java applets, and ActiveX controls:

- *Web Developer's Secrets* by Harold Davis (IDG Books)

Index

Index

Index

Index

Index

Index

Index

Index